The Magpie's Companion

The Magpie's Companion

A GUIDE TO THINGS FOUND

Steven Banks

Illustrated by Nicholas Griffiths

JOHN MURRAY
LONDON

Printed in Great Britain by
Jolly & Barber Ltd, Rugby, Warwickshire

0 7195 3491 7

Contents

FOR ELMA-LOUISE

Acknowledgments

To the Curator and staff of the Salisbury and South Wiltshire Museum, first and foremost my most grateful thanks for facilities to examine and illustrate many things from the extensive collections in that museum. Then my sincere gratitude to Nicholas Griffiths for his willingness to tackle every strange object I asked him to draw, producing hundreds of illustrations with unfailing art and cheerful regularity.

Many of the things people find are donated to museums, which is largely where I have sought them, receiving help and encouragement from Directors, Curators and other members of staff, which I acknowledge with many thanks:

E. J. W. Hulse, Breamore Countryside Museum; John Hoyle, Dudley Metropolitan Borough; N. W. Bertenshaw and P. Robinson, City Museums, Birmingham; D. C. Norton, Norton Museum, Bromsgrove; J. F. L. Narwood, Hampshire County Museum Service; J. H. Lavender, Red House Museum, Christchurch; D. P. Dawson and Miss G. Plowright, City of Bristol Museum; Miss Dyer, Museum of Costume, Bath; Norman Cook, Wells Museum; Mr and Mrs B. Jarvis, Rockbourne Roman Villa; D. J. Penn, Imperial War Museum; H. L. Blackmore, Tower Armouries; Dr R. G. W. Anderson, Miss S. Cackett and F. A. Alflatt, Science Museum, London; C. Blair and C. H. Truman, Victoria and Albert Museum; M. G. L. Thomas, Avoncroft Museum of Buildings, Bromsgrove; M. J. Watkins, City Museum, Gloucester; J. H. Andrew, Museum of Science and Industry, Birmingham; N. Walden, Black Country Museum, Dudley; G. L. Shearer, Worcester County Museum, Hartlebury; L. C. Hayward, Yeovil Borough Museum; J. D. L. Fleetwood, Taunton Castle Museum; F. W. Holling, Guildford Museum; E. M. Perry, Horsham Museum; Miss M. J. Waller, Preston Manor Museum, Brighton; Miss F. M. Greig, Brecknock Museum; Richard Hagen, Luton Museum; H. J. Turner, Bedford Museum; Miss L. Davies, City Museum, St Albans; D. G. Davies, Verulamium Museum, St Albans; I. G. Sparkes, Wycombe Chair Museum; G. C. Lamb, Aylesbury

Museum; H. N. Savory and G. C. Boon, National Museum, Cardiff; T. R. Whitney, Cyfarthwa Castle Museum, Merthyr Tydvil; C. Barnett, Newport Museum; M. Fendall, City Museum, Worcester; C. Hajdamach, Museum and Art Gallery, Dudley; S. J. Woodward, Great Western Railway Museum.

There are individuals too numerous to mention who have given me assistance in various ways, such as by letting me illustrate the things they have found, or by allowing me to reproduce an illustration of theirs. Among these I record with particular gratitude:

Mr and Mrs Michael Carey, J. Lloyd, Stanley Moody, R. Heaton, the late Hugh Shortt, R. A. Lewis, R. L. Thomson (The Patent Office), Dr R. F. Tylecote, Master Hugh Studholme, Mrs Jess Foster, Professor Leslie Alcock (for permission to reproduce the 'A' from Cadbury), Mrs Jo Petersen, Messrs Renlane and Co, Commander John Smallwood RN, J. Abnett, Martin Green, John Collins, Major J. G. Rollins, Dr A. K. Huggins, Messrs. Stanley Gibbons, H. Wheeler (The Gemmological Institute of Great Britain), M. L. Pearl (The Metals Society), A. V. Ware (Messrs. Hardy Bros.), Mrs Cressida Ridley, Mrs N. Yeatman-Biggs, John Bingham, Frank Sykes, Desmond Banks, J. Beavan and Mrs H. Cumberland (Needles Industries Ltd), and Ms Jane Carver (The Royal Warrant Holders Association).

Finally, my thanks to Miss Jean Hunter for her accurate and expeditious typing.

Illustrations not captioned are identified in the text.

Things in General

The Quest Defined

One of my friends has never ceased to be amused by my fondness for small and broken things; another has re-marked on my store of useful and useless knowledge. This book is for those who have the same liking for things, and wish to learn from them. In our researches we will use only our five senses, a magnifying glass, and simple measuring instruments.

The French expression *objet trouvé* has been taken into English, but it means not just things found but natural objects which chance to have some artistic value. Eminent painters and sculptors have been inspired by them. The drawings show two *objets trouvés* from my own mantelpiece: the flint 'madonna' comes from a Wiltshire field, and the twisted piece of root was picked up while swimming underwater off the south coast of Turkey. These natural curiosities are of interest and give pleasure, but they have no further place in this book. Here with a few exceptions only the works of man are discussed.

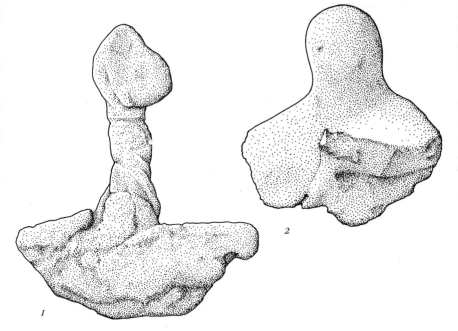

1

2

As to these exceptions, they include natural objects which have been related to man, such as round pebbles collected as sling shot or for games; spire shells used by children as tops, such as the one shown, which was found on a site where people had lived some miles from the sea; even natural curiosities so long as they have evidently been collected. A large pebble of brilliant red jasper down at the floor level of a medieval tower comes to my mind: it must surely have been admired and collected by someone before me. Natural objects may look as though they have been made by man. A pebble may swirl round under water and form a perfectly round depression, even a hole, in a stone lying beneath it. Fossils are for ever being brought to museums in the belief that they are artefacts of some kind. The natural 'twinned' crystal called staurolite looks very like a carved cross.

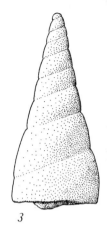

3

The subject of this book is the things found while walking the land, swimming in the sea, digging in field or garden for practical purposes, exploring attics or cellars or hollow trees. 'The land' includes town and country, even the pavements of London, from which it was possible to gather a fine collection of hair-pins a few years ago. But this book is not concerned with finds brought to light in the course of archaeological investigations of any kind; such digging is above all a search for knowledge, and the 'small finds' encountered are just one part of the knowledge gained. Nor are we seeking for treasure, so that, for instance, copper coins are of more interest to us than gold because they are more likely to be found. There must be some limitation on size, and here I am concerned that my subjects shall be portable. Archaeologists speak of 'small finds' without any specification. It seems fair to say 'no bigger than a rat trap'.

4 Staurolite

The things we find have either been thrown away, lost by accident, or hidden and not recovered. Buckles are thrown away when the belt wears out; most keys are lost by accident; Samuel Johnson's story of the five guineas he carefully hid, and forgot where, is a common tale of woe.

Broken and worn-out things are not excluded. A fracture can expose the inner material to judgment, and show the nature and depth of surface treatment. Further, identification of the whole from a surviving part is a fascinating pastime. Many of the things we find will have been worn down while in use, and the nature of this wear will lead to conclusions about their history.

Before the days of municipal rubbish dumps, that is to say in the early nineteenth century, every householder disposed of his rubbish as best he might. He threw it on his own rubbish dump, from whence it could be spread with the compost on garden or field, or he used it to fill up a cess pit which had become too smelly for its original purpose. The cess pits we must leave to the archaeologists, but the bits and pieces scattered over cultivated land are very much our concern. One evening in Scotland, returning from shooting on farmland, I picked up a shard of pottery on the infield near the farm and found to my delight that it was part of the well of a plate, printed with a view of the 'high girders' of the Tay Bridge which collapsed so disastrously one stormy night in 1879.

As to the acceptable age of things found, let us say pre-plastic. The synthetic materials known generally as plastics have come very rapidly into use and given the metal and wooden things they replace the status of antiques. A few years ago 1830 was accepted as a good upper limit for antiques to qualify as such, on the basis that by that year the craftsman's individual workmanship had yielded to the soulless repetition of the machine. Not so these days, when anything with pretensions to age is sold under the sign 'Antiques'. It was only about twenty-five years ago that modern thermosetting plastics were first made in bulk in this country. At that time, as always, the introduction of a radically new material imposed strains on the designer and the user. Many thousands of years ago the first clay pots had a baggy shape, with marks like stitching on them, to reassure the user that they were legitimate descendants of leather vessels: so too were plastic table-cloths impressed with the patterns appropriate to linen and lace. The archaeologist calls these copies 'skeuomorphs', and they can be very helpful when placing a group of things in order of date.

Having excluded plastics, the only other materials I have deliberately omitted, with certain exceptions, are textiles and paper. This I have done with some regret, because, for instance, a splendid collection of old hats was recently found in a papered-over cupboard of a former hatter's shop in Salisbury; and the newspapers used to line the drawers of old furniture can be a rewarding study. But the subjects are too wide, and the materials too perishable, for inclusion here. Leather, however, lasts surprisingly well under favourable conditions. A family I knew bought an old manor house in Kent and set about restoring it. Up came the old floorboards, and under one of them, in the hall near the foot of the stairs, was a child's shoe, which the local museum dated to the seventeenth century. It was well preserved though much worn; a little chaff was embedded in the insole, which was impressed with a set of small toeprints. When they spoke of this locally, people said, 'But haven't you heard the story?', and went on to tell them about the ghost which walked their house, a small girl weeping piteously, who three hundred years ago had been sent to bed in disgrace for losing her shoe, and had got up in the night to look for it and fallen to her death down the stairs. So now the little shoe was left out on a window ledge at the top of the stairs, and after that the ghost was never heard nor seen again.

Our quest will lead away from the objects to mentions of them in writing. The novels of the last two centuries can add to our knowledge, and so can the works of Chaucer, Shakespeare and other early writers. Wills and inventories contain interesting lists of possessions. The seventeenth-century inventory of a certain Scottish castle included 'two laim dishes standing high' on a dresser, and recently fragments were found which might well have been from them. Unfortunately, however, people seldom write intentionally for the benefit of posterity and there are curious gaps in the written history of ordinary things. For instance, the first reference to port wine is from the late seventeenth century, when it is recorded that certain traders were shipping wine from Bordeaux through Oporto and passing it off as port: clearly the wine was already known and appreciated at that time. Such frustrations should not prevent us keeping our ears open, as it were, for useful references in our general reading.

Books may also be useful for their illustrations. The early editions of Charles Dickens' works, which largely deal with the lives of working people, were plentifully illustrated, so that we may see in them pots and pans, children's toys and many other things of the period.

Beware, however, of novels such as *Lorna Doone*, which, though set in the past, was written in the nineteenth century about events in the seventeenth, and is full of anachronisms. Paintings and prints in art galleries and elsewhere will show the objects of everyday life known to the artist when he was illustrating scenes from his own days. Sometimes these may convey a message; for instance, a table with porringers and spoons would indicate poverty, but if furnished with plates, knives and forks it would suggest riches. The wealthy could afford flesh: the poor had porridges and suchlike 'spoon-meats'.

If you are interested in finding things you must cultivate the gentle art of observation. In general, men only see what they expect to see or have been taught to see. The axe heads carved during the Bronze Age on the great stones of Stonehenge went unobserved for hundreds of years, but since they were noticed twenty years ago we can all see them. Here a natural advantage lies with the young and, in my experience, not those most gifted in reading, writing and arithmetic. Two incidents come to mind. At the site of the port of Tahiri, on the Persian Gulf, which was laid in ruins by the Mongols in the thirteenth century, I made a small collection of pottery shards from those lying in plenty on the surface of the ground. The local children had only to be shown a piece of Early Islamic pottery or Sung stoneware and they soon brought others, seldom bits of modern pots in error. Coming nearer home, a few years ago the authorities levelled the area known as Bugmoor, south of Salisbury, where the medieval pest-houses and later rubbish dumps used to be. The plan was to create public pleasure gardens in this neglected locality. While the ground was open I went with some unacademic fifteen-year-old lads from a local school, and here again they soon picked up the more interesting pieces of, in this case, moulded glass candlesticks, slag-ware dishes and so forth. But not only the young have sharp eyes: a distinguished amateur archaeologist in his middle age selected from among the pebbles on a beach in Tahiti a rare and perfect example of the polished black stone mirrors which the native people used before they had glass.

A keen eye may be to some extent natural, but the sense of touch needs to be cultivated. Some years ago there was a television programme called 'Animal, Vegetable, or Mineral', in which a panel of experts was invited to identify objects of interest. One of these was shown to the audience and described to them as 'a flint knife made by a flint jack', that is to say a fake. When Sir Mortimer Wheeler came to it, he turned it round in his hands and then, without so much as a glance, judged it to be modern work on the evidence of touch alone.

A great deal of expert judgment depends on handling objects: it is not just the feel of the surface, but also the weight and, for tools and weapons particularly, the balance. Most things in a museum are, for good reason, kept out of the hands of visitors, but the objects we find may be handled and fully examined: in them the ring of glass, the absence of smell from ancient peat, the saltiness of a stone from the sea shore will exercise our senses of hearing, smelling and tasting: and that elusive sixth sense will from time to time add itself to complete our judgment. This sixth sense is compounded of experience, devotion to the subject, and something more. An archaeologist may know the exact place on a site to excavate without being able to explain exactly why; the assistant in a good shop can distinguish real from artificial tortoiseshell without fail, but he knows of no test available to our normal five senses.

Only some of us may have a sixth sense, but surely we can all savour the romance in things found. A gardener drove a pointed iron bar into the lawn to prepare it for a post, and when he brought it up there was a gold signet ring around the point which had been lost by the grandfather of the owner of the house many years before. This was a case of a re-discovery restored to where it belonged, but not all valuable things lost are returned providentially to the owner or his descendants. Recently another gold ring was found in a medieval privy, and I wondered if the reputation of some unfortunate servant all those years ago was also lost, unfairly. There is a display of ancient keys in Salisbury Museum, dredged from the mud in the street channels of the city when they were cleared out and filled in last century. Keys being what they are, and pockets few in the old days, almost every one must have been not only a lost key but a lost temper too. But the most eloquent 'thing found' that I know was a severed hand and a single playing card, an ace, walled up behind the panelling of an inn parlour.

No need to speculate about that: the fraudulent fifth ace and the hand that dealt it lay there together.

The second and fourth sections of this book are for reference when something is found. The section on materials is an historical review of the processes applied to the materials used in durable artefacts: much can be learnt from the material of an object and the way it has been worked. 'Things Found' is a brief encyclopedia of those objects within our terms of definition: it will usually be possible to give a name to the thing found, whether it be a nail or a doll's head or whatever, as well as to say broadly of what it is made.

The Maoris of New Zealand have a saying '*ahakoa iti, he pounamu*' ('although it is little, it is of jade'), and Marlowe's 'infinite riches in a little room' conveys the same thought. Let us accept those things which, although little and commonplace, and often damaged, yet have riches in them to be discovered.

The Rules of the Game

The first rule is not legal, but moral: don't touch anything which from its position may have some archaeological value. This at once precludes us from digging in, or removing surface finds from, archaeological sites. Carried to its logical conclusion, this rule would forbid any collecting at all, for who is to say what place is not an archaeological site? I do not propose, however, to be absurdly logical, and if I find a flint scraper while walking the downs, or a Georgian penny while digging my garden, I will keep it, and invite you to do likewise. What to take and what to resist taking will be, in some cases, a matter of judgment which will develop with knowledge and experience. One of my favourite finds is a chip of bluestone taken one day in 1953 from the earth at Stonehenge under the place where Stone 58 had long lain before being lifted upright again, a few minutes before, by a giant crane. The archaeologist in charge of the restoration work was standing nearby, and I asked his permission before picking up the chip. On cleaning it at home, I was delighted to find a flat and weathered surface on one side only, evidence that the chip had come from a stone which had been part of some monument. It is known that there is a layer under Stonehenge with plenty of bluestone fragments in it, so the removal of one of them was of no significance.

Before considering the law of the land, let me mention the metal detector, illegitimate offspring of the soldier's mine detector. The use of this bastard device should be illegal except by special licence, for it can be damaging to buried structures and other non-metallic things in the ground when something of metal is retrieved by it. Moreover, because the metal detector is 'blind' to non-metallic objects, any survey done with it will be defective, like a picture seen by a colour-blind person. The detector may have its uses in straight treasure hunting, such as the search for a chestful of Spanish doubloons left by a pirate on a desert island, but it has no place in the gentle art we are considering.

So we come to legal matters, and first let's deal with the simple case of something which belongs to the finder because it was found on his own property. Obviously no problem here, but note that should you have a scheduled Ancient Monument on your land, neither you nor anyone else may disturb it or take from it without the permission of the Royal Commission on Historical Monuments, which does not grant such permission lightly.

Anything on publicly owned land, or on private land that doesn't belong to you, cannot be taken if it possesses 'economic value' and thus qualifies as a 'corporeal chattel'. You may say that even a chip of flint or a discarded medicine bottle has some worth, but if you think that the owner would not object to your taking and keeping a find of marginal value, you are not committing an offence. Beware, however, of deceiving yourself, or you may have to answer some very awkward questions in court. Money, jewellery or other valuables must be taken to a police station. If the owner doesn't claim them within a few months, the police will usually give them to you. I remember a steward who swept up a diamond ring after a dance aboard ship, and declared it. Six months later it was his, but I always wondered why the wearer of the ring never turned up.

Above the level of single diamond rings we come to treasure trove, defined as 'money, coin, gold, silver, plate or bullion' found hidden in the earth or other private place. The operative word is 'hidden', that is with the intention of eventual recovery, and the law requires an inquest to be held by a coroner to try and find the owner, failing which the treasure belongs to the Crown. In practice, unclaimed treasure trove is sent to the British Museum, and the Trustees will normally compensate the finder. But if you do not declare the treasure trove and this is found out, it will be confiscated without compensation. The definition of treasure trove includes all money, even paper money, but other precious things only if they contain silver or gold. Note that things deposited in the ground to accompany the dead or for other ritual purposes are not treasure trove, but belong to the owner of the land, just as do things casually lost or discarded in the past.

Finally a word about trespass in the sense of 'entry on land in the possession of another without lawful authority'. The person in possession of the land is he who has the use of it, as owner or lawful tenant, and he has the right to eject the trespasser, if necessary 'laying gentle hands upon him'. He may sue him for trespass too. If the trespasser causes actual damage to the property, the owner may also bring an action against him on that account, but the common belief that a trespasser cannot be sued by anyone unless he creates damage is false. Not so long ago it was the general custom for farmers to allow all and sundry to enter on their land, but with the increase in population, and easier access to the countryside by private car, this is no longer so. Public rights of way are now required by law to be indicated by signs, and it is advisable to keep to the path unless you have obtained permission to leave it. Under all circumstances, gates must be left as you find them, either open or shut, and you must keep off growing crops. As to fierce beasts, you may reasonably expect not to be confronted by them when you are on a right of way, but if you stray elsewhere it is at your own risk.

Let's now suppose that you have some object that you have obtained with a clear conscience. This book and other sources of information should help you to identify, label and retain it. If, however, you think it may be of more than passing interest, or if you want further information or a second opinion about it, then the professional staff of museums are very willing to give advice on things found by the public. The first responsibility of a museum curator is towards his museum's own collections, so you may have to be patient, and when you do get his advice it will not include valuation. Your find may be of great interest but of no monetary value; or worth a fortune but of no interest whatever to the museum. In any case, museum staff are not valuers.

Most countries have museums with general collections, usually in large towns, and some of these specialise in the natural history, industry and antiquities of the locality. In addition, there are highly specialised museums, either in capital cities, such as, for instance, the Wellcome Museum of Medical Science in London, or in areas of particular interest, such as the Black Country Museum in Dudley, a town in the industrial midlands of England. There are also the great national museums, such as the Metropolitan Museum in New York or the Louvre in Paris. You will probably find it most convenient and best to start with a local, general museum, and only in exceptional cases will you need to go further. The usual procedure is to take your find to the entrance counter, where you will be asked to fill in a form giving your name and address, saying where the find comes from, and when you intend to come and collect it. The attendant will advise you how long the find should be left, and when you return to recover your property you will be told the verdict of the museum staff. Exceptionally you may be invited to donate the object to the museum, or told to seek further advice at some specialist museum. This quite often happens in the case of ethnographical things, that is to say artefacts from outside the main Western and Eastern world cultures. Whatever the outcome, you should keep the object, with the information given, for a few months at least, just in case the museum needs to see it again. In one case a coin was brought to a curator, himself a considerable numismatist, and he took a great deal of interest in it and wrote detailed notes for the owner. A few months later a similar coin turned up, but by then the curator had died and the owner of the first coin had thrown away the report. So knowledge was lost, something just as bad if not worse than if the coin itself had disappeared. This cautionary tale leads to the final rule: keep your finds and the information you gather concerning them referenced together and intact.

Style and Sequence

The word 'style' is used here to mean the certain sameness in expression and proportions that things made in the same place or at the same time tend to have. Style is easier to recognise than to explain, but an obvious example is the 'rococo', with its swirling asymmetric waves, which flourished in Europe from 1730 to 1760 and has been revived since but with little of its original vigour. Every style has a reason for it, though it is seldom so well defined as the rococo, which originated at the court of the gay young Louis XV and his mistresses as a feminine reaction to the ponderous formality of the previous reign.

The rococo style is clear-cut in appearance, and the style of the Renaissance is astonishingly clear-cut in time. From its origins in Florence during the early years of the fifteenth century it spread through Europe and carried away the gothic style completely. Compare the two pieces of silver shown: both of them were made in

7 *Gothic salt-cellar*

5 *Rococo bookplate*

6 *Renaissance salt-cellar*

London and there is only fifty years between them, but one belongs to the old pious medieval world and the other to a new generation which saw the virtues of humanism reflected in the art of classical Rome.

As a general rule, the more materially developed a society becomes, the more closely defined will be the style its members prefer, and the more the style will permeate and affect architecture, furniture, clothing, pottery and everything else. It is to many people a depressing aspect of the culture of Imperial Rome that, from Uriconium in the north of England to Palmyra in Syria, a fine, uniform, impressive but uninspired architecture proclaimed the worldly success of Rome. But the effect of these ruins, associated in the minds of Western people with departed grandeur and glory, was to stimulate revivals of classical style from the first renaissance in the fifteenth century onwards.

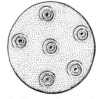

8 *Saxon disc*

9 *Date unkno*

In contrast to the regular and uniform style of Rome, consider the cave paintings at Lascaux. Here in the Old Stone Age men drew realistic animals being hunted by men who are shown in a different style, like the 'matchstick' men children draw. Moreover the groups are unrelated, so that one scene is painted over another. Clearly these primitive people were not concerned with a scheme of decoration: they were probably inspired by the belief that in painting the death of their quarry they would bring about the actual event.

Roman architecture and cave paintings are not 'things found', but they illustrate the rule of civilised regularity compared to barbaric abandon as in the two copper alloy discs of about the same dimensions shown; one of them was found in a Saxon grave and securely dated thereby, the other was a surface find. The decoration of both is scribed and punched, but is the second disc Saxon? Most unlikely, because the scribed circles and punched diamonds are altogether too exactly placed. Of course, like all good rules there are exceptions; for example, see the plan of Fyrkat, in Denmark, where there existed in Viking times four buildings within an earthwork. The plan is of an extreme regularity, a most surprising thing to find on any medieval site. We can, at least for the moment, only suppose that it was the design of some individual of great strength of will, whose ideas of strict rectitude may also be seen in an exactly straight section of the Dannevirke, the defensive wall across the southern end of Jutland. I use the word rectitude to suggest not the ability to survey or scribe straight lines and true circles, but the wish to do so. When Bishop Poore laid out his new city of Salisbury in the early thirteenth century, he did so with streets running north and south, crossing others running east and west, to form a chequer pattern. His surveyors could surely have laid out the streets exactly straight if they had wished to do so, for his cathedral has a properly squared plan, but they preferred to let the lines wander a little. We have cause to thank them to this day, as we see the house façades gently and restfully curving away in the distance, unlike the stark straight canyons of down-town Melbourne.

Roman brooches of the same period, like Roman buildings, are remarkably similar wherever found. By contrast, although brooches of the safety-pin type continued to be used extensively in Europe during the Dark Ages, they vary in style locally. Here we have the re-assertion of local styles after a period in which they were overlaid by more powerful influences. People have a strong tendency to retain their individuality in their artefacts down to the simplest things, so that we can say of a door handle 'that looks French' or of a drinking glass 'surely that is Scandinavian'. But the belief that there is an ideal sequence for any style, from the primitive through its fully developed prime to decline and extinction, is no longer the article of faith that it used to be. Recent discoveries in natural history have indicated

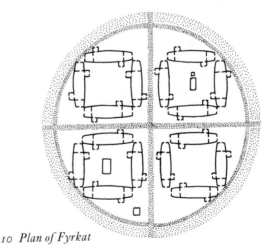

10 Plan of Fyrkat

otherwise; for instance, the flying rudder of the ptero-dactyl was situated on the back of its head so that it always flew the way it looked, and was superior from the flying safety point of view, and probably the aerodynamic also, to the tail rudder of the bird developed later, and its derivative the aircraft rudder. Most progressions in time, and that of styles are no exception, may be seen as a series of ups and downs, of improvements and fallings off, that are related to natural circumstances, political and social history, to technical invention and perhaps to influences outside our knowledge. A simple case is the thin impracticable silver table-ware made in Britain around 1815, after many years of impoverishing warfare against France. Within a few years the country revived, and silver spoons again became as substantial as in the middle of the previous century, though perhaps not so elegant.

A larger and much more complex question is how and why artefacts from the nineteenth century, no matter where they were made, have a common air of fuss and strain as distinct from the relaxed and satisfied appearance of most things from the eighteenth century, whether French or Chinese, Polynesian or African. Some astrologers would say that the universal influence of the stars is the cause, and so it may be. As the century progressed, patterns tended to be ever more close-textured, as shown in the head of the silver paper-knife which dates from 1885, until the inevitable collapse, around 1900, into that free expression of plant forms which came to be called 'art nouveau'. The crowded character of late nineteenth-century design is found in the academy paintings of the times, of which it was said 'every picture tells a story': here the threadbare carpet or the silver on the sideboard each had their significance. Even poetry was not outside the fashion, as may be seen from the works of Lord Tennyson or Rossetti with their spate of material allusions.

The nineteenth century saw the triumph of industrialisation in the western world: machines allowed endless repetition of intricate designs, and individual good taste and craftsmanship were rare. In other times, however, when the pace of life is less hectic and circumstances such that designers and makers of useful and decorative articles are able to make a good living without too much effort, they will tend to produce work of good

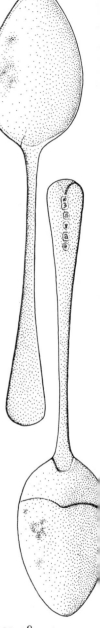

11 *1815 spoon*

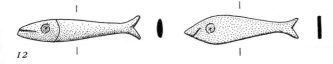

12

form and quality, and this was generally so before the Industrial Revolution. Compare the two bone counters shown: on the basis of superior form and workmanship it is safe to place the carefully made, well polished counter of superior material as from the eighteenth century, while the other is from the nineteenth. It is known from their history that both are at least ninety years old. A more subtle difference appears between the glass-cutting workmanship of the drinking glass and the toilet water bottle shown. The eighteenth-century glass has a well designed, nicely cut leaf pattern on it; the nineteenth-century bottle has perfunctory and meaningless slashes on its shoulder. The technique of grinding and polishing would have been the same in both cases, but one cutter worked with pride and care, the other did not.

*13 Silver paper-
knife*

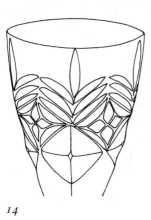

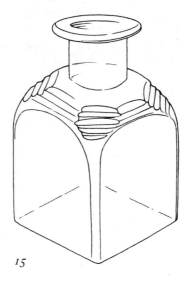

14   *15*

The early years of this century are now distant enough to be coming into focus for a study of their styles and fashions. In the western world, life was overshadowed by the prospect of a disastrous war, and somehow this gave a flimsy air to many things, from filigree silver to spindly furniture, as though they were made only to last a short time in contrast to the confident solidity of former years. The particular style of the 1900s was inspired by plant forms; it has been named Art Nouveau and extensively studied. More recently we have come to recognise the succeeding style, that of the years between the World Wars. Its sparse, abstract and often jagged designs have been dubbed Art Deco. An example is the monogram on a silver ladle bought second-hand twenty years ago; it seemed to have no interest at that time and I was intending to have it erased. Now in the 1970s Art Deco is appreciated and the monogram will remain.

16

We sometimes speak of 'fashion' in reference to clothes, and indeed other things tend to follow their styles. For instance, the fat 'cup and cover' on the legs of late sixteenth-century English tables echoes the padded breeches worn by gentlemen of fashion in those days. We will not be directly concerned with tables and breeches, but the outline of a candlestick may suggest its own date by reminding you of a contemporary form in clothing. Not only date but nationality too may be indicated by an outline. For some reason the people of North America like long and low proportions: an eighteenth-century settee from the United States and a large mid-twentieth-century automobile have the same drawn-out look, and so did a Baltimore clipper.

17 Neolithic mace

Things made by or for women tend to be small. Pots thrown on the slow wheel bear the marks of their small fingers; Chinese snuff bottles made for courtly ladies were of suitably reduced size; and the Neolithic mace shown, only three inches long, was surely intended to be supported on an elegant rod by a woman of queenly rank. The Roman glass bottle, its dimpled sides convenient for delicate fingers and its flared mouth against which excess liquid could be returned from a brush, has the appearance of being for some cosmetic in an ancient beauty box.

18 Roman bottle

It would be commonplace to point out the obvious difference between the 'stout ashplant' used by the countryman as a walking stick and the elegant cane of the dandified city dweller. But now go further and consider a recent improvement in the stick of a blind person: formerly he tapped his way with the aid of a rough, short, cheap stick converted to his use by a lick of white paint; now he wields a long white wand specially made for him. Not only is this a practical improvement but also a great boost to his morale. Indeed sighted people, on seeing a blind person feeling his way around with speed and confidence, might well speculate how much better able he would be to take the lead in the dark. The style of the blind man's wand has been consciously, deliberately imposed for a set purpose, unlike most styles, which are derived from current taste and fashion.

Let us now consider the relations between art historians and archaeologists, both of whom are concerned with the style and dating of artefacts. Art historians tend to agree with Dr Johnson that 'a mere antiquarian is a rugged being', and archaeologists suspect art historians of using their imaginations too freely. Both seek to analyse the past from the works of man left to us, but owing to imperfections in the two disciplines they sometimes give different answers to the same question and fall to quarrelling. It is not so long ago that archaeologists dated the sarsen structures at Stonehenge to the Wessex Culture, coexistent with the Minoan civilisation, and parallels of art and style were suggested between the two. Then revised Carbon 14 datings put the whole Stonehenge sequence back five hundred years, leaving these theories suddenly discredited. Such setbacks are unavoidable in the field of prehistory, but happily the art and archaeology of China, a country with a strong literary tradition over thousands of years, have a more harmonious relationship. There the findings of archaeology are supported and confirmed by the copious literature on most subjects, including descriptions of technical processes used in remote past ages.

So much for style as an aid in placing an object in time. Admitted to be a broad and fallible method, it can establish a reasonable sequence and often a country of origin. Archaeologists can support or contradict theories based on style from the report of the excavation of the find, if available, and from scientific tests upon it. In our study of things found we will not have the resources of a library containing learned books and periodicals, nor access to expensive sophisticated processes of dating such as Carbon 14 or Thermoluminescence, but our objects contain information to be read by the five senses. Technical considerations will be discussed in the next section: here we will deal with inscriptions.

The easiest thing to place with accuracy is a coin. Almost all those we are likely to encounter will be clearly marked with the date of striking and enough information to establish the country of origin. Next in order of simplicity come British silver and gold, which from the Middle Ages have been 'hallmarked', that is to say every piece made in this country has been and still is required by law to be submitted to the 'hall' of an Assay Office, there to be tested for purity of metal and marked with a series of punches if found satisfactory. These marks are usually in the following order:

1. First the Assay Office mark of origin. Here are the more common ones:

Assay Office	Mark	From
London	Leopard's head	Late 14th century
Edinburgh	Castle with three towers	1552
Dublin	Crowned harp	1638
Sheffield	Crown	1773
Birmingham	Anchor	1773

The offices at Sheffield and Birmingham were instituted to assay silverware, much of it small and largely machine-made, when it started to flow from those rapidly expanding industrial cities. It aids the memory to recall that, according to legend, the silversmiths from the two towns met at an inn called the Crown and Anchor to decide upon their marks, and shared the inn sign between them.

2. Next the assay mark. That of a lion passant (striding along, looking at you, with one front paw raised) has been used on English silver since 1544 to signify that the piece is 'sterling', that is, 92.5 per cent silver. Between 1696 and 1720 the figure of Britannia was used instead, to indicate a compulsorily higher standard of 95.8 per cent. This was imposed to prevent the silver coinage, which remained at 92.5 per cent, being melted down and

made into silverware during a current shortage of the raw material. In 1720 the legal standard reverted to sterling, but since then silverware of Britannia standard has sometimes been made, and marked with her figure. Edinburgh uses a thistle as an assay mark, and Dublin the figure of Hibernia, like but not to be confused with Britannia. Hibernia has a harp by her; Britannia a shield.

3. The exact year of any piece of British gold or silver is shown by a date letter, which can be looked up in reference books, or in a useful little booklet called *British and Irish Silver Assay Office Marks*, published by J. W. Northend Ltd, West Street, Sheffield. If you are without a reference book, here are two good tips: the leopard's head is crowned up to 1820, bare-headed later; and a 'duty mark' of the sovereign's head, clearly distinguishable as either that of a Georgian gentleman or a Victorian young lady, is stamped on British silver from 1784 to 1890. So if you see a crowned leopard's head together with a man's head, you can say at once 'it is London made, and late Georgian', which indeed a great deal of commonly met silver is.

4. The remaining mark on British silver, of lettering normally, is that of the maker, and it is seldom of interest except to a specialist on the subject.

Much foreign silver is marked with three figures, such as '900', which indicate the purity expressed as the number of parts in one thousand.

Heraldic inscriptions are often made on gold and silver, less commonly on other materials, and of course can be an aid to identification and dating.

Heraldic colours, called 'tinctures', are shown conventionally when inscribed on gold, silver, book plates etc., as follows:

GOLD (OR)   SILVER (ARGENT)   RED (GULES)

BLUE (AZURE)   BLACK (SABLE)

Heraldry is a wide subject, so here just let me recommend the standard works in which you can learn to trace the previous owner of the achievements adorning things found:

Papworth's *Ordinary of Arms* . . . to identify a coat of arms.

Berry's *Dictionary of Heraldry* . . . to find the coat of arms of a person or family.

Fairbairn's *Crests* . . . both purposes for crests.

The Royal Arms of Britain have varied throughout the years, and can therefore be helpful in dating. Sometimes the arms are shown out of unalloyed patriotism, but since 1911 Royal Warrant holders have been permitted to display the Royal Arms on their goods and trade cards. For many centuries the Lion and the Unicorn have, unaltered, maintained their support of the shield, but the 'quartering' of the shield itself is significant and reflects the descent of kingship as shown.

The British royal crown, as depicted, for instance, on the buttons and badges worn by soldiers, sailors and other 'Crown servants', differs according to whether the reigning sovereign is a king or a queen. Note that Queen Victoria reigned from 1837 to 1901, and Queen Elizabeth II ascended the throne in 1952.

Coronets also appear, inscribed on silver, painted on coaches or elsewhere, over the crest or monogram of titled persons. Fig. 22 distinguishes the ranks of the British nobility: if a coronet not pictured here is seen, or a crown other than those shown, it is a foreign one or merely decorative.

From the year 1842 all articles of British manufacture, including ceramics, metal, textiles and glass, could be registered at the Patent Office in London and granted a mark to protect them against imitation. The diamond mark system (Fig. 20) lasted to 1883, after which date a number, usually of six figures, will be found preceded by the letters 'Rd. No.'. The Public Record Office (Kew branch) has information enabling registrations to be traced, and search may be made there on application. Things found often have registration numbers on them from which interesting information may be gained.

The registration of an article gives limited protection to its design: much greater security can be obtained by a patent, but this is only granted to a new invention if it is agreed to be such by the Patent Office.

To trace an early British patent, consult the *Alphabetical Index of Patentees of Inventions 1617 to 1852* by Bennet Woodcraft (reprinted by Evelyn Adams and Mackay in 1969). For a patent after 1852 you may need to visit the Patent Office to consult the original records. The address is The National Reference Library of

17th-century

1707–1714

1714–1801
19 *Royal Arms*

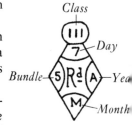

20

Science and Invention (Holborn Division), 25 South-ampton Buildings, London WC2A 1AY. A number of large reference libraries outside London have the official publications of the Patent Office, and it is worth making enquiries locally before coming to London.

It is useful to know that up to 1916 British patent numbers started afresh each year, for example 334/87; then from 1916 patents are numbered consecutively from 100,000. Patents lapse after about twenty years but may continue to be quoted on the product, for prestige. The bottle of 'Cephalic Snuff', a medicine, was patented in 1776, and the patent number is shown on the side not illustrated.

21

If you can see the name, address, or mark of the manufacturer or retailer on a thing found, you should be able to track down information concerning him. Pottery is quite commonly marked, usually on the base, and the standard reference work is Chaffers' *Marks and Monograms on European and Oriental Pottery and Porcelain*, now a scarce and expensive book since its latest edition in 1946; however copies can be consulted in public libraries.

Drinking glasses are seldom marked, but glass bottles and jars made during the last century or so are found cast with the maker's mark, but seldom the full name, on the base.

Small metal objects, notably toys, are cast or stamped with the maker's name.

Once a maker's name is known, the years during which he was in business can be found from trade directories. Among them, *Kelly's Directory* has been produced yearly for two centuries, with separate volumes for principal cities and groups of counties. Large public libraries should have a long run of their local volumes, in which the first and last appearance of a maker's name can, with sufficient time and patience, be found. Much the same applies to retailers, whose names

appear in particular on containers for food and medicine, but here the books to study are the local Post
Office directories, a run of which, with any luck, may be
found in a library not far from where the retailer's name
turned up.

Changes in currency, in weights and in measures,
may be recorded on things found, thus adding to their
interest. Even quite recent happenings, such as the
alteration from shillings and pence to new pence in
Britain, can be significant, and will become more so.
Books priced in the old currency are already being
collected for their 'antique' value. As to weights and
measures, this book is written in the throes of metrication, which will in time establish a latest date for
anything marked under the old system. Meanwhile the
last significant change in Britain was the alteration from
the old gallon associated with the late fifteenth-century
Winchester bushel, to 'Imperial' measure in 1829, so
that a gallon of water was to weigh exactly ten pounds.
All measures of capacity had to be calibrated anew, or
replaced, so that for a number of years after 1829 we find
for instance the words 'Imperial Pint' stamped on pewter tankards. The U.S.A. did not follow the British
move, so the American gallon remains a little smaller
than the British. Personal inscriptions are usually informative only by their style, but around the eighteenth
century the initials of a married couple are to be found
on possessions of theirs, be it a house, a piece of furniture or of silver, placed in a triangle which, once the
convention is understood, can be helpful.

We now come to the form and style of letters and
figures, a subject distinct from the information con-
veyed by words and numbers.

My interest in lettering was first aroused in Beirut, in
the days when it was undeveloped as a holiday resort and
happily also unshattered by civil war. What it did have
was a fine museum. In this and also about the city were
to be seen antiquities of the familiar 'provincial Roman'
style. There was a first century A.D. inscription to
Berenice: stout letters clean cut in white marble, striding
round the inside of a dome. Very different was the
lettering in a nearby cemetery on tombstones of the sixth
century, when Syria lay between the contending great
powers of the Byzantine and Persian empires: here the
lettering had become thin, the cutting uncertain and

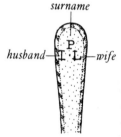

24 *Owners' initials*

wobbly, for all the world as though the letters themselves were surrounded, poor, and without confidence.
Far away in Britain, a single bronze letter 'A' in similar
style came from Cadbury Castle, a hill fort in Dorset
believed to have been a stronghold of the British in the
same perilous times, when the Roman Legions had left
Britannia to her own defences.

So lettering can indicate an emotional state; it can also
suggest a lack of emotion, as in the marking on a piece of
cloth somehow retained from a war-time gas mask.
The 'dead pan' effect of the letters come from lines of
equal thickness, with no effort towards graceful proportions, and quite unadorned. The notice reading
'Bristol Crematorium' outside the cemetery of that city
has the same character, as though to say 'read me only if
you must'.

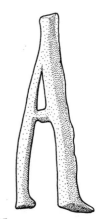

25

The emotion expressed by lettering on things found
may be significant: for instance, compare the inscription
moulded into a medicine bottle from an infirmary with
the style on a patent medicine bottle (Figs 154, 21).

There are two basic methods of applying letters or
numbers to materials: they may be drawn in contrasting
colour by pen, brush or spray; or they may be formed in
or on the material itself by stamping, raising, moulding,
engraving, or by attaching letters made separately. If the
letters are raised above the surface as in printing, or sunk
below it as in engraving, they may be inked and the
impression transferred to another surface. The letters
formed by pens, brushes and engraving tools tend to be
rounded and cursive; those cut by the chisel will be
composed mainly of straight lines, and the letters separate. The ancient Middle Eastern form of writing
known as cuneiform is typical of chiselling, being entirely made up of cone-shaped depressions, and the little
tail on some of our lettering, known as a serif, originated
as a neat way of ending a line chiselled in stone. Founts
of type are cast from letters first cut in steel dies, so
printing follows the work of the chisel rather than the
pen. On the other hand the engraver, when he works
with tools which scoop out a sweeping line of varying
thickness, will form letters similar to those made by the
pen.

The work of the engraver on metal may stand by
itself, as on an inscribed piece of silver, or it may be inked
and printed on paper. During the eighteenth century the

27 *19th-century wheel engraving*

26

title pages of books and the trade cards of merchants were elegantly engraved, and visiting cards are still printed in 'copperplate' style. One further step was taken in the middle of the eighteenth century, when engravings were printed on absorbent paper in enamel colours and transferred to the glazed surface of pottery.

Engraving can be done on glass with a point of diamond or steel, or with a revolving wheel of stone or metal. 'Diamond-point' engraving was a speciality of the Venetians, and is only seen on some rare early English glasses in the Venetian style. The Dutch used this technique for calligraphic inscriptions early in the eighteenth century. Such engraved glass as we are likely to find, however, will be English or Irish, of the eighteenth or early nineteenth century, done by the wheel on the strong lead glass of that time with the steel tools which were then available. The example shown is typical: the style of lettering in wheel engraving follows that of printing rather than writing.

28 *Calligraphic inscription*

Turning to consider styles of writing in relation to time, examples will be more helpful than detailed explanation:

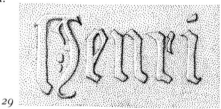

29

Fig. 29 'Black letter' inscription cast on a bronze vessel of the late fifteenth century. In the next hundred years this style gave way to our familiar Roman lettering except in Germany, where it persisted until quite recently.

Figs 30 and 31. Two late-seventeenth-century inscriptions, one in silver and the other on stone. Notice the loose and florid character, also found in printed books of the period.

William Areley 1681

30

31

Figs 32 and 33. During the course of the eighteenth century, inscriptions became increasingly elegant.

God blefs Queen Ann

32

Robᵗ Gomery 1759

33

Fig. 34 is a dedication painted in enamel colours on a jug. The 'eclectic' manner, combining several styles of writing, is typical of the middle of the nineteenth century.

James & Sarah Gordon Was Married 1844.

34

As to numbers, Fig. 35 shows figures from a clock face of about 1740. Notice the squashed appearance, especially the '5', which looks as though it had been written then pressed down. Numbers have this air from the seventeenth century through to the middle of the eighteenth, when they became tall and elegant (Fig. 33).

Fig. 36 shows the date aperture on the same clock face; the stylised wreath surrounding it is very typical of the early eighteenth century.

0123456

35

36

Materials

Manufacture and After

In this chapter we will be considering in general terms the composition, manufacturing processes and subsequent history of the things we find. The following chapters will deal with particular materials, so that having decided that something is of wood, or metal, or whatever, we then examine it and comment more closely.

Composition. Let's admit at the start that often it's not possible to identify the composition of a manufactured object, other than to distinguish it simply as wood or metal or whatever, without the facilities of a specialist laboratory. For example, it takes a microscope and an expert eye at the Jodrell Laboratory in Kew Gardens to say with certainty the species of tree from which a given piece of wood was cut. Again, although a large weathered piece of wrought iron, for example part of the framing of an old tilt hammer, can be identified by its exposed grain, smaller pieces cannot be distinguished from steel by our unaided senses.

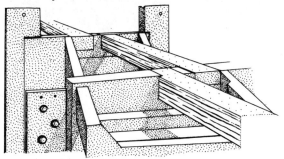

37 Wrought iron

Manufacturing processes. These start with the raw materials and end with the finished article in its pristine state. From the new and lively subject of Industrial Archaeology we are learning more and more each year, but much remains to be discovered by the study of old industrial sites. Also, the scientific examination of old artefacts is teaching us that our ancestors, without reading the dials of instruments, could make sophisticated materials such as high carbon steel for weapons.

The making of pottery and glass will be left to subsequent chapters, but the processes applied in general to metals are considered here in order to avoid repetition when dealing with particular metals later. In brief, metals can be cast by pouring into a mould; they can be shaped by forging with hammer blows when either hot or cold; they can be rolled into plates or bars, drawn into wire, stamped into coins or spun into thin-walled vessels. They can be cut, filed and polished. Some can be welded by heat and pressure, or electrically. They can

38 *Piece mould*

40

39 *Turkish brass bell*

also be joined by soldering or brazing, that is by running another metal between them. All these processes will leave evidence for our information.

Casting. At first castings were made in open moulds of stone hollowed out to the required form, but one side was simply the flat surface of the liquid metal. Such things as daggers, axes and chisels could be made in open moulds, and they long continued in use for the casting of small ornaments. Two improvements, however, were made in the course of the Bronze Age; first a two-piece mould was invented in which objects shaped on both sides could be cast; then the core and print was devised, which allowed simple hollow objects to be cast.

Moulds continued to be made of stone or metal until the second millennium B.C., when the two processes of sand-casting and lost-wax casting were developed.

For sand-casting, a pattern of some durable material, usually wood, is embedded in sand in such a manner that it can be removed and metal poured into the mould to take its shape. The drawing shows the elements of this process, which has the advantage of being repeatable, using the same pattern again. The alternative process is by 'lost wax', which is the preferred method for works of art, whereas piece moulds are suitable for a run of industrial products. First a full size core, known to sculptors as the 'anima', or soul, is built up and baked hard. It shrinks uniformly, and is then restored to its original size by a coating of wax upon which the artist will then add such detail as he chooses. He is not restricted by the pattern having to be designed for withdrawal from the mould. Fireclay is now applied over the wax, and this so-called 'camisia' (the clothing) is pinned through to the anima, thus uniting them. Holes for the pouring of metal and the escape of gases, known as runners and risers, are made in the camisia. The assembly is now inverted and baked, thus running out the wax and hardening the camisia. It is now ready to be placed right side up in a pit and filled with molten metal.

If castings by the two processes were left as they came from the mould, it would be easy to distinguish them by the 'flash' along the parting line of the piece mould, and by the ends of the wires on the lost-wax casting. Unfortunately for us castings are carefully finished so as to eliminate these tell-tale features. All the same it is sometimes possible to find a corner where a seam has been allowed to remain on pieces not of the best quality, such as the small Turkish souvenir bell shown. Fine castings, on the contrary, are not only cleaned up but detail is added by engraving. Ancient Chinese bronzes were of excellent finish, and until recently it was assumed that they were made by lost wax. Now patterns have been found proving that they were cast from piece moulds. Many lost-wax castings, however, do declare themselves by their complexity and a softness of outline that comes through from the wax modelling. The figure of the Chinese lion from the cover of a censer must surely have first been formed in wax. To compare the two processes

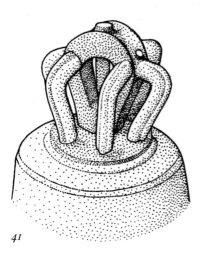

41

42 *Injection moulding*

together, examine a bell of the larger sort found in belfries. The body was shaped in clay by rotating a contoured board round a post. The mould for the loops at the top was made by lost wax, and this so-called 'canon' plugged into the top of the bell like a cork in a bottle. The slack appearance of the canon contrasts with the strict curves of the bell itself. An additional point of interest on a church bell is that the scars left by runners and risers on the crown of the canon can be seen. It is to be supposed that they were not worth the trouble of cleaning off, being hidden by the trunnion when the bell was slung in place.

The casting of metal by injection while fluid into a die was developed late in the nineteenth century for the setting up of print. Injection moulding was greatly improved during the Second World War for the mass production of such things as bomb fuzes, with their delay and booby trap mechanisms. The fully automatic injection of metal at high pressure produced large numbers of complex small castings with fine detail. After the war injection moulding was used for toys, greatly to the benefit of children interested in model cars, cranes, tanks and so on. A flash line and a small circle left by the runner remain to identify injection mouldings. The process known as electro-typing is another child of the printing industry, and was first shown at the 1851 Industrial Exhibition. An object requiring to be copied, such as a plate of type or a gold medal, is dusted with blacklead to improve conductivity, then copper is deposited on it by electrolysis. The thin shell of deposited metal is removed, backed with a lead-tin alloy, and the surface gilded or otherwise finished as required.

Forging. This is chiefly associated with iron and steel. Alloys of copper can be forged, but this had no advantage once the metallurgy of iron was understood, except for special circumstances such as tools for gunpowder mills and magazines, where struck sparks must be excluded. The forging of aluminium was developed during the First World War for aircraft engines, in which low weight is critical, and it is now also used for parts of fast cars.

Rolling, drawing and spinning. The early, tedious and inaccurate way to make metal sheet and wire was by hammering. Squeezing between rollers is easier, faster, and produces sheet of more constant thickness; likewise drawing wire through a plate is a great improvement upon hammering it out of forged bar. Small hand-operated rolls and draw-plates have been used by the goldsmith since ancient days, but the drawing of wire for general use dates from the tenth century, and the rolling of workaday metals was not undertaken until the seventeenth century, when it was done by water power in Germany. From then it was not lack of power which delayed the bulk production of rolled metal, but lack of rigid cast iron beds for large machine tools, and improved lathe tools to shape the rollers. Both these became available in Britain in the eighteenth century, when brass and iron were rolled into plates and bars of quality and quantity enough to supply a rapidly expanding industrial country. These dates are of interest, because the irregular thickness of hammered wire and sheet can be measured by the micrometer and sometimes even seen by the unaided eye. Rolled metals of normal thickness, say a millimeter, are constant within .002 millimetre, but if hammered they vary up to .01 millimetre.

The spinning of metal sheet into moulds was known to the Romans, and also used around the sixteenth century for making such things as large brass dishes for display rather than use. Until powerful machine tools were available, spun metal could not be made of thick enough sheet for practical use. In the U.S.A. around the year 1840, a process of industrial metal spinning was developed whereby circular discs of brass and copper, and in later years other metals, were spun in a lathe and pressed into shape against wooden formers. Spun vessels can be distinguished from those cast by their lightness, and from those hand-raised by circular marks on the side the tool was applied. Much modern copperware brought back from the Near East, or made in this country for decorative use, is lightly spun.

Stamping. The stamping of metal between dies has long been used for minting coins. In the late eighteenth century, it became a practical method for the mass production of such things as fittings for furniture and motifs of silver to be worked into silverware.

Chasing and repoussé. Relief patterns may be formed on metal sheet by hammers and punches without the removal of any material: this is known as chasing if worked from the face of the material, and repoussé if from the back. In either case the metal is supported from the opposite side, usually on a bed of pitch. Oriental beaten brass has been made all over Asia for centuries, and imitated in Europe for the last hundred years. The imitation work is stamped from dies or impressed from wheels, so that details of the design appear exactly repeated. This applies to even small defects in the die or wheel itself, as shown in the brass pattern below. Genuine oriental work will show small variations in a repeated element of the design. It has been well understood by craftsmen of different times that chasing on thin sheets of precious metal makes a passable imitation of solid gold and silver, particularly if the back is filled with some heavy and cheap material. Much late-eighteenth-century silver in the classical style is of thin chased metal, backed with pitch.

Engraving and etching. These are processes which remove metal, either by sharp tools which cut and scrape, or by acid which dissolves it. Both these processes were developed in the Renaissance for the decoration of ar-

43 Defective wheel-impressed pattern

mour, and spread to other metal surfaces. Engraved and etched copper plates are used for prints, and much silver plate is engraved with decorations or written inscriptions. A special machine tool called a rose-engine engraves a pattern of interlacing circles known as engine turning, and this is found on small objects of gold and silver, such as watch cases made since the early nineteenth century. It can be crudely copied by stamping, but then the ridges will be found blunt to the touch.

Inlaying. The inlaying of one metal by another is sometimes called damascening, but this term is best avoided as it is also used for a number of other techniques originating in the city of Damascus. Inlay is achieved either by roughening the surface of the ground metal and beating a thin sheet of the other metal on to it; or it can be done by engraving the surface, preferably with an under-cut, and hammering in wire or narrow strips of the other metal. The first way gives a mass effect, the second a line effect, and both may be found on the same object. If pieces of the inlay have become detached, the treatment given to the ground metal should be clearly visible. Like engraving and etching, the craft of inlaying metals was first practised by armourers, and was later used for trinkets and even for furniture. It remains an expensive minor art, not very likely to be encountered in things found. European armourers probably learnt the art of inlay from the East, where it has been practised for many centuries, notably by the Persians and the Japanese. The Japanese have been skilled for the last two centuries in applying shaped pieces of precious metal to their bronzes, giving a low relief effect. There is also a variant of inlay called niello, whereby a recessed pattern done by etching or engraving is filled with a composition of silver sulphide which is fused to give a black colour. Niello was known to the ancient Egyptians, and has been used by silversmiths of various nations and times since, in particular by Russians working for the Imperial Court in the last century or so before the Revolution. Finally the inlay of metals on wood, tortoiseshell, ivory and bone, which is known as piqué, should be mentioned. This originated in France and came to England with Huguenot craftsmen, to flourish here in the first half of the eighteenth century for the decoration of small boxes and the like.

After an object leaves its maker's hands it may suffer accidental damage, wear, corrosion, or some other form of attrition. It may be repaired 'in antiquity', as they say, or it may reach our hands still damaged and sometimes incomplete. There is a peculiar fascination in trying to identify the whole of an object from a surviving part. Fig. 44 shows a piece of bronze which, after lying in a museum collection for years, was recently identified as part of a medieval horse trapping. Here we have a simple case of fracture and separation; of greater interest can be the incomplete state of an object caused by some part of it having perished. For instance, in deposits of Saxon date, iron bars with looped ends have been found, and are believed by some people to be purse mounts and by others to be steels for use with strike-a-light flints. And there is a general difficulty in distinguishing the handles of cosmetic brushes, if they no longer have any trace of bristles, from needle cases. Both turn up in a feminine context, such as the burial of a woman or around a domestic hearth.

Many useful articles and some decorative ones, such as jewellery, become worn down during their active life. They may be further abraded after being discarded or lost, if they chance to lie in running water or on a beach. The action of a river or of waves is to roll an object about and to grind down all the exposed surface, removing surface detail, sometimes with curious results. This wear is arbitrary; the effects of wear in use are commonly of more interest. The grip of fingers will wear away the handle of a tool; boots and shoes will scuff depressions in the stretchers below furniture; and the purpose of the tool itself may cause it to wear away in use. Take for instance the paper knife shown. This is of Mauchline ware, a popular line in Scottish souvenirs, made in Ayrshire last century from local plane wood decorated in tartan designs. If you hold the knife as if to open an envelope, your thumb fits over an area of wear on the hilt, and there are other worn areas around the point and sides of the blade. It seems therefore to have been in use for opening letters over a considerable time. You may speculate, if you wish, as to why the owner treasured this cheap little souvenir so long. Incidentally, the wear also shows that the tartan pattern was applied by a transfer not by printed paper. This, and the shape of the knife, suggests a date around 1850 for its manufacture. Now

47 Paper knife

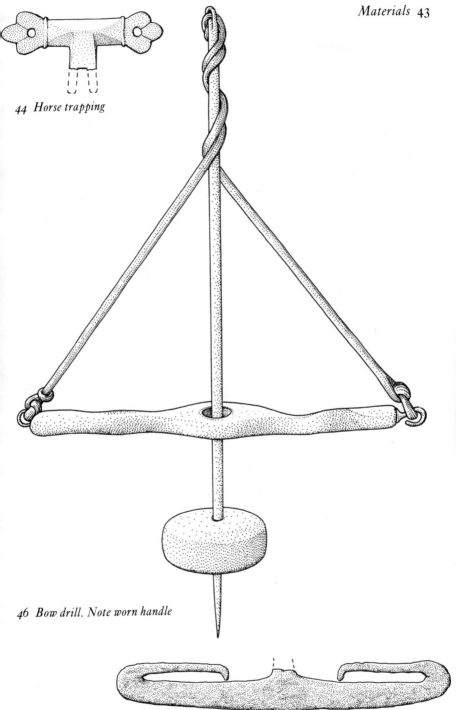

44 Horse trapping

46 Bow drill. Note worn handle

45 Purse mount or flint steel

look at the truncheon of a Victorian policeman. Notice how the paint has been worn off the end, presumably by constant prodding of members of the public, accompanied by the traditional advice to 'move along there, please'. The shaft of the truncheon, however, is in good condition, with sound paintwork, suggesting that it was little used as a cudgel. Thus worn objects may make personal or social comment.

The state of preservation of things found will vary with the surroundings in which they have lain since being lost or discarded. An impressive example of this was the Swedish battleship *Vasa*, which sank on her maiden voyage in the seventeenth century in fresh water, so that her timbers were not attacked by the dreaded ship-worm. The whole ship remained complete, though waterlogged, so that it could be lifted, and she is now in dry dock in Stockholm. To take another case: some time ago they were excavating in London on what had been the banks of the Fleet River, now long confined in a sewer; the soil has remained damp, and is free from the acids and oxygen which destroy metals. So an excavated Roman crane hook was picked up by a contractor's workman and used again for its original purpose, which it performed adequately after so many hundreds of idle years. Not only metal, but the soft parts of men and animals may be preserved under favourable circumstances. Tales of complete mammoths emerging from melting polar ice are well known, but less so is the story of a woolly rhinoceros, also a creature of the Ice Age, which had the misfortune to fall into a well of natural tar and was thus embalmed complete. On the contrary, if conditions are adverse, even bones may disappear from the earth without visible trace: it is still uncertain whether the rich funeral trappings in the ship found buried at Sutton Hoo in East Anglia surrounded the body of a king, or if the ship and its contents were his cenotaph.

On the general subject of metallic corrosion, two rules may be stated. First, a pure metal resists corrosion better than an alloy. Thus copper keeps better than bronze, and wrought iron better than steel. The depot ship in the naval base at Auckland, New Zealand, used to be an old warship, H.M.S. *Philomel*. Every three years she was docked and a prodigious quantity of mussels and seaweed scraped from her bottom, but underneath the metal

48 *Truncheon*

was sound as a bell, year after year – her plates were of wrought iron: the pure metal. The second rule is that if two metals are in contact and moist, an electric cell will be set up, resulting in severe corrosion of one metal and protection from corrosion of the other. The Roman steelyard weight shown was originally of lead cased with bronze, but the lead has completely changed to a white powdery oxide. Without the presence of bronze, it might have survived as metal. Another example is illustrated under the entry BELLS: there an iron suspension ring has protected the bronze bell. Which metal corrodes, and which is protected, depends on their relative 'nobility'. This term refers to the way in which metals are listed in descending order from gold, the most noble, to lead the least. Certain alloys are subject to corrosion between their constituent metals; thus brass can lose its zinc and turn to a friable copper. The electrolytic cause of corrosion is exploited in laboratories to change the products of corrosion back to the original metal, and can almost completely restore some objects in an advanced state of decay.

Between the extremes of perfect preservation and complete loss there is a wide range of deterioration suffered by things lost, thrown away, or otherwise uncared for until found by someone.

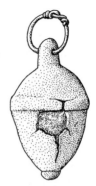

49 Steelyard weight

Copper and its Alloys

Nuggets of native copper found in the Near East were in very early times hammered out to make tools and idols. Even in those days the process of annealing must have been known, whereby from time to time in the course of working copper is heated to 'cherry red', as the coppersmith calls it, and cooled, to prevent it hardening and splitting.

About the year 5,000 B.C. copper was first smelted from its ore by the people of one of the first great civilisations that dwelt around the Tigris and Euphrates rivers. Smelted copper forms a spongy mass which can, like native copper, be worked into simple shapes. The next step was the discovery that at a somewhat higher temperature than for smelting, copper could be melted and cast. But the supreme invention of early days was bronze, in which the addition of a small amount of tin to copper made a greatly superior metal with a lower melting point – therefore easier to cast – which was above all harder and only a little less malleable than plain copper. Now excellent tools and weapons could be manufactured. These were left in the 'work hard' condition, that is without a final annealing, and the edges were ground: ancient bronze implements in good condition show the marks of hammering and grinding. When the edge became blunt or damaged the bronze could be softened by annealing, then reshaped and rehardened by hammering. At last when beyond repair it could be melted down and the metal used again. No wonder that the early bronze-smiths guarded the secrets of their craft and traded their products far afield. Moreover they had to travel to find the sources of their raw materials, in particular tin ore which is not as widely distributed as copper ores. Thus the making and use of bronze spread east and west, to reach the western confines of Europe and the eastern confines of Asia at about the same time, in the first half of the second millennium B.C. In China they loved this metal, and used it with great refinement to make ritual vessels in the Shang Dynasty (1766–1401 B.C.). One of these, a handsome footed bowl, turned up among Roman remains in the city of Canterbury; it must somehow have been brought to Rome, perhaps after theft from a temple in China, and then carried to far Britannia by some cultured soldier or administrator. In Europe also bronze must have been highly regarded, to judge by the carvings of bronze axes on the stones of Stonehenge. These are all shown without a haft, suggesting that it was only the bronze blade, not its replaceable handle, which they wished to depict in this hallowed place.

A good bronze may be made from one part of tin and nine of copper, but the amount of tin in early bronze varies according to the skill of the founder and the availability of that metal. Less than a tenth of tin and the bronze is brittle; more than that percentage is a waste of the more expensive ingredient unless some special quality is required, such as in the brightly reflecting tin-rich bronze called speculum, which is used for the mirrors of telescopes. Ancient bronzes sometimes also contained small amounts of other metals by chance, brought through from the ores, until the Greeks in classical times learnt to control these additional alloys for their qualities. Thus silver increases the fluidity of the molten metal, and is used in statuary bronze. The small bronzes of classical inspiration for which the sculptors of the Renaissance are famous were cast from bronze formulated to give fine detail and beautiful patina. Sometimes they may go unrecognised; recently one was left as an ornament, thought to be of no particular value, on the mantelpiece of a bungalow and sold complete with its contents.

The addition of antimony to bronze, and to other metals, greatly increases their hardness. Before the Second World War a fine Chinese cannon stood outside the Officers' Mess in Devonport Barracks. It was in the shape of a dragon, and of a dull silvery colour that was much admired. Alas, at the beginning of the war, shortage of metals decreed that it should 'go for salvage'; but on trying to saw it in half for the melting pot, nothing could be found to cut it. Analysis by the dockyard laboratory showed that it was of a bronze rich in antimony, the main source of which was China.

The first large objects other than statues to be made of bronze were church bells, which were made as early as the ninth century. The favoured material for them has always been a tin-rich alloy, four of copper and one of tin being typical. This is supposed to give a superior tone to the note sounded; it certainly makes the bronze paler than normal, as may be seen on an old polished hand-bell. The very first guns were made up like a barrel with iron staves and hoops, but soon the bell-founder was called in and guns were cast; the material used was the standard nine to one of copper and tin, which came to be called gun-metal to distinguish it from bell-metal.

In 1870 it was discovered that a small amount of phosphorus added to bronze made it more tough and resistant to wear, and this alloy has since been favoured for engine bearings under the name of phosphor bronze. Another newcomer is aluminium bronze, in which the tin in bronze is replaced by aluminium to give a metal with improved tensile strength; this is used for the moving parts of internal combustion engines. It is also resistant to corrosion and therefore good for such things as the propeller shafts of sea-going motor-boats.

Under favourable circumstances a hard, olive green surface, both good looking and protective, forms on bronze. Even a bronze object that has lain in the ground for centuries may have this so-called 'patina', which should on no account be removed: even to scratch the surface may start corrosion where the metal is exposed. However if the surface of a bronze is flaking and erupting it needs immediate skilled attention.

All these various alloys of copper must not make us lose sight of the pure metal which since antiquity the coppersmith has taken in the form of sheets and worked with shears and hammers to make all sorts of things, mostly vessels of one kind or another. Plain copper cannot be welded, does not make good castings, and is not as strong as its alloys, but it is supremely malleable and ductile.

The coppersmith has a coke fire blown from a hand bellows or mechanical fan. He works the metal cold, with hammers of various weights and faces, over small anvils, called stakes, of which there are many shapes. For special purposes he may use suitable blocks of cast iron. Much of his work consists in 'raising from plate', that is to say by alternate hammering until the metal becomes hard, and annealing by heating to red heat and cooling, he makes the metal 'flow' into the forms of kettles and pots of all kinds, pipes for machinery, and other useful or ornamental things. He exploits the ductility of copper to create deep and narrow shapes (Fig. 50) that could not be made from any copper alloy. However, he must join some pieces together after working them, and this he does either by the cheap and easy method of soldering, which leaves a silver coloured line, or by brazing, which leaves a brass coloured line. Solder is an alloy of tin and lead, so it melts at a low temperature and is unsuitable for copper kettles and other vessels that will be exposed to the heat of the fire. So-called 'spelter' for brazing is supplied as granules of a fifty–fifty copper and zinc alloy. The objects to be brazed together are strongly heated to run the spelter and the subsequent join is much harder than a soldered one. Fig. 50 shows an old copper kettle with a joint line indicated: others are clearly visible on the kettle itself. The only soldering is on the lid, which is not intended to come into contact with the heat of the fire. Solid fittings, such as the handles and lid knob on our kettle, are made of an alloy of 94 per cent copper and 6 per cent zinc, which shows a slight yellow tinge against the plain copper body. Vessels built up of thin copper sheet with tinsmith's joints are described under 'tinplate' in the next chapter.

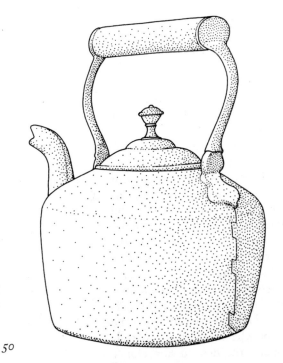

50

The final process of making a copper vessel for food
or drink is to tin the interior by heating until a stick of tin
melts against it and then wiping with the molten metal.
Do not use a copper vessel unless the inside is soundly
tinned, or you may be made ill.

Brass, which is the easiest copper alloy to cast, and
cheaper than bronze, is not so easy to work under the
hammer as pure copper. It was not known until the first
millennium B.C., when it was made among upland
tribes in the Caucasus mountains. Darius the Great is
said to have had a cup which looked like gold but had an
unpleasant smell, and this was probably of brass. The
comparatively late discovery of this simple alloy was due
to an unusual characteristic of zinc, which comes off as a
gas from its ore. Only in the sixteenth century was it
captured from the vapour by distillation, and metallic
zinc became known. All early brass had to be made by
smelting zinc ore in liquid copper, so that the copper
took up some of the zinc as it gassed off from the ore. It
was an uncommon metal in the ancient world, and was
used principally for the lower denominations of coinage;
only late in the Middle Ages did it become plentiful,

with the discovery of good sources of the zinc ore calamine in central Europe.

Brass has never earned the regard accorded to bronze, perhaps because of its unpleasant tarnish; or maybe its unfortunate ability to imitate gold is part of the reason. Yet well kept brass has beauty; with constant polishing a smooth glowing surface develops, which gives pleasure equally by the fireside at home or set against scoured woodwork on the bridge of a ship. Moreover by varying the amounts of the two constituents a wider range of alloys is available than with bronze. Whereas 10 per cent tin and 90 per cent copper is just a plain optimum, zinc and copper combine up to 30 per cent zinc as a solid solution with certain qualities; and in a different manner up to a high limit of 40 per cent with other qualities. Above that percentage the metal is unworkable. Brasses low in zinc can be worked cold, and those high in zinc can be hot rolled and forged. Zinc tends to be cheaper than either tin or copper, so brasses have a cost advantage over bronze, which is maximised by using the high limit of 40 per cent zinc where practicable. Metallurgy, economics, and finally the desired appearance combine to produce the following range of brasses:

% Zinc	Uses	Appearance
5–20	For deep drawing, cold, of cartridge cases and tubes; also jewellery for subsequent gilding.	Yellow, tinged red.
20	'Pinchbeck' metal, formerly used for cheap jewellery, watch cases, etc.	Like gold, but lacks its lustre.
30	The cheapest and strongest brass which can be cold worked. Ancient brass is around this constituency, and recent brass for stamping, drawing, spinning.	Full yellow.

'Muntz' metal, for hot
rolling chiefly in
engineering context.
Naval brass is similar,
with a small amount of
lead to help in machining it.

Pale yellow.

The brass used for casting is often the 30 per cent zinc mix, to match the normal brass used for cold work on those many things, such as candlesticks, that are made up of pieces, some of them cold worked. Cheap brass castings contain as much zinc as will still give a brassy colour (about 50 per cent), and cheap tinned brass castings will be found pale beneath the tin.

A commercial process for the production of zinc as a metal, so that brass of constant quality could be made from measured amounts of copper and zinc, was invented by James Emerson in 1781. It is sometimes claimed that this new 'Emerson' brass can be distinguished from the old 'calamine' brass by its appearance, but the truth is that only the constant full yellow colour of Emerson brass is observed, compared to the chancy tinge of calamine brass.

The words 'maslin' and 'latten' are used in old documents for brass. Maslin implies a mixed metal, a 'mash', and latten means something flattened, like a lath. Until the late seventeenth century, when rolling mills started to take over, brass ingot was reduced to sheet by hammering, and this was latten as distinct from maslin, which was cast brass. Thus a latten candlestick or 'take a quart of sweet wine, and do it in a clean maslin pan'. This would be a skillet as in Fig. 372, a valuable chattel often bequeathed in wills: by contrast early sheet brass vessels were made of thin sheet, riveted and with folded seams, so very few have survived. These days the word latten is used to imply a certain composition, and the word maslin is forgotten. Both remain useful if confined to their original meanings.

The process of beating out the ingot was known as 'battery', and this term was also applied to the shaping of sheet metal over a former. A number of cooking pans of graded sizes could be made by hammering out several discs piled together, hence the expression *'batterie de cuisine'* for the array of saucepans in a French kitchen.

'Spelter' originated as the name for zinc imported from China, where the secret of its distillation has been known far longer than in the West. Now the word is used for decorative objects of zinc. The word brass is also sometimes avoided: at the end of the Second World War the British campaign medals were officially described as of 'copper-zinc alloy'.

Brass can be soldered or brazed the same as copper. The line of a braze on brass is, understandably, hard to see: if breathed on, it may show up in the condensation. The only major limitation to brass is that it is not as malleable as copper, silver or gold, so it is not raised from the plate as readily as they are, and the alternative process of building up from sheet makes brass vessels somewhat light and fragile.

Brassware is associated in the minds of most people with Birmingham. This used to be a small place, with small workshops making small things such as nails and spurs, until in the late eighteenth century a series of inventions to stamp, press and roll brass coincided with the presence there of skilled workers driven out of Europe by wars and persecution. Since then the factories of the Birmingham district have turned out brass furniture fittings, buttons, frames for miniatures and the like, in plentiful supply.

The Chinese smelted an ore containing nickel and copper to which they added zinc and exported the resulting malleable silver-coloured alloy to Europe in the eighteenth century under the name 'paktong'. Nickel was first isolated in Europe in 1820, but by an expensive and limited process. Nevertheless it too was alloyed with copper and zinc and used under the name 'German silver' for small articles imitating silver. Its extended use for cutlery and plate became possible in 1890, when the Mond extraction process gave ample and reasonably cheap supplies of nickel. From then 'Electroplated Nickel Silver' (EPNS) has been a household word. Brass plated with nickel is known from 1860, but its great days were in the early years of this century, when it was used for the surfacing of motor car and bicycle parts before chromium plating took over in the 1920s.

Iron and its Alloys

Before men learnt to smelt iron, they occasionally encountered it on the surface of the earth as something strange and magical, to be used by the Egyptians as beads and by the Chinese as amulets. This was meteoric iron, rich in nickel, which had fallen from the skies.

Iron was first obtained from its ore, in a furnace basically similar to that used for copper, among the Hittites in the great days of their empire in Asia Minor, around 1500 B.C. At a temperature of about 1500°C. iron ore smelts into a spongy mass of iron grains in slag, from which bars of iron can be forged. During the process of forging, the slag is squeezed out of the 'bloom', as it is called, and at the same time a fibrous structure is imparted to the metal. Wrought iron was extensively used until recently by blacksmiths for workaday things such as horseshoes, door hinges, the tyres of carts; it has also been employed for decorative gates, grilles, door and chest mountings, and a limited amount of wrought iron is still available for such purposes. It is an agreeable metal to work at the forge, being malleable over a good range of temperature from white hot down to cherry red; it is not easily spoilt in the fire, and is readily welded under the hammer.

Iron ores are plentiful, so the manufacture and use of wrought iron spread rapidly, ousting finally the flint and obsidian which had continued in use during the Bronze Age for such expendable items as arrow heads, and replacing bronze for tools and weapons. The economics can be explained by an example: an iron axe could be given a loop for its handle by forging and welding, a cheap and easy process, but the hole in a bronze axe had to be made by casting, a more advanced technique requiring special apparatus. It was from a homeland in what is now Austria, that bands of warriors bearing cheap and effective iron weapons spread the benefits of the Iron Age throughout Europe in the eighth century B.C.

The technology of iron reached the East, where the Chinese learnt to cast iron a thousand years earlier than in the West, having the advantages of superior bellows developed for their ceramics, and iron ore with a low smelting temperature.

The production of wrought iron from ore, and its

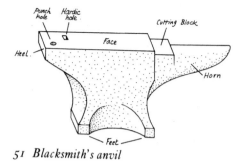
51 *Blacksmith's anvil*

52 *Scroll wrenches*

forging and welding, continued in Europe throughout the Iron Age, then in Roman, medieval and post-medieval times without interruption. Any occupation site of these periods will yield iron spikes, straps, pintles and other such fittings. These simple and useful things look much the same wherever and whenever they come from; only if there was some visible development, as in the case of horseshoes, will an entry be found later in this book. It was not until the middle of the last century that the making of mild steel in quantity became possible, and this led to the factory production of 'builders fittings' and the great days of the ironmonger. Glance through one of his catalogues from the second half of the nineteenth century, and wonder at the serried ranks of drawings that depict, in order of size, ranges of washers, nuts, ring bolts etc., all very uniform and dull products of the drop forge.

Compared to these the plainest thing made by a blacksmith is of interest, and if we examine the way he worked, the things he made will be better understood. On the face of his anvil, which is of tool steel welded to a wrought iron body, he will do most of his hammering into shape and welding. Here also he will 'upset' a red-hot iron bar, striking its end so as to make it swell out. The horn of the anvil provides a rounded surface for curves of decreasing radius towards its point, and the cutting block is of soft iron so that cutters and chisels will not be dulled against it. In the hardie hole he fits the stem of a hardie, a cutting tool, or a bottom fuller for use with a top fuller, held in a withy handle to form channels; also various sorts of swages to round up a bar, form a collar, or a hexagon for bolt heads and nuts. Off the anvil he will have, of course, a range of hammers and tongs and, if he has any artistic pretensions, wrenches to make scrolls and twists. The blacksmith-made stable door hasp shown has a decorative twist that also gives added strength. Fig. 54 is a piece of decorative iron work known to have been made for a church by the village blacksmith a hundred years ago. The modern blacksmith welds steel by oxy-acetylene torch and electric arc, but these processes were not used by him, or in factories and workshops to any large degree, before the First World War. Not until the Second World War did the technique and inspection of gas and electric welds allow highly stressed parts to be joined by such means.

Let us now take up the story of steel. The crucial difference between it and wrought iron is that steel contains carbon combined with the iron in certain ways according to the amount of it and the treatment given to the steel after manufacture. Let us expand this statement in the form of a table:

53 *Door hasp*

54

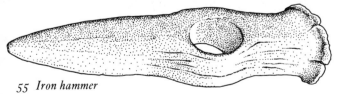

55 *Iron hammer*

Name	Percentage of Carbon	Use	Treatment
Mild Steel	0.15 to 0.30	Structural sections, builders' fittings, wire.	Cannot be hardened.
Medium Carbon Steel	0.30 to 0.50	Machinery parts.	Cannot be hardened.
High Carbon Steel	0.50 to 1.50	Cutting tools and weapons, springs.	Hardened and tempered.

High carbon steel is 'hardened' by quenching in water from a red heat to cold. This makes it very hard, but too brittle for any purpose. In order to get the required combination of hardness and strength for the intended use of the tool or weapon, it is 'tempered', that is reheated to an intermediate temperature, and quenched again. The temperature for the second quench is indicated to the smith by colour changes on the surface of the steel, from a pale straw good for the stout, hard tools to cut steel, up to a dark blue for springs. Glimpses of these 'temper colours' may be seen on the finished article, but the blue on coil springs and the brown on armour are improved by burning on a coat of special oil.

The above facts and figures are now well known and applied, but this was clearly not the case before the science of metallurgy developed last century. Under certain accidental conditions steel, even of high carbon content, was produced directly from the smelting of iron ore, and isolated examples of tool steel correctly heat-treated by ancient smiths have been found. They probably accepted the steel as a 'gift from the gods' with due gratitude but little understanding. More importantly, at some time not yet determined during the Iron Age, the secret of 'cementation' or 'case hardening' was learnt, whereby iron is kept in contact with some material high in carbon under heat for a long time and thus given a skin of high carbon steel, which can then be tempered. Such treatment could be given direct to tools and weapons to harden their cutting edge. The Romans improved this 'steeling' of iron by removing the case-hardened skin, forging to shape, and welding it to a backing of wrought iron or mild steel. The welding of tool steel to wrought iron or mild steel, to give a composite tool, has continued even to the present day for axes, scythes, ploughshares, and so on. These are described as 'edge-tools'. Spades and hoes require a tough rather than a sharp blade, and may be found marked 'solid steel' since the mass production of steel in the second half of the last century.

Classical writers speak of Gaulish swords being notched and bent against Roman weapons, so it seems that there was a considerable range in the quality of 'steeled' weapons at that time. During the Dark Ages, notably among the Vikings, high carbon steel was introduced into the interior of swords by what we call 'pattern welding'. Bars of steeled iron were laid together and welded, then folded, twisted and forged to give a blade with a characteristic rope pattern to be seen on an exposed surface. A parallel development took place in Damascus, where it got the name 'damascene'. Here swords were forged from cakes of pure Indian steel, made by the 'crucible' process to be described later. The swordsmith worked the cakes of steel together to produce the effect of rippled water on the finished blade, comparable with but not the same as pattern welding. It seems possible that the renowned swords of those days, such as Excalibur, Joyeuse and Durendal, which came to be made at Toledo and other places as well as Damascus, were of this very superior kind.

From the early Middle Ages the ironworkers of central Europe and Sweden, using iron ores of suitable composition available there, deliberately produced a limited amount of high carbon steel direct from the smelting process. This was traded as an expensive commodity to countries, such as England for example, where the native ores were not suitable for direct smelting into steel.

However case hardening and pattern welding by hand remained the principle means in the West of achieving tempered steel until, with the harnessing of water power in the seventeenth century, it became practicable to cut up case-hardened iron bars and forge the pieces together. This was known as 'shear steel'. If the process was repeated, to get an even more homogenous metal, the result was called 'double shear steel'. Then in Sheffield in the early eighteenth century came the making of 'crucible cast' steel by melting together measured quantities of iron and charcoal, in much the same way as the Indian steel of antiquity mentioned above. This was a high carbon steel of constant, controlled quality, and it was the foundation of Sheffield's fame for knives, scythes and other such tools. An early use of these excellent tempered steel implements was for cutting fine detail on the intensely hard Cuban mahogany that became fashionable for furniture about the year 1720.

The last great step in the story of steel was the production, in the last half of the nineteenth century, of structural steel in quantity. This was made possible by two inventions, the Bessemer Converter and the Open Hearth Furnace, both of which worked on the novel principle of burning the carbon out of cast iron to make steel. Although the principle was new to the West, the Chinese had made high carbon steel by these means since the early Middle Ages, and their technique spread to Japan, making possible the famous swords of that country, that were said to be so sharp that a silk handkerchief allowed to fall on an upturned edge would be cut in half by its own weight.

The copious supply of mild steel, at first from South Wales and then from elsewhere, was quickly taken up by shipyards and factories to make plates, girders, chains and all manner of structural parts previously of iron. The triumph of mild steel is vividly demonstrated in the Cyfarthwa Castle Museum, a nineteenth-century South Welsh ironmaster's stately home on a hillside above the valley where once stood his ironworks with their roaring converters. Here in the museum are locomotive rails twisted like barley sugar, slabs folded over and over like pastry, and other such delights, all of cold worked mild steel, remaining from the demonstration pieces made soon after he installed his Bessemer Converters in the 1860s. From those days onwards, only the village blacksmith held faithful to wrought iron, which works hot better than mild steel, and he had not the power to work the steel cold. The last production forge for wrought iron in Britain closed in 1960.

It is not easy to determine whether a thing found is of wrought iron or mild steel. The only certain evidence is that some weathered things of wrought iron, especially if large, will show the fibrous nature of the material. Otherwise, we can only guess by the contorted appearance of many wrought iron things, or associate the rough finish of blacksmith's work with his favourite material. See Figs 55 and 56.

Cast iron, the remaining basic alloy of iron, is composed of iron with carbon in it as a mixture, not chemically combined as in steel. Not until the late fifteenth century were tall blast furnaces built in Europe that created enough heat to bring down liquid iron. This was then run into channels to form in fancy a sow with her litter of 'pig iron', or even a gun cast direct from the furnace mouth. Cast iron is strong in compression, and suitable for pillars and arches in buildings; it is also used for naturally robust things about the house and garden such as stoves, grates, flat irons, door stoppers, railings, garden seats. Parts of these may be found, with the 'sugary' fracture typical of that material; if the object is whole, the heaviness and blunt granular surface will declare it. Cast iron is notoriously weak in shock and tension, so small things that receive rough use are not made from it. Cast iron became available in quantity in Britain in the early eighteenth century. It coincided with the increased use of coal as a domestic fuel, and one result was the basket grate in the middle of the eighteenth century, and the first cast-iron cooking stoves a few years later. Now the so-called 'down hearth', with its andirons, jacks and other apparatus necessary for roasting meat in front of it, or boiling pots and kettles over it, became unfashionable, but not extinct for another hundred years.

During the years 1830–1850 cast iron was much favoured as a material, and good design went into the

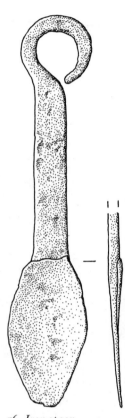

56 Iron spoon

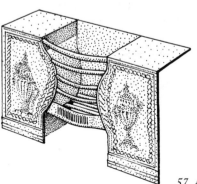

57 Basket grate

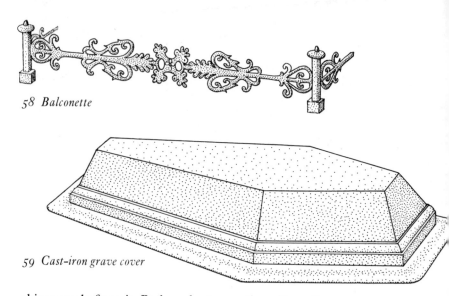

58 *Balconette*

59 *Cast-iron grave cover*

things made from it. Perhaps best were the railings for the balconies of houses, or the smaller 'balconettes'. One can also find cast-iron grave covers, and screens for urinals on un-modernised railway stations.

The strength of cast iron can be considerably improved, so that it can be used for such things as fire irons, if the castings are heated in contact with a substance which will absorb some of the carbon out of it and leave a steel surface. This is the reverse process to the 'steeling' of wrought iron. The making of this 'malleable cast iron' dates from the late eighteenth century to modern times. Cast iron was also turned into wrought iron before the mass production of mild steel superseded that material, by a process called puddling, whereby molten iron was stirred until the carbon burnt out of it.

So much for the plain alloys of iron and carbon, but the story would be incomplete without some mention of stainless steel. It was in the 1930s that a stainless steel containing chromium, which had been developed for engineering use, spread to the food preparation and dairying industries, being more hygienic than the tinned or galvanised steel plate previously used. From the dairy stainless steel came into the house, and in the years just before the Second World War it was fashionable for cooking utensils (see Fig. 373). This material is difficult to weld and was expensive, so articles made up of stainless-steel plate never became popular, but with the development of deep drawing during the war, the pro-

duction of stainless-steel domestic vessels without welds
has continued to this day.

Stainless steel does not corrode, as the name implies, but other iron alloys suffer from rust if left without a surface finish. Protection is commonly given by paints, either of the ordinary kind that dry in air, or 'stove enamel' that is fixed by heating in some kind of kiln. This process has been applied in the last eighty years or so to utensils and apparatus required to be hygienic, such as saucepans and cooking ovens. A 'black japan' derived from asphalt and linseed oil, and also fixed by heat, forms a thinner and cheaper surface on lanterns and the like made during the nineteenth century. Ever since the quantity production of mild steel last century, steel goods intended for marine or other severely corrosive conditions are 'galvanised', that is to say given a coating of zinc. More rarely than zinc, in the past copper has been applied to iron by painting with a powder of brass suspended in some kind of oil that dried out. This is known as 'bronzing', and no doubt the intention was to counterfeit the more expensive material. Between 1800 and 1850 some small articles such as knife blades were covered with silver foil by a process known as 'close-plating'. It will usually be found to have chipped away from the edges.

Of greater importance to us than these treatments is that of tinning. Alloys of copper as well as of iron can be tinned and have been since antiquity, either to improve their appearance, to preserve them, or for reasons of health. The object is either dipped in a bath of molten tin, or heated and the tin run on from a stick of that metal. A bright coating results, and although this dulls in time it continues to protect the metal body from corrosion. Equally important it allows copper and alloys of copper, which have a poisonous tarnish, to be used safely for food and drink.

When in the late eighteenth century the great water-driven rolls of South Wales started to turn out thin iron plate in quantity, it was tinned by immersion at the works and supplied as tinned plate, or 'tinplate' as it came to be called. In the factories of Britain and abroad it was worked up, at first largely by hand-operated machines, into cheap utensils and containers by the thousand. The tinning of tinplate by electrolysis superseded immersion during the Second World War. The

60 *Bucket with folded seam*

typical seam on tinsmith's work is folded, the edges being bent to grip each other and, if water-tightness is required, solder is run into the seam (see Fig. 60). Seams made automatically are thinner than those made by the tinsmith on hand-operated machines. Even after the introduction of stainless steel plate, much tinsmithing was still done by hand until the Second World War. Interesting old tin kettles and such like may turn up in attics, but those consigned to the ground will have corroded away to nothing.

In the middle of the eighteenth century, a special process was invented by Thomas Allgood whereby things made of tinplate in and around Pontypool were given a hard, lustrous surface of lacquer. This lacquer was derived from coal tar, and a number of coats were carefully painted on, slowly baked, and well rubbed down. Good early 'Pontypool ware' is of a dark reddish brown, often with some gilding. Later, a black and blue ground was decorated with flowers. Utensils for the kitchen, such as spice boxes, were extensively produced, but coffee pots, trays and so on enjoyed some popularity also. The works at Pontypool closed in 1822, but an offshoot at Usk carried on, in the face of competition from Birmingham and abroad, until 1861. The lacquered tinware made in Birmingham, and in France and Holland, is similar to Pontypool and Usk but generally inferior.

Lacquer was applied to tinned iron and steel sheet

things of some permanence, but the lightly made 'tins', as we in Britain still call them, used for packaging and meant to be discarded when empty, have been labelled by transfer printing since the process was invented in 1860. In 1875 an improvement allowed transfers to be applied to shaped tins, leading to biscuit tins in the form of delivery vans, and other extravagances popular until recent years. (See the entry TINS for more details.) It also permitted cheap mechanical toys to be made of tinplate (see MECHANICAL TOYS).

Meat was first canned in the early nineteenth century; the containers were large and of thick tinplate, and had to be opened with a hammer and chisel, and probably also much swearing and some loss of blood. Around 1860 the tinplate was made thinner, and now the first tin-openers appeared. These were robust instruments with a blade that could be removed for sharpening. The bull's head suggests 'bully beef': but there is a good story about one of these heads, detached from the opener, being for long accepted as a Roman antiquity!

61

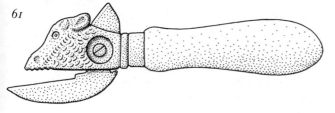

Alloys of Tin and Lead

Tin is an ancient metal that was mined in Cornwall long ago and traded from thence to the Mediterranean. The pure metal is a shiny bright silver colour, malleable, but soft and lacking in tensile strength, so it is only suitable for the occasional decorative object. It is, however, rolled into the well-known 'tin foil', used for wrapping sweets and pills and also, until 1840, for the 'silvering' of mirror glass. Tin foil is called silver paper, but there is none of that metal in it.

Lead has also been used since antiquity, and is obtained with ease from its sulphide ore galena, which is well distributed throughout the world. It is proverbially heavy, hence it is used for weights, but its important quality as a pure metal is softness and ease of working. Roofs can be covered with sheet lead worked by wooden tools, and pieces can be joined by melting together at a low heat, without flux. Lead pipes, extensively used for water systems until the last few years, are joined end to end with solder in a softened state, by a process known as 'wiping'. These joins have the appearance of a bulge on the pipe, and can be seen in the back quarters of most old houses. As to things found, however, fishing weights or the occasional counter are all you are likely to come across.

So much for tin and lead separately: they are more important when alloyed together, either into solders or pewter. As to solders, it is sufficient to note that they come in a range of compositions, but are all called soft solders, as distinct from hard solders of silver with copper and zinc. Soft soldering has been used since antiquity, largely in the construction of copper and copper alloy vessels which do not have to withstand heat. The craftsman will try to make his soldered seams as inconspicuous as possible, but if you breathe on them they will often show up on something such as a brass candlestick.

Pewter is essentially an alloy of tin and lead, but as to the proportions it has been said that there were as many recipes as for rum punch. Lead being the cheaper constituent, the pewterer will include as much of it as he dares. A satisfactory pewter can be made from 70 per cent tin and 30 per cent lead. If more lead is included, an exposed edge of the metal will mark paper like a lead pencil, and furthermore be dangerously poisonous to eat or drink from. If more than 70 per cent tin is included, a hard metal of bright appearance results. The addition of a few per cent of copper was often made to the metal for beer-drinking vessels, plates and dishes, to increase their hardness.

It was the Romans who invented pewter, but the art was lost and only revived in the twelfth century, when pewter was used for the chalices required to be buried with dignatories of the Church, and for pilgrim badges. From these limited beginnings pewter spread into common use until by the fifteenth century the pewterer was a well established craft, with guilds in cities throughout Europe. In 1503 the London pewterers made the marking of their wares compulsory, in an endeavour to control standards of material and workmanship. The important mark to look for is that of the maker, known

62 *Pilgrim badge*

as his 'touch'. The touch of Thomas Bennet, a London pewterer of the late seventeenth century, is shown. In addition you may find other marks, signifying the place of origin or the quality of the piece. Finally there may be devices which are deceptive, such as an animal's head remarkably like the leopard's head of the London assay office for silver and gold.

63

Pewter was cast, raised, pressed and soldered, but never riveted or spun. If in good condition it has an attractive 'moon glow' sheen, but if neglected it corrodes rapidly, so found objects of pewter may be in a sorry state, with ugly scale which it is best not to try to remove as no sound metal may remain underneath.

During its heyday, between the late seventeenth and the early nineteenth centuries, pewter was the accepted substitute for silver, and it generally followed the fashionable styles of the superior metal with a lag of twenty years or so. All the things made of silver such as plates, tankards, salt-cellars, spoons etc. were made of pewter, except forks, because it was not strong enough for the prongs.

Pewter flat-ware was driven off the market in the late eighteenth century, largely by Wedgwood's improved earthenware, but tankards, mugs and measures were still made for inns and taverns right into the nineteenth century, and have been avidly collected from pubs in the last few years. These late vessels are coarsely made, and can often be positively distinguished by being stamped

64 Britannia metal hot water jug

'Imperial' pint or half pint or as may be, to show that they were in accordance with the new capacities introduced in 1826. Measures, which are bellied vessels ranging from $\frac{1}{2}$ gill to $\frac{1}{2}$ gallon, were marked with the sovereign's head to certify capacity when made, and if in use after 1877 by a portcullis when periodically checked. Measures earlier than 1810 have lids, but genuine ones are rare as they were called in to be destroyed when Imperial measures were introduced.

Britannia metal, an alloy of 90 tin and 10 antimony, was invented in 1770 and in Victorian days was extensively used for such things as tea-pots and hot water jugs. Unlike pewter it can be spun, and it is distinctly harder, giving a tinny sound when tapped. It was commonly electro-plated, and if so may be marked EPBM, for Electro Plated Britannia Metal. Until recently it was disregarded by collectors, but it is now respectable to own early pieces of Britannia metal. Modern so-called pewter is a sort of Britannia metal, and so is the 'white metal' used for costume jewellery.

Lead and tin go into the composition of type metal for printing, and bearing metal for machinery, usually with some antimony to improve resistance to wear. The composition of type metal has not radically altered since the invention of printing in the fifteenth century.

The New Metals

Aluminium This light and useful metal was first isolated in 1825, but it remained a curiosity until the early years of the present century. The difficulty was that although a process for its bulk production from bauxite ore was invented in 1886, it required high power electricity, the technology of which was little developed at that time. Moreover it was not until 1907 that the alloying and hardening of aluminium was mastered, allowing the production of forgings and extruded sections for the construction of aeroplanes and airships, notably the German Zeppelin airships of the First World War. Things found of aluminium will be bits and pieces from aircraft, or modern pots and pans mostly post World War II.

Nickel When a process for the commercial production of nickel was invented by Ludwig Mond in 1889 the result, so far as we are concerned, was the extensive use of Electro Plated Nickel Silver as a cheap substitute for real silver table-ware. 'Nickel silver', also called 'German silver', is an alloy of nickel with copper and zinc. The more the nickel in it, which is the most expensive ingredient, the more silvery it looks; conversely a poor EPNS, when worn, shows yellow under the silver plating. Nickel has also been used in coins: the U.S.A. coin of five cents, known as a nickel, contains one part of that metal to three of copper.

Pure nickel, a fine metal like stainless steel, may be encountered in vessels made for laboratory use.

A variety of nickel silver, known as paktong, is used in the Far East as a substitute for silver in the making of cheap decorative objects. It is a dull whitish silver in colour.

Pottery

The word pottery is used here to include all materials thrown or otherwise shaped by a potter, although it is sometimes taken to mean everything except porcelain, as in the title *English Pottery and Porcelain*, a well-known book by W. B. Honey.

Pottery is made from some kind of clay, defined in the *Oxford English Dictionary* as 'stiff viscous earth'. A large amount of aluminium silicate in clays will make them plastic, or 'fat' as the potter says, and capable of being thrown on his wheel. Clays poor in aluminium silicate tend to tear like short pastry and are only good for tiles and bricks. There are two kind of additives used in potters' clays. Firstly, those known as 'fillers', which are fragments of grit, shell or previously fired pot, mixed with the clay to prevent it collapsing on the wheel or in the kiln, and to reduce shrinkage. Secondly, 'temper' of straw or grass is needed for thick objects fired at a low heat: the temper burns out in the kiln, leaving small channels which conduct heat into the interior of the piece to improve its baking. The archaeologist relies on a knowledge of fillers and tempers to identify pottery. There is an old adage that you cannot make bricks without straw, which applied to the large and low-fired building bricks of antiquity, with their necessary straw temper.

Clays vary in colour, both in the raw and fired states, owing to the presence of impurities. The commonest of these is iron, which gives a black colour when fired with only a little oxygen in the kiln, and red if there is excess oxygen. There is a famous kind of ancient Chinese stoneware called Chun Yao, which has patches of purple on a lavender glaze. The story runs that when these patches, caused by certain stray oxides, were first seen, it was feared that a devil inhabited the kiln, but later the potters learnt to activate the purple colour at their will.

The quality of pottery depends on a process known as vitrification, in which under considerable heat a sort of glass is produced which binds the particles of the pot. The first pots produced by man, around 5,000 B.C., were baked in an open fire; this went no further than driving off the water in the clay, producing a fragile and porous earthenware. When the kiln was invented about a thousand years later, the increased heat caused by induced draft was sufficient to vitrify the outer surface of pots and a good earthenware, impervious to liquids, was made. The Chinese developed efficient double-acting bellows in the first millennium A.D., and with their forced draft produced stoneware, which is vitrified throughout. It was then not long before they discovered porcelain, which is made of china clay and china stone, the first being refractory and the second fusible: the Chinese call china clay the bones and china stone the flesh of porcelain. Porcelain is resonant when flicked with the finger nail, and translucent when held up to the light. Stoneware is resonant but not translucent. Earthenware is neither.

The occasional piece of Chinese porcelain found its way to Europe. Its name came from the likeness of this hard shiny material to the shell of the cowrie, itself called 'porcellana' from its shape like a little pig. The secret of the manufacture of porcelain was eagerly sought, but it was doomed to failure until kilns equal to those of the Chinese were available. Late in the sixteenth century, however, an imitation of porcelain, consisting of glass mixed with white clay and certain fluxes, was made for a short time in Italy, but the secret of it died with its inventor. These whitened glasses are called 'soft paste porcelains' because they required a low or 'soft' heat to fire them compared to the true 'hard paste' Chinese porcelain which needed a higher temperature. The making of soft paste porcelain was rediscovered in the middle years of the eighteenth century in England

and France and used for useful and decorative things of great charm. Meanwhile the secret of firing china clay and china stone together at a high temperature had been discovered by alchemists working for the Elector of Saxony early in the eighteenth century, and his factory at Meissen had the monopoly of making figures and useful wares in true porcelain until the secret was leaked, first to Vienna in 1720, and then to a number of German factories. By the end of the eighteenth century hard paste porcelain was being made all over Europe, and soft paste porcelain was in decline. It is easy to distinguish a piece of hard paste from soft paste if there is a chip or break to show the interior, which is like a broken flint or sea shell in hard paste, but chalky or sugary in soft paste. If the piece is unbroken, you must rely on the appearance of the enamelled decoration, which tends to sink into the surface of hard paste. However this distinction requires some experience to observe. The invention of bone china, a porcelain fluxed with ground bone to reduce the firing temperature, was made in Staffordshire late in the eighteenth century, and the material is still used, particularly in the potteries of that county. Bone china has a high glaze, with a stark whiteness unlike the melting tones of old porcelain. Modern porcelain produced in Europe has by contrast a dark thin look. Appearances are difficult to describe and impossible to illustrate: the best way to learn the differences is to examine known pieces of the various sorts of 'china', which can easily be done on view days in an auction room.

Pottery is of paramount importance to the archaeologist, because although pots are broken the fragments do not decay, though the glaze may do so. Moreover pottery has been made since early times, and being fragile but composed of inexpensive material a great deal of it has been produced, so it is usually plentiful in the ground of excavation sites. Clay is easily formed and decorated, and so pottery tends to reflect accurately the current styles of the culture from which it comes. Finally, pottery is not harmed when removed from the earth, washed in water and dried, unlike some materials which need special attention when they are brought to light.

The potter's wheel was invented in the third millennium B.C., but it has never been universally adopted.

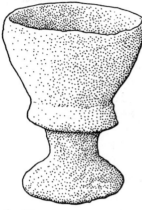

65 *Thumb pot*

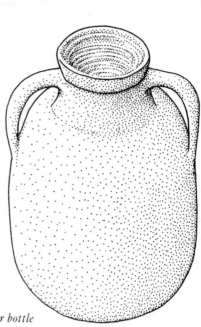

66 *Water bottle*

The story runs that an African art student, on being shown how a pot could be built up of coiled clay without a wheel, remarked that this was how his grandmother always made pots. It is significant that before the potter's wheel, which requires a man's strength to work, was adopted in any culture, pottery was generally made by women. Thus in prehistory or in later primitive societies the pots of a vanquished people will tend to continue to be made in the fashions of the vanquished, because the mothers will instruct their daughters in the old ways even when they have passed into the households of their conquerors.

Wheel-turned pots are of course more regular in section than those coiled up, and much more so than the primitive small vessels called thumb pots which are made out of clay pressed into shape by the fingers. A well made coiled pot, however, has an even surface with all outward visible signs of the coils smoothed away, whereas a thrown pot often shows the lines made by the potter's fingers, particularly on the inside.

It remains to consider the surface finish of pottery. Low-fired earthenware will, if left as fired, be so porous as to allow water to seep through it, which is intolerable except for water bottles, in which evaporation through the walls cools the bulk of the contents, or for flower pots, which if porous are said to keep the soil in them from souring. The earliest and simplest way to seal the surface of a pot is by burnishing, before firing, with a piece of stone or bone. This is effective, but tends to be ousted by glazing whenever that process, with its greater possibilities, is made possible by the use of a kiln.

The word glaze is the same as glass, and glazes for pottery are made from ground sand or quartz fused into glass by heating and adding lime, potash or soda. Lime or soda has been used on common European pottery over the past thousand years, with lead oxide to improve the coating quality. Colour was obtained by adding other oxides: light browns and yellows from iron, green from copper, and more rarely a purple-brown from manganese. From the fifteenth to the eighteenth century an opaque white glaze was obtained from tin oxide, and this tin-glazed earthenware is variously called delft if Dutch or British, faience if French, maiolica if Italian or Spanish. It was mostly made in imitation of the blue-and-white porcelain then being imported into Europe and greatly admired, but any chip through the glaze of earthenware will expose the material of the pot itself. Not so the glaze on genuine porcelain, which is derived from china stone, one of the ingredients of porcelain, and so becomes perfectly united with it. In contrast the thick translucent glaze on much Middle Eastern pottery remains quite distinct, and a piece of such ware will show sheets and pools of glaze over a granular body. These glazes use soda as a flux, like Middle Eastern glass, and the range of colours given by oxides is different than with lime or potash, so that copper gives a turquoise blue and iron plus manganese a black. These Middle Eastern pots are often 'slipped', that is to say after drying in air but before firing they are dipped in a mixture of clay and water, which gives an improved colour and texture to the subsequently fired surface. Slip may also be applied as a decoration, by brushing or dribbling it on the pot.

The pottery we find around the house and garden and elsewhere will mostly be parts of broken and discarded things. If enough of the shape and decoration remains, we shall be able to judge what it was by considerations of style, but if only a fragment is discovered, the size and shape of the whole vessel will be more or less apparent from the curvatures of the 'shard'. To an archaeologist a piece of rim, handle, or base angle are the most helpful fragments, so collect these if there is any choice. This is just an outline of the basic facts about pottery; if you want to know more about special techniques, such as throwing into moulds, lustre glazing and so on, see the bibliography.

Glass

Pottery and glass are romantically called 'the arts of the fire', because fire hardens pottery and softens glass, but is necessary for the working of both materials. Glass is less helpful to the archaeologist than pottery for two main reasons: it is younger by about 2,000 years, and broken glass can be remelted for use again so fewer fragments are found. Also, although it does not perish utterly in the ground, glass can 'degrade' into a dark crumbling substance that falls away from a glazed pot or an enamelled surface. The first onset of decay in glass shows as an attractive rainbow effect, called iridescence, which appears after only a few years in the earth. The enamels used on metals (but not the enamel paint used on furniture), the glazes on pottery, and the 'paste' of artificial jewellery, are all no more and no less than glass.

The essential ingredient of all glasses is silica (SiO_2) in the form of sand, flint or quartz. It is possible to make a glass of silica only, but this requires a very high temperature, and so from earliest days a flux has been added to reduce the temperature at which silica fuses into glass. The fluxes used are alkalis, either potash or soda, largely dependent on availability. In Egypt, sodium carbonate in the form known as 'natron' is to be found in certain salt lakes and the soda-glass derived from it is typical of that country and the Near East. Elsewhere it is generally true that by the coast people made a soda-glass from seaweed or glasswort fluxes, and inland they relied on potash from wood or bracken. Potash gives a glass that is easy to blow, but the impurities in bracken and wood give it a dull or even dark colour, whereas soda gives a clearer glass but one that is not so easily worked. In the sixteenth century, the Venetians introduced manganese to produce a clear, so-called 'crystal' glass for superior purposes, but plenty of dark-glass bottles continue to be made until the present day. The final constituent of glass, also an optional one, is lime or lead as a stabilizer. This makes it stronger and in addition prevents glass, which is a supercooled liquid, from crystallising as it ages.

The tools and methods used by glassworkers have remained much the same since the blowing of glass was discovered, probably in Syria some years before the birth of Christ. Liquid glass is held over a fire in a crucible, with holes in its cover through which the worker can gather blobs of glass on an iron tube or rod, or insert partly finished workpieces for reheating or for the slight surface melting which gives 'fire-polish'. The blob of plastic glass may be blown, rolled or flattened on a plate, formed with tongs or cut with pincers, and pieces stuck together.

The history of glass-making before the invention of the blowing tube is given under BEADS, for they were the principal product of those early days, although small bottles could be made by winding glass round a core.

The Roman world welcomed the new blown glass with enthusiasm; the first centres of production were in Syria, but later bottles and bowls were made all over the Empire. The typical Roman bottle was shaped by blowing into a mould, then the lip was formed and a strap handle stuck on. Vessels were also free blown and shaped with tongs. The material was a fairly clear soda-glass, sometimes coloured or with trails dribbled on. This was the ordinary glass of the Romans; it often had simple decoration but was not in the luxury class. In Alexandria, however, the skills learnt in hardstone carving were applied to the moulding and cutting of very special coloured glass, and extremely fine objects of art were produced, such as the Portland Vase now in the British Museum.

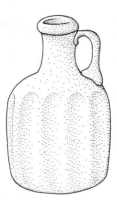

67 *Roman bottle*

The Romans had some window-glass, but it was cast in moulds and not ground flat, so St Paul could well write in one of his Epistles, 'now we see through a glass, darkly'. Roman window-glass is slightly rougher on one side than the other. With the fall of Rome, glass-making went on in a restricted and rustic way throughout Western Europe, and fine glass continued to be made in the Byzantine and Ommayad Empires, where in particular the glass mosaics used to decorate churches and mosques remain to delight us.

The revival of fine glassware in the West started in thirteenth-century Venice. A 'cristallo' glass was developed from local kelp and quartz pebbles, and this was suitable for the creation of the 'frail ethereal shapes' associated with the fame of Venetian glass, at its height in the fifteenth century. Renegade workmen spread the making of cristallo glass to the Netherlands in the sixteenth century, and to England. Meanwhile the potash-fluxed 'forest glass' of central Europe, with some technical aid from Venice, developed a separate tradition and produced stable and capacious vessels such as the roemer suitable for northern beer-drinkers' thirsts.

68 *Roemer*

Flat glass was made in Normandy from around the twelfth century by the surprising method of spinning an opened bubble of glass in the heat of the crucible until it flashed out into a disc under centrifugal force. The size of the panes cut from this so-called 'crown'-glass was limited but sufficient for leaded casement windows, and it was used for them until the end of the eighteenth century. Clock faces were also glazed with crown-glass. Such glass is thin and of good clarity owing to the fire-polish imparted during the 'flashing' process. The bulls-eye in the middle of the disc could be used for some purpose where transparency was not required, and now some 'olde worlde' cottages display a wealth of imitation bulls-eyes in their windows. A sure sign of genuine crown-glass is the curved striations or chains of bubbles seen against a favourable light.

A second method of making flat glass, known as 'broad'-glass, is associated with the glass-makers of Lorraine, who employed this method there from the fifteenth century though it had been practiced earlier in Bohemia. A cylinder of glass is blown, the ends cut off, and the cylinder slit along its length and flattened. Large sheets can be produced, but they do not have the handsome fire-polish of crown-glass. Any imperfections will, of course, be straight not curved.

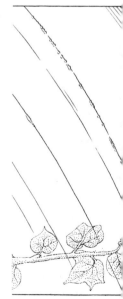

Although crown-glass was made in England from the thirteenth century, it was considered inferior to that imported from France. When the religious wars of the sixteenth century drove glass-workers from Lorraine to England, they continued to make their broad-glass, but found a strong tradition in favour of bright, clear crown-glass. This only gave way slowly during the course of the eighteenth century to broad-glass for the large panes of the sash windows then in fashion.

The third method of making flat glass is to cast it in plates thick enough to be ground and polished. This was

69 *Crown-glass*

most desirable for mirrors, to give a clear reflection, but coach and house windows of superior quality were also made of plate-glass. The first commercial plate-glass dates from the late seventeenth century, and a mirror with its original glass is now highly valued. Since 1840 the reflecting surface on mirrors has been applied by a chemical process: previously tin-foil with mercury was used. The use of plate-glass for windows developed during the first half of the nineteenth century, largely for shops but also for the houses of the rich and great and for public buildings. When the Crystal Palace was erected in Hyde Park for the Great Exhibition of 1851, however, it was glazed with broad-glass, as this was cheaper.

Let's now return to the story of glass vessels, with particular attention to developments in England. In 1615 wood as fuel for industrial purposes was forbidden, in order to conserve the timber used for shipbuilding. Coal was therefore brought into use, but the impurities in it, notably sulphur, made the covering of crucibles necessary. The consequent reduction in direct heat required more flux to reduce the fusing temperature, but this in turn caused the break-up of the finished glass by 'crisselling', somewhat like a shattered windscreen. George Ravenscroft, a glassmaker of London, solved the problem by including lead oxide in his glass. This also had the effect of strengthening it and increasing its refraction of light, so that lead-glass shines and glitters, especially when wheel cut.

Two other improvements contributed to the eminence that English, and later Irish, glass was to enjoy for many years. Firstly, the refining of wood ash was perfected, so that potash could be used as the flux instead of soda. As already mentioned, this made the glass easier to blow. Secondly, the grinding of flint in mills driven by water power provided a good supply of suitable silica for glass. Because flint was adopted as the basic ingredient of fine English glassware at about the same time as lead oxide for its stabilizer, the glass became known confusingly as 'flint-glass', and is still so called today.

During the eighteenth century, and well into the nineteenth century, English and Irish lead-glass was of excellent quality. Fig. 70 shows a typical example of English glass from the first half of the eighteenth century. The cutting of glass on the wheel had not yet been adopted, but tongs were used to good effect in displaying

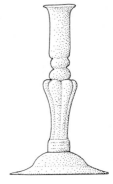

70 Glass taper-stick

71 *Glass salt-cellar*

72 *Victorian*

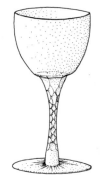

73 *Edwardian*

the heavy, bright glass, rich in lead. In 1745 a duty was imposed in England on glass, by weight, and doubled in 1777. This first caused a reduction in lead content, and then eventually drove English glassmakers to move their business to the south of Ireland, where the duty was not levied, and free trade with Ireland was permitted after 1780. Thus during the last quarter of the eighteenth and the first quarter of the nineteenth century, after which the tax was levied in Ireland also, Irish glass in the English tradition was extensively made. The fashion then was for thick glassware faceted on a grinding wheel. The Irish factories were inclined to be uncertain in the use of manganese to take out the colour, so old cut glass with a dark tinge is commonly ascribed to Ireland. The blue tone associated with old Waterford glass is, however, a myth.

As the nineteenth century progressed, British and Irish cut glass became coarse, heavy and without inspiration, but it has continued to be made until the present day. Much Victorian and later glassware for the table is, by contrast, made by machine and is thin, with perhaps some shallow cutting as decoration. Edwardian glass is positively flimsy, with a prewar 'it'll last our time' air about it.

Early English glass has been extensively faked, and there is no positive way to distinguish the genuine from the false. The base of an old glass will have the scar (known as the pontil mark) where the iron was broken away, but so will a modern reproduction. The base will also have a ring dulled with minute criss-cross lines where it has been scratched in contact with furniture and shelves, but this pattern takes only a few years to develop.

During the eighteenth century and later, ordinary glass without the expensive ingredient lead continued to be made, for common bottles, hour-glasses, and other expendable articles. Much of this glass has the brown or green colour produced by unrefined flux without the addition of manganese.

Another kind of crystal glass, with chalk as the stabilizer, has been made in central Europe, notably in Bohemia (now part of Czechoslovakia) from late in the seventeenth century up to the present. Characteristic pieces are of clear glass cased with coloured glass, which is then cut and ground to display both clear and coloured areas. Much Bohemian glass was inscribed in English, for export to Great Britain, but phrases such as 'The Industrial Exhibition for 1851' on the piece illustrated, are somehow not the words of a native English speaker.

One final 'advance' has been the commercial production of pressed glass, first achieved in the middle of the nineteenth century in the United States. This is made by dropping molten glass into a mould and forming it with a plunger. The mould is made in parts and opened to release the finished piece, which may be given a superficial similarity to cut glass. However the sharp feel of genuine cut glass is lacking, and often the seam can be observed. The plunger must be plain and have at least a slight taper, so that it can be drawn from the inside of the finished piece. Fig. 76 shows a typical pressed glass jug, with a beaded effect in clear glass. Pressed glass is also found coloured, either plain or swirled.

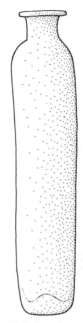

74 *Medicine bottle*

75 *Bohemian glass*

76

Animal

We will be considering only those things made from the durable parts of animals, that is ivory, bone, horn, tortoiseshell, sea shells and leather. Sometimes the original shape of these materials is retained, for instance in a whistle cut from the bone of some creature's limb, or in a box formed from the complete shell of a tortoise. Ivory carvings frequently follow the line of the tusk. Mostly, however, although we can easily say that something is of ivory or bone, horn or whatever, it is not possible to go further and say what kind of animal it is from without expert analysis.

Ivory deserves to be taken first, because it is a rare and beautiful material. It is by definition the large teeth of certain animals. When fully developed within the living body, a tooth is solid and inert; we can chip one of our teeth without pain, but it will not heal. By contrast bones are living; if broken they are painful, but will knit together again. In this distinction lies our best chance of telling a piece of ivory from one of bone, because only bone has minute channels in it to convey vital fluids, and these often appear as black dots. Two other aids may help: ivory has a grain which shows up on a good flat surface, and when cut across the grain a milled effect appears. Both the grain and the milling are coarser in African than in Indian ivory.

Besides elephant ivory we may occasionally find tusks of the walrus used for small carvings, such as chess men. Walrus ivory is lighter in weight and less opaque than that of the elephant, and it has a peculiar silky feel, but these distinctions are not easy to follow without experience. Only if part of the outside of the tusk is seen, will its oval section declare walrus ivory without doubt. Other than elephant and walrus, the single twisted tusk of the narwhal may be found made into a walking stick, or the very hard dull white tusk of the hippotamus met in the form of false teeth from the eighteenth century. The teeth of the sperm whale are technically a kind of ivory, and were a favourite material for whaling men to carve and inscribe.

Ivory and bone are readily stained: often green for knife handles or furniture inlay, red and green for chess men of opposite teams, or pink for the tint of flesh in carvings. In Europe ivory has not commonly been

77 *Indian ivory chess pawn*

78 Sperm whale tooth

painted, the colour and texture of the exposed surface being too much appreciated, but Oriental ivories may be found completely covered.

The simplest work done on bones by man is chopping, sawing or smashing them in the course of preparing meat for food, and archaeologists derive information about the diet of past peoples from the meat bones they leave on living sites. The bones worth our attention will have been cut less casually, and in the process their original shape much altered. Remembering, however, that all bones are either more or less hollow rods, or more or less flat plates, we can understand an object made of bone. Fig. 79 shows a crucifix figure clearly formed from the end of a limb bone.

79

The horns of cattle are a useful by-product of their slaughter for meat, and the ancient craft of the 'horner' is not yet extinct. A drinking vessel or equally well a bugle was the simplest thing he made by trimming and decorating a horn, which is naturally hollow for most of its length. A further step was to make a beaker, by turning down a horn at its wide open end and inserting a round cut piece as a base. These horn beakers have been made and used until recently, mostly for the refreshment of hunting or shooting parties, horn being light to carry and fairly strong. Many of these beakers are quite plain and hard to date, but the author has seen one with an inscription dated 1835.

Horn can be opened up and pressed between hot plates to make windows for lanterns, and this must have been a very usual practice in old days or the common mis-spelling 'lanthorn' would not have arisen. Sheets of horn for this purpose are much thinner than glass, and it should be possible to judge from the depth of the housing for the leaves if the windows of an old lantern were meant for glass or horn.

The rims of spectacles were formerly made of horn, and we still speak of horn-rimmed glasses in this plastic age. We also still have shoe horns.

The horns of sheep are generally too small for use as raw material, but a well known class of snuff box, known as a 'mull' and attributed to Scotland, is not uncommon.

Much of the craft of the horner consists in cutting horn so as to take advantage of its natural shape, for instance to ease the putting on of shoes, but even more usefully it can be pressed into shape when hot and this quality enables practical things such as horn spoons to be made. Horn is not often used for artistic work, but an exception is the plaques and box covers of horn pressed into moulds, made by John Obrisset early in the eighteenth century. The subjects of these are British but the taste is French: probably John Obrisset started life as Jean, but came to England as a refugee from France.

80 *Pressed horn box*

Tortoiseshell is another 'natural plastic', capable of being shaped when hot. It is scales from the carapace of certain turtles, and these scales can be united by the use of hot irons into sheets of two or three millimetres in thickness. Tortoiseshell has been used, notably by the French in the seventeenth century, for veneering boxes and mirror frames; in the nineteenth and well into the twentieth century it is found as the sticks of fans, as combs, on the backs of hair-brushes and on many such small, useful and decorative articles. The usual colour of brown flecked with yellow is familiar to all, but there was a blond tortoiseshell of much lighter hue, and another sort in which the flecks were red. The magnifying glass shown has the rim of the lens made from a section of horn and the case of tortoiseshell.

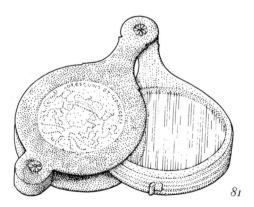

81

Since the eighteenth century horn has been stained to imitate tortoiseshell. In the 1920s and 30s celluloid, a material derived from plant cellulose, was coloured in imitation of tortoiseshell and extensively substituted for it. Celluloid is heavier in the hand, does not have the silky feel of tortoiseshell, can be made in any thickness, and above all is highly inflammable.

Mother-of-pearl is a commercial material from the shells of large tropical oysters. The shiny 'nacreous' appearance of mother-of-pearl can be imitated in plastic, but the greater weight of the genuine material distinguishes it. It is still fairly cheap and has therefore remained in favour for buttons. In the last century mother-of-pearl was in fashion for trinkets, and for the handles of fruit knives and forks, which were often carved.

82 *Fruit knife with mother-of-pearl handle*

A large kind of cowrie shell, traded into Europe from the Indian Ocean since very early days, has a good appearance and a capacious interior. It has therefore been frequently converted into a snuff box by cutting away the opening and mounting a lid. Cameos are made from the helmet shell, and the nautilus makes a fine drinking-cup. Otherwise, sea shells are collected for their beauty and rarity, but little used as raw material.

For the sake of completeness it remains to add a few words about leather which, if kept entirely dry, or conversely soaking wet but with oxygen excluded, will last remarkably well. Boots and shoes (see FOOTWEAR) may thus be preserved and found. Leather has been and still is extensively used for purses, pouches and belts, which may also be discovered, and are usually in need of treatment: see section on conservation. Ancient harness is uncommon considering the large amount that was made. Perhaps when discarded, it lies around in tack rooms and stables until the day comes for a great clear out and burning.

Vegetable

The word 'treen' is used nowadays to comprise the variety of small things made of different kinds of wood and nut. It is a popular subject, and a good book on it is *Treen* by Edward Pinto (Batsford, 1949).

We can usually say, by the evidence of touch, weight, colour, the appearance of growth rings, and how the material has been worked, that a thing is made of wood. But it is not possible to go further, and say what wood it is, without the resources of a specialist laboratory. There identification will depend on examination by expert eyes of a minute slice of the wood under a microscope. However there are some woods that can be guessed with a fair degree of probability. Ebony and lignum-vitae are the only commercial woods heavier than water, so if a solid piece is available, we have only to see if it sinks to isolate our specimen as one of these two. The dense black of ebony is well known as a wood favoured for piano keys, the backs of brushes, carved elephants and so on. Lignum-vitae, which curiously has no common name, is rich brown in colour with lighter swirls, and quite unmistakable when once recognised. It is intensely hard, so seldom carved, but it is turned to make coffee grinders, spinning tops etc. One interesting use for this wood is to line the stern-tubes in ships, as bearings for the propeller shafts. Ebony and lignum-vitae are tropical woods; the only wood from temperate climes that almost sinks in water is box, which is used for good quality drawing instruments and for small carvings. It is yellow, with no visible grain.

83 Oak

Leaving these unusual but identifiable woods, let us consider those we are more likely to find, and what may be done to name them.

First of all must come oak, which has been used in Europe from earliest times, both for large things such as the frames of ships and houses, and for smaller things such as implements and playthings. On large surfaces of oak, so-called 'rays' may be seen as light silvery paths running across the grain. These will not be visible on small pieces, but even they should show the well marked lines of pores in the softer wood between the annual rings. These pores will be more or less elongated according to the angle of cut. As to colour, oak is naturally a light brown, but it is readily stained darker, or bleached lighter, and will often be seen so 'improved'.

The other two famous woods for furniture, walnut and mahogany, will be found made into boxes to contain bottles, or gloves, or what you will, chiefly according to their fashion in furniture, that is to say walnut from 1660 to 1720 and mahogany from then until well into the nineteenth century. When polished and aged, these woods are not easy to distinguish. To see undoubted

84 Walnut

pieces of walnut, examine the stocks of shotguns in a gunsmith's shop: note the bright lustrous surface and the characteristic dark lines running along the borders of the annual rings. Walnut has been, and continues to be, much used for carvings, the handles of cutlery, and other small things of quality. Mahogany, on the other hand, is too soft for such purposes, if we except the kind from the West Indies, which was used in early Georgian furniture and soon all cut down. Mahogany, when matured and polished, is of a rich coppery colour, but it fades to a greyish brown if exposed to the sun. Unlike oak, the pores are evenly spread throughout the wood.

Besides these furniture woods we may find several other woods used for small things. There are lime and field maple, both close-grained, light coloured woods that have been used for decorative objects throughout the centuries. Then we have pearwood, formerly made into large drawing instruments, such as T-squares, and drawing boards themselves; it is also a favourite wood for sculpture. It is of a purple-brown satiny appearance, with no visible grain, and noticeably light in weight. For some reason it is called 'fruitwood', though it is not the only wood used from fruit trees. Cherry wood is not unlike that of the pear, but without the purple tinge and with a distinct grain. It is used for furniture handles and even buttons. Tobacco pipes made of cherry wood give a delicious scent to the smoke, but soon burn through.

Finally in this short and selective account there is rosewood, which actually comes from a tree of the pea family growing in Brazil. As well as a furniture veneer, it is used for the handles of superior craftsman tools (Fig. 85). The appearance is distinctive: a warm reddish brown with patches of golden and violet-brown stripes.

As well as wood itself, nuts have been made into small articles or decoratively carved. Most common is the coconut, which needs no description. Others are the coquilla, the fruit of a Brazilian palm, which like the coconut has three 'eyes' at the end that can be made to look like a face, and 'vegetable ivory', the nut of another South American palm, which was imported in quantity in the last century for making buttons.

There are also such curiosities as walking sticks made of cabbage stalks, but even the toughest material from herbaceous plants such as this will not prove durable enough for us to find.

85 *Gold-leaf burnisher*

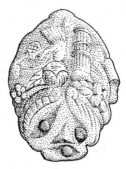

86 *Coquilla nut*

Few small things are veneered, but among them are the mahogany boxes already mentioned. Early veneers were handcut to thickness of about 2 mm: from 1860 veneers have been pared by machine and are considerably thinner. If a veneer is not a plain slice of one wood, but is made up of pieces of different woods, cut and laid into a pattern, it is known as marquetry if the effect is pictorial or parquetry if it is geometric. A special kind of parquetry was applied to small boxes, small picture frames and suchlike in the town of Tunbridge Wells, Kent, from the eighteenth century until 1900, and then again as a revival in the 1920s. Tunbridge ware is wood covered with slices of canes made from strips of different coloured woods, some stained and some natural. It was at the height of fashion about 1850 when the best work was done, and some canes were sliced at an angle to give a long rectangle. Another kind of fancy work was Mauchline ware, also at its most popular about 1850 and dying out around 1900. It was made in and around the Ayrshire town of Mauchline, of local sycamore wood, with black transfer prints varnished, or covered with tartan designs, or varnished black, with ferns.

Small decorated lacquered objects will usually be oriental, judged by their style and also the superiority of the lacquer, which was laid down in coat after coat, each with the greatest care, and finely polished. The imitation 'japanning' practised in Europe from the late seventeenth century was too coarse for use on anything other than furniture. Japanning was often done by amateurs, and so was 'penwork', in which a light-coloured, close-grained wood was drawn on in ink, largely during the eighteenth century. In the same class is the scrolled-paper work mostly to be found covering wooden tea caddies.

89 Penwork pattern

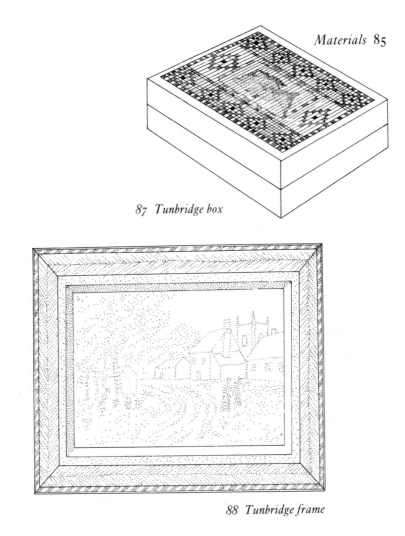

87 *Tunbridge box*

88 *Tunbridge frame*

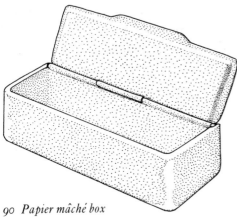

90 *Papier mâché box*

Papier mâché is not strictly of wood, but of a substance reconstituted from it. We find it as cheap little boxes dating from the eighteenth and early nineteenth centuries and often showing at broken edges the pulped paper from which they were made. The papier mâché is varnished, and sometimes inlaid with lines or motifs in pewter, or it may be splashed with paint to give a passing likeness to tortoiseshell. I have seen a box painted with a young girl in 1860 costume, with the then fashionable 'pork-pie' hat. Superior to these are the boxes, letter racks and so on of black, deep green or red papier mâché, gilded, painted, and inlaid with mother-of-pearl. These were made for a century or so following the method invented by Henry Clay of Birmingham who, in the late eighteenth century, formed a hard and durable material out of sheets of paper, glued and pressed together, and then lacquered.

Mineral

Having already dealt with ores, the only group of minerals left to us is those known as 'hardstones', the natural decorative stones not used in jewellery. This definition has an area of uncertainty: jade is basically a hardstone but is used in jewellery; topaz is a gem but a large one can be carved into a box.

The most common hardstones which may be found are varieties of quartz, the general name for crystallised silicates. If pure, it is clear and colourless rock crystal, and the crystals are visible and often quite large. Rock crystal may have needles of a reddish-brown mineral in it, or fern-like intrusions which turn it into moss agate. If coloured with oxides, it can still form large crystals: the light purple amethyst, citrine the colour of dry sherry, and smoky quartz. But a quartz with considerable impurities will have solidified into small crystals not visible to the eye, and according to its colour will be one of the following large and popular class of hardstones:

1. Chalcedony is uniformly grey, with possibly some shadows of lighter or darker colour.
2. Agate is striped in a circular or wavy fashion.
3. Onyx is striped black and white in flat layers like a layered cake. An onyx striped brown and white is a sardonyx. The distinction between onyx and agate is

that only onyx can be cut into a cameo, forming a low relief of contrasting colour.

4. Impure quartzs of one colour throughout are the red-brown cornelian, the dark green plasma, the light green chrysoprase, and the dark brown sard. Plasma with specks of red is bloodstone.

5. Jasper is an impure quartz of variegated colour.

Impure quartz can be stained to improve its colour, and this is extensively done when preparing onyx for use as a cameo.

Quartz of good quality is widely distributed in igneous rocks, and has been worked ever since metal tools enabled it to be cut. Moreover modern lapidaries use the same tools and methods as did those in former ages, so a good modern carving is much the same as an ancient one.

Jades are complex silicates, notably hard, tough, heavy and beautiful, but the word includes two distinct minerals. Nephrite has a greasy lustre, a granular structure, and a wide range of colours; it is found in Turkestan, New Zealand and South America. Jadeite has a bright lustre, a fibrous structure, is green and white in colour, and rarely blue or lilac; it is found in Burma and Normandy. With some experience gained in museums and auction rooms the difference in appearance between the surface of nephrite and jadeite is distinguishable. The Chinese have always admired jade above all other material, and have carved large pieces of it into works of the highest art, but small things of jade were made to be kept on the person and handled from time to time, such as the disc with rice-grain pattern shown, and should be

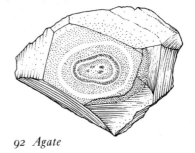

92 *Agate*

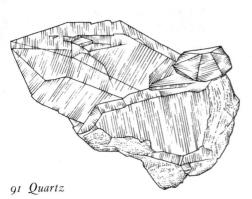

91 *Quartz*

93 *Chinese jade disc*

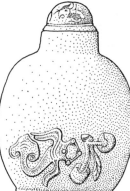

98 *Chinese snuff bottle*

94 *Hand-drilled tiki*

95 *Machine-cut tiki*

recognisable if found. The Maoris of New Zealand also loved their 'greenstone' from the streams of the South Island west coast. The illustration shows two of their *tikis*, an old one with hand drilling and cutting and one that was recently cut on a grinding wheel. One of these people was lifting a boulder of jade from the water when he noticed a pocket of golden flakes where it had lain. This was of no interest to him, but it started the New Zealand gold rush of the 1850s by Europeans.

Another complex silicate, lapis lazuli, is of blue flecked with the silver of iron pyrites. The ancient civilisations of the Middle East traded it from far-off Afghanistan, and another kind is found in Chile.

A limited variety of small practical things are made of hardstones, such as the agate lid of a small box, a mortar of chalcedony for an apothecary, and a Chinese snuff bottle. Carvings of men and animals are found in hardstones, notably the realistic figures made in the workshops of Carl Fabergé in Russia before the Revolution. He used different coloured stones with great skill but his work is not comparable in beauty to Chinese carving.

96 *Box with agate lid*

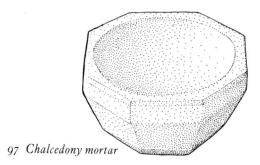

97 *Chalcedony mortar*

The brightly variegated calcium fluoride known as Blue John was mined in Derbyshire by the Romans and again from the eighteenth century. It is too soft for figures, but it can be turned into urns and vases, or cut into veneers for the sides of boxes. The name is a corruption of 'bleu jaune', and indeed blue and yellow are the principal colours in it, with white and touches of brown. Another soft decorative stone is malachite, a favourite material for the Russians to turn and veneer in much the same way as Blue John.

The various coloured calcites known as marble, and the alabasters formed of gypsum, are outside our range as they are generally made into large objects such as the tops of furniture and basins. However a greenish marble with brown markings is nowadays carved into small things and sold under the deceptive name of 'onyx'.

Keeping the Finds

Conservation

This will not be a long chapter because there is little that can effectively and safely be done on a 'do-it-yourself' basis to conserve things found. Laboratory processes start with a detailed analysis of the material and go on to employ sophisticated techniques, apparatus and chemicals far beyond our means.

The objects we find and bring home have usually been in the same place for many years, and have achieved a balance with their environment. Otherwise it stands to reason that they would already have rusted, rotted or somehow faded away. When we remove them from that environment into another, they may suffer considerable damage before achieving a new balance. A simple case is that of a shoe found in a river. Soaking wet, it is nevertheless still fairly supple and has remained its full size. Taken home and put in the oven to dry, you will find in the morning a hopelessly shrunk and hardened relic. At the other extreme, however, a flint axe may require no attention at all, and may remain perfectly unchanged in any normal surroundings.

The following notes refer to materials in the same order as earlier.

First a general rule applicable to all metals: resist the temptation to 'see what it is made of' by scratching or filing the surface. Even a small scratch will open up the interior to corrosion, and in the case of coins the value and interest of your find will be severely reduced.

Bronze and Brass These metals, particularly if they have previously been polished, are often found with a smooth grey-green patina, which is much better left as it is. Coins should never be polished, and indeed it is best to leave all old metal objects unpolished. The medals from recent wars which their recipients were pleased to keep bright, may be polished afresh if in sound condition. The dreaded 'bronze disease' appears as a light blue powder in the presence of acid and oxygen, and it requires expert attention. It is a comfort that attacks are unlikely if things are kept in the atmosphere of a normal house.

Iron and its Alloys   Most wrought iron or steel objects come out of the ground heavily corroded, some to the extent of being unrecognisable. Generally speaking the older the iron the better it will keep, but nobody should attempt to retain iron objects of more than passing interest without their receiving expert treatment. As to what is interesting, your local museum will advise. The best way to preserve iron is to paint it, but if this is not acceptable there are preparations such as Plus-Gas Fluid A that will soften the rust, though they will not inhibit further corrosion.

Lead and Tin Alloys   In the context of conservation, this means pewter, and the only treatment advised is to wash with warm soapy water. If the surface is corroded there is nothing to be done, but in my experience a moderately corroded piece of pewter exposed to the ordinary atmosphere of a house will get no worse over the years. Old pewter should not be polished.

Pottery   Washed in warm soapy water, it is remarkable how improved even the most ordinary shard appears. Use up the last slivers from cakes of toilet soap this way, but avoid detergents. I once had success in cleaning black deposit from a Roman pottery lamp by using salt and vinegar, thus exposing a figure in low relief previously unseen. Even a weak acid, however, would damage some pottery, such as certain Bronze Age clays which were mixed with chalk. If a pot is to be restored by gluing together fragments, do it in a bed of sand and use a reversible glue in case for some reason you want to have it in pieces again. There is more than one adhesive which has a solvent, but a suitable pair is the polyvinyl acetate sold as 'Uhu', which is melted out by acetone.

Glass   Wash with soap and water, but definitely not with detergents. It is important to keep old glass, which may have partially crystalised, quite dry after washing.

Animal   Dry leather can with advantage be treated with neatsfoot oil. Wet leather will require expert treatment to replace the water in it without permanent damage.

Vegetable Wood soaked in water is also a subject for expert treatment. Sound wood will benefit from furniture polish but be sure that it is the right colour. A simple 'reviver' for neglected wood is made from 2 parts of linseed oil and 2 parts of methylated spirit made up with 8 parts of vinegar.

To read an inscription cut in any hard material, if it has become blurred by wear or otherwise difficult to see, take a sheet of metal foil from a roll in the kitchen and press it carefully into the surface with an old, stubby but soft paintbrush. Then shine a light in various directions upon it and you will often be able to read in the reflecting surface of the foil what was otherwise undecipherable.

Many things found will be dirty but perfectly sound underneath. If so, a great deal of satisfaction can be gained from careful and thorough cleaning accompanied and followed by studious handling. The exhibits in a museum are quite rightly only there to be viewed, often from one angle, but interesting old things found may be examined from all angles and their surfaces explored by the sense of touch. Moreover, most materials in sound condition will benefit by being handled, or kept in a warm pocket of one's clothes if a suitable size. The only caution necessary here is to avoid finger-marks on polished metal surfaces because they can cause corrosion.

It is not only when things have been recently acquired that you should examine them, but also from time to time as long as they are in your possession. If you get to know a thing, it will in some strange way tell you about itself. Looked at from various angles and under different lights, and handled when you feel like it, a certainty about some detail will establish itself. I have in mind a small terracotta figure of a dog which I have had for many years on a shelf in my house. This object is of a class from the ancient Near East which is still under dispute, some people thinking that they are cult objects and others believing them to be toys. Knowing the figure as I have come to do over the years, I am quite convinced that it was a child's toy.

Many things found will be interesting enough to be kept, and how to do so is largely common sense. Clearly the ideal is to display finds in a well-lit glass-fronted case, not crowded with objects, and each of them labelled. But display is not as important as keeping the thing found, together with all that is known of it, complete and permanently referenced to each other. That is what this short chapter will mainly be about.

When you find something, make rough notes about where you found it. If you have an Ordnance Survey map covering the location, write the grid reference, otherwise a description will have to suffice. Not only where on the surface is important; you must also note if it was on the surface or how far under it. And the immediate surroundings may relate to your find: parts of clay pipes may be plentiful near an inn; or special implements near to some place of work, such as a tannery.

As soon as possible give the find an 'accession number', and enter it in a suitable book or card index system. Transcribe your rough notes and add anything else to the record that you have learnt since the thing was found. Use a simple system, such as numbering from one every year, so that your sixth find in 1974 would be 6/74. Indian ink and a mapping pen are best for marking the object, and you will need a bottle of both black and white ink, for contrast on light or dark surfaces. Mark in what you judge a suitable place, neither spoiling the best view of your exhibit, which museums used to do frequently, nor writing in such an obscure place that it is difficult to see. When the ink is dry, put a dab of nail varnish over it.

Labelling should be done on thin white card, preferably with an electric typewriter, but an ordinary typewriter is almost as good. Be brief but informative, saying what the thing is and its date. If you are unsure, put a question mark in brackets, but a whole case full of queries would give a poor impression. Cut the card so that it can be shaped as an inverted 'V', and aim for a long low shape rather than a tall one. Avoid using those machines that print by hand on plastic tape: they have their uses, but one of them is not for labelling exhibits in cases, where the effect is coarse and assertive, as well as expensive, and the tape tends to come unstuck in time. While on the subject of what not to employ, be warned against sticky tape, particularly the clear pressure-adhesive kind, which leaves indelible marks on many surfaces at best, and at the worst may lift paint or other treatment.

You may have to keep some things in reserve storage, indeed it is said that a good museum is one quarter display and three-quarters storage space. Have your reserve finds wrapped in acid-free tissue paper (which can be bought from a large stationery shop or a museum supplier) with a temporary label secured to the outside by a rubber band. Stow the wrapped objects in drawers, only one layer deep.

(In dating finds I have tended to use periods rather than specific dates. This table gives some dates for the periods.)

Reference in text	Dates
Old Stone Age	approx. 500,000 B.C.
Middle Stone Age	approx. 12,000 B.C.
New Stone Age or Neolithic period (dawn of civilisation in the Near East)	8,000 B.C.
Ancient civilisations, antiquity, the ancients, the ancient world, ancient days	4,000 B.C. to A.D. 500
Bronze Age (in Britain)	
Early	2,000 B.C.
Middle (Wessex Culture)	1500 B.C.
Late	1000 to 500 B.C.
Iron Age (in Britain)	500 B.C. to A.D. 40 (Roman invasion)
Classical times, classical world	600 B.C. to A.D. 500
Ancient Egypt, Egypt of the Pharaohs	5,000 B.C. to 30 B.C. (death of Cleopatra)
Hellenistic world	331 B.C. (death of Alexander) to 50 B.C.
Roman	265 B.C. (Rome supreme in Italy) to A.D. 500
Imperial Rome, Roman Empire	A.D. 27 (Augustus becomes Emperor) to A.D. 500
Saxon (in England)	A.D. 450 to 1066 (Norman conquest)
Dark Ages (in western Europe)	A.D. 500 to 800
Byzantine	A.D. 500 to 1453 (fall of Constantinople)
Middle Ages, Medieval	800 to 1350
Renaissance	approx. 1350 to 1550
Post-medieval	1500 to 1750
Restoration	1660 (accession of Charles II)
Industrial Revolution	1750 to 1850
Georgian	1714 (accession of George I) to 1830 (death of George IV)
Victorian	1837 to 1901 (reign of Queen Victoria)
Edwardian	1901 to 1910 (reign of Edward VII)

Things Found

Aircraft Parts

Aircraft and parts of aircraft have been scattered over most countries in wartime, and accidents continue to happen. Most aeronautical material that comes to earth is recovered almost immediately, but some remains to be found and deserves comment on dating and identification. In the past many detachable parts such as clocks and control columns have been taken as souvenirs from aircraft about to be scrapped, and some of these may be discarded to be found again by us.

The structure of early aircraft was made of wood sticks, braced with wires with screws to tension them, and covered with painted canvas. In the 1930s this form of construction gradually gave way to riveted aluminium sheet and bars, but even today there are still a few of the old 'box-kite' type of aeroplane flying.

The development of aluminium casting in the early years of this century contributed more to the development of the aeroplane than any other single factor. This light material was used even before the First World War for the crankcases of aero engines, and during that war it was trusted enough to be made into cylinders. During the First World War also the forging of aluminium made possible the manufacture of connecting rods and other moving parts from it. By 1918 brass and copper had been almost eliminated from the engines of aircraft.

A less important but interesting material was bakelite, a synthetic resin invented in 1909 and largely developed for the ignition systems of aero engines. Vulcanised rubber was also used, but it dated from the 1860s.

You are unlikely to find parts of airships but if you do the aluminium alloy bars of larger section than used in aircraft will be a good indication of their identity.

Parts of aircraft from the Second World War will not be identifiable from their materials, which were much the same as at present.

There is a fine collection of old aircraft and engines in the Shuttleworth Collection, Biggleswade, Herts. See also *Aviation* by C. H. Gibbs-Smith (The Science Museum, London, 1970) and *Aviation Archaeology* by Bruce Robertson (Patrick Stephens, 1977).

Amulets and Talismans

An amulet exerts magical protection against evil in general, whereas a talisman provides some particular virtue or affords protection against some specific ill, such as drowning or insobriety. The usual talisman is a ring, brooch or pendant set with a gem, but a plain copper ring worn to relieve cramp is by definition a talisman rather than an amulet. An amulet is marked with words, figures or a design, writing being regarded by the illiterate as magical in itself. The ancient inscribed seals to be found in Western Asia after the seasonal rains have washed them out, were collected and ground into powder for medicine. For the literate, words of prayer or invocation from the Bible or the Koran, magic diagrams such as the pentacle or the early Christian sign of the fish (the Greek for fish is ICHTHYS = ' the initial letters of 'Jesus Christ, Son of God, Saviour' in Greek) may be written on suitable material to compose an amulet.

99 Talisman

Amulets and talismans came into Christianity from the pagan world, and persisted in use despite the disapproval of the Church. Even in our day birth-stones and medals with zodiacal signs are still popular, even if few people believe in their powers. It follows that amulets and talismans of all ages may occasionally be found.

100 Flint 'eye'

One particular amulet, the 'eye bead', deserves special attention. If some natural stone has layers of two or more different colours, and a pebble of it chances to break in a slightly domed form, a circle of one colour may be shown against the background of another, and looks like an eye. These natural eyes are readily reproduced by cutting, and easily copied in glass (Fig. 101). Whether natural or man-made, eye beads have long been widely accepted as amulets to watch over their wearers, who may be human or animal. To this day working horses in Turkey are adorned with eye beads of blue glass, and so are small children in Greece.

101 Glass eye

This is no place to list all the properties ascribed to gems, which range from protection against sudden death of various kinds and illnesses, to loss of chastity. It is safe to say, however, that the gems in any piece of jewellery from the fall of Rome to the Renaissance had some talismanic reason for being there. The toadstone is of particular interest. It was in fact some natural curiosity such as a piece of fossil tooth or a pebble of grey

102 Toadstone ring

chalcedony, but it was thought to be from the head of a toad and to afford protection against poisons. The theory was that the toad, itself believed to be venomous, carried its own antidote. The author saw a friend wearing a grey chalcedony in a ring; she had no idea of its significance, but had found a strange round grey stone and liked it well enough to have it mounted.

Armour

Armour is the protective clothing worn in war. It may be of leather or any other stout material, but here we will only consider metal armour of the kinds that might possibly be found as pieces discarded or lost. The oldest specimens of armour we might perhaps find are the small tinned bronze plates that were wired in overlapping rows on to the leather cuirasses of Roman auxiliary soldiers. The legionary wore a steel cuirass instead.

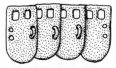

103 Roman 'lorica' armour

Mail armour is commonly called chain mail, a needless repetition as the word mail means 'meshed'. The process of making mail was indeed like that for chain: iron wire was wound on a bar, and the coil then cut along its length to form a number of open rings. The ends of these were then flattened, the rings linked to one another and the ends riveted or welded together.

Worn over padded clothing, mail resisted sword blows well, but those of maces less effectively, and the angles of the body such as the knees and elbows were particularly vulnerable, so from the thirteenth century pieces of plate armour were added. By the middle of the fifteenth century plate armour reached perfection and covered the whole of a knight's body, though he still might wear a coat of mail under it.

104 Mail armour

Pieces of European mail are unlikely to be found, but in the Near East and in India mail armour continued in use until the end of the nineteenth century, and was acquired by soldiers and travellers and brought back to the West. Eastern mail is often of large links, with the ends prominently flattened and riveted.

Plate armour was made by working plates of iron or steel over formers; the marks left by this process will be evident inside, though smoothed away on the outside. Much of the armourer's skill lay in making different areas of the piece of an exact thickness, to avoid unnecessary weight. Thus a sleeve for the forearm, known as a 'vambrace', will be thinner on the side nearest the body. Modern reproduction armour for stage use is generally lighter, but of constant thickness. The use of the micrometer and calipers is recommended, although the general air of solidity and good workmanship in a genuine piece of armour should suffice to identity it. Even so, old armour varies greatly in quality, from the superb productions of the sixteenth century – after which armour was made mostly for show – to the roughly made pieces for continental mercenaries in that century and even in the next.

Armour was too valuable to be left lying about after a battle, and it is a long time since it was worn, but pieces might be found in some neglected corner of an old house.

There are fine collections of armour in the Tower of London and the Victoria and Albert Museum, London. A good introduction to the subject is *Arms and Armour* by A. Cimarelli (Orbis, 1973); a more advanced book is *European Armour* by C. Blair (Batsford, 1958).

Arrowheads

It is now generally agreed that the bow was independently invented, in different parts of the world, in Upper Paleolithic times (say 20,000 B.C.), when men learnt to trim bone or stone neatly enough to make heads for arrows. The other two essential parts of an arrow, the shaft and the feathers, are perishable and need not be mentioned here, but arrowheads survive in large numbers widely scattered where they fell to earth.

Early arrowheads, usually made either of flint or obsidian according to availability, are found in five common varieties (see Fig. 105).

The leaf shape and tranchet arrowhead are natural forms to be made in stone; the leaf is formed by flaking all over, and the tranchet by trimming a 'slice' struck from a core. The hollow-based and barbed forms are copies of bronze arrowheads, which were latterly in use together with stone ones. Both were finally superseded by those of iron. Arrowheads were made of bone by some primitive people, but they are unlikely to be found by us.

The use of metal for arrowheads allows a distinction

Barbed

Hollow-based

Leaf

Tranchet

Tranchet

105 Flint arrowheads

between heads for hunting birds and small animals, which are broad to increase the chance of disabling the quarry which can then be caught and killed, and heads for warfare or hunting large beasts, which are stubby to penetrate armour or hide and pierce to the vitals. The flint tranchet arrowhead may also have been for hunting small game.

According to Marco Polo, the broad arrow was used for short range in warfare by the soldiers of Kubla Khan in the thirteenth century. The illustration shows a Persian 'broad arrow' of bronze.

So far we have written of arrows for the long bow made of wood, or horn, or of several materials; it was basically a simple weapon, drawn by the power of a man's muscles directly applied. The Romans had a military engine for discharging arrows: it was called a *catapulta*, and nicknamed 'scorpion' by the soldiers. We hear of it also as a *ballista*, but that was properly for throwing stones. We do not know exactly how the *catapulta* worked, though it was probably on the principle of a crossbow, but its boltheads are found in forts besieged by the Roman armies, such as Maiden Castle, where one was left in the backbone of a defending British warrior.

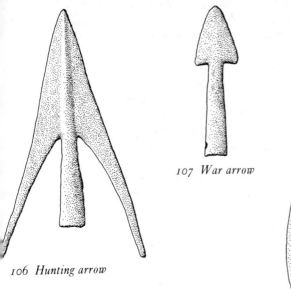

106 Hunting arrow

107 War arrow

108 Bronze Persian arrow

The hand-held crossbow or arbalist was a medieval weapon favoured on the continent of Europe but little used by the English except at sea, or for hunting. The basic difference between the longbow and the crossbow was that the latter had a short stiff bow to be drawn by the power of both arms applied to a hook over the string, or by a windlass. It was harder hitting at short range than a longbow, but the rate of fire was slower. The crossbow fired a bolt of wood shorter and thicker than an arrow, with an iron head. It is the greater diameter of the shaft hole (about 15 mm compared to about 8 mm), and its often square section head (from which it is sometimes called a 'quarrel'), that distinguishes a bolthead from an arrowhead.

The conventionalised mark of a hunting arrow, known as a 'broad-arrow', which is used to mark British government stores and which it is a felony to obliterate or deface, was originally the badge of Viscount Sydney, Master-General of Ordnance 1693 to 1702. No doubt it was generally adopted because it is distinctive and easy to cut.

Axes

An axe has its blade in line with the haft: its near relative, the adze, has its blade at right angles to the haft.

Axes and knives have this in common: both are for cutting and both can be used for peaceable or warlike purposes. Just as a man can cut up his meat or stab his enemy with the same dagger, so he can chop down wood or his foe with the same axe. However a purpose-made battleaxe tends to be slimmer and therefore lighter than a wood axe, because it must be wielded against a moving target; whereas the heavier a felling axe is, within the limits of the woodman's strength, the better.

The axe of the Old Stone Age was a crude implement; it was chipped into shape by blows of another stone, unpolished, and held in the hand without a haft. We cannot tell exactly how it was used; it may at times have been held like an adze and drawn through the ground to grub up roots.

In the New Stone Age axes were made of good hard stone, such as quartzite or even jade; they were well shaped and polished, and some were provided with a carefully drilled shaft hole. The distinction between the

109 Ballista bolt

110 Crossbow bolt

battleaxe and the wood axe was, at this time, quite clear. *Things Found* 103

Axes of the Bronze Age have long been a favourite
with archaeologists. They demonstrate progress from
the simple flat axe through the palstave to the socketed
axe, a well defined series of advances in the bronze
founder's craft (Figs 115–117).

With the Iron Age we reach axes of forms like those

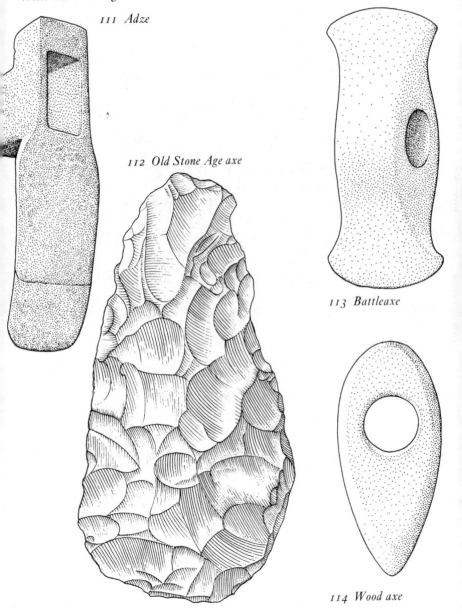

111 Adze

112 Old Stone Age axe

113 Battleaxe

114 Wood axe

we still use, except of course the battleaxe. This was a hard-hitting weapon, but it had the disadvantage of exposing the warrior to a quick thrust with sword or spear as he lifted his axe to strike. Despite this, the northern barbarians of the Dark Ages favoured it. The Vikings carried a large hand-held iron axe, no doubt steeled at the edge, and the Franks who poured into Gaul from the north-east as the Roman Empire failed, bore a throwing axe called a *francisca*. Notice how the blade is set at right angles to the line of flight as it whirls in the air. Franciscas are found in graves and also in the ground where they fell and were not for some reason recovered.

Fig. 120 shows an axe from the grave of a Saxon warrior, who was buried with a sword and a spear as well. The axe looks too stout to be a weapon: perhaps its owner was a famous tree feller of his day (such as can still be found in Australia), and his favourite axe was intended to go with him to the next world.

More likely to be found than any form of battleaxe are the medieval, and later, axes for use with wood and stone. From the illustrations in medieval manuscripts we can distinguish many types including:

Fig. 121. A woodman's axe, stoutly made and often with a hammer end that was no doubt useful when setting up posts.

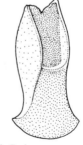

115 Flat axe

Fig. 122. A carpenter's axe. This is the tool of a craftsman, with the shaft hole drifted through the solid iron, and a flat top edge so that the carpenter can see to keep to a scribed line on his workpiece.

Fig. 123. A trimming axe of light form for work on the side of riven timber. Trimming axes may be flat on the side used against the wood.

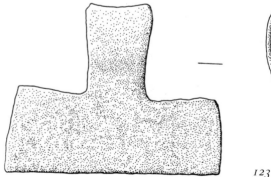

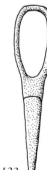

123

116 Palstave

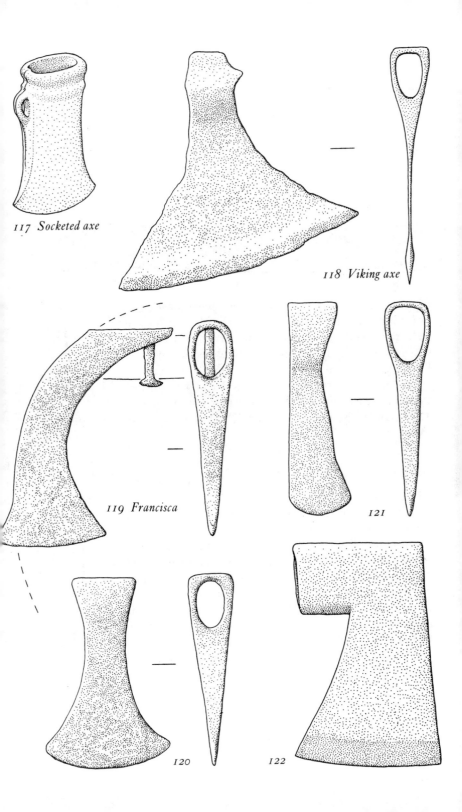

117 Socketed axe

118 Viking axe

119 Francisca

120

121

122

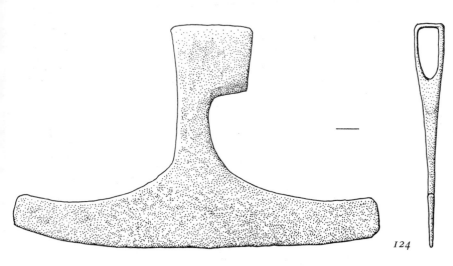

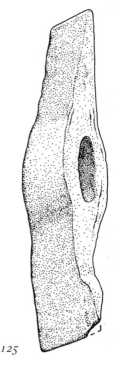

Fig. 124. A so-called 'bearded' axe for general use. The beard is the downward extension of the blade. This axe lacks the quality or weight of the carpenter's axe; the socket is made by folding over and welding down.

Fig. 125. A stonemason's axe, with a pick at the end.

It was not until the factory production of drop-forged axes in the early nineteenth century that axes became of a few standardised sorts and shapes, and thus they have remained.

Badges

The dictionary defines a badge as 'a token or cognizance worn in allusion to the wearer's occupation, position, preference or achievements'. The Royalist badge dating from the English Civil War is typical. It differs from a medal in not being awarded, and unlike medals and medallions (see the entry MEDALS) does not celebrate public events or deeds. Badges and medals alike may be pinned to the clothing, or provided with a ring so as to be suspended from a ribbon. Badges but not medals are to be found with a flat hook at the back, so that they can be worn on headgear, or the smaller ones in the lapel of a coat. Since the eighteenth century some military badges have been given two small rings at the back for a split pin (Fig. 127).

The heraldic device known as a badge is a special emblem worn by members and servants of a particular family. A well known badge in this sense is the three

126 Cap badge

127 Collar dogs

128 Coal-seller's badge

129 Helmet plate

ostrich feathers of the Prince of Wales. Unlike a crest they are not part of the coat of arms.

The earliest badges likely to be found are pilgrim badges from medieval shrines; these were bought to be worn, often in the hat, by those who had made the pilgrimage. They are flat castings of what appears to be pewter, and have a pin and clasp at the back, like a modern brooch, unless this has been lost. Pilgrim badges turn up in the ground, in the bed of a river, or in the neighbourhood of famous shrines visited by many pilgrims. Some of these devout travellers would wear the badges of other places they had visited – rather like the stickers on modern tourists' cars – and could easily drop one without noticing.

In the Middle Ages and later, people such as licensed watermen operating ferries across the Thames, and even beggars in the streets of London were required to wear badges. These badges were decreed to be '. . . with th'arms of London in the midst, to be stricken with a stamp in metal of pure white tin . . .'. The municipal coat of arms on the coal-seller's badge is typical.

Most of the badges found will be recent, and either military or denoting membership of some society. The

130 Royalist badge

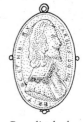

131 Lapel badge

132 First World War badge

badges of societies will declare themselves by the writing and emblems on them: some masonic badges are of gold and enamels, and are worthy relatives of the jewelled badges worn by member of orders of chivalry.

Early soldiers' badges and the badges of officers until modern times were made of embroidery, including silver wire, and will seldom have survived. Metal badges were introduced late in the eighteenth century, first as a large 'helmet plate' that survived until the peaked cap, which required a smaller badge, took over between 1880 and 1914. Small badges, known as collar dogs, usually with split pin attachment, were provided in pairs for tunic collars, and badges of rank (small crowns and stars) for shoulder straps were all of metal until in the 1930s cloth badges of rank came in. Brass was the universal material, but in very recent years metal coated plastic has outmoded the daily polishing of buttons and badges. Brass military badges are commonly found, in great variety. Identification depends largely on the history of the regiment or corps concerned, but the distinction between the King's and Queen's crown (see p. 29) can be useful, and the style is also a clue. As with many things, older badges tend to be more substantial than later ones.

A particular badge that turns up regularly is that for 'services rendered'; it was given to men and women who were honourably discharged from the Forces during and after the First World War (Fig. 132).

Brighton Museum has a good general collection of badges, and King's Lynn Museum, Norfolk, has a selection of pilgrim badges. For military badges, see *Regimental Badges* by T. J. Edwards (Gale & Polden, 1966).

Beads

Beads were surely among the first personal adornments, for a string of brightly coloured stones, or even seeds, effectively graces a woman's neck, arm or waist. Among early beads must have been many that have perished away, like the hips and haws, the sloes and barberries still used to make rustic jewellery.

Beads are usually strung, but to judge by their position in some ancient graves they were also sewn on to garments.

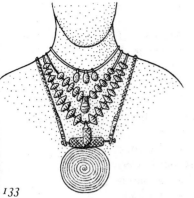

134 Egyptian beads

133

Casual finds of beads may be single or a group. If a group is composed of similar beads, or ones that go well together, they may be assumed to have been strung together, but it is not unknown for a bag of unrelated beads to be lost or deposited. Some years ago a boy brought a fine blue glass bead to a Kentish museum, saying he had found it with a number of others in a hollow tree. When questioned he blithely admitted that he had kept only one bead and used the others in his catapult. He had presumably found a complete Jutish necklace. Another bead story comes from Skara Brae, a prehistoric village on the coast of the Orkney Isles, where the excavators found a trail of amber beads on the path leading out of the settlement. They had been dropped by a woman from a broken necklace in her precipitate flight as sands finally engulfed her home.

Among the earliest beads found are those made from bone or teeth, from amber, or from some brightly coloured but soft stone such as the apatite necklace from Çatal Hüyük, the site in Turkey of one of the earliest towns in the world. These may have been bored using an obsidian drill, for they show the characteristic conical hole bored by a non-metallic bit.

Many early beads were made from small shells or pieces of larger ones, and these together with seeds were copied in gold by the goldsmiths of the ancient world. The necklaces of the Phrygian goddess now in the museum at Izmir in Turkey are formed in pottery as is the rest of the figure, but the originals were probably of precious metal, which there was no shortage of in the Midas dynasty (Fig. 133).

The discovery of metal enabled hardstones to be worked, so that the attractive range of quartz – agate, cornelian, onyx, etc. – as well as other hardstones such as turquoise and lapis lazuli, became available for beads among the people of ancient civilisations. The Egyptians of the pharaohs desired to make durable monuments, and for this purpose they developed the cutting of granite and other hard rocks, using bronze tools and abrasive sand. Using similar tools, their lapidaries cut and engraved hardstones to make many small things, including seals, amulets and beads. These beads were turned, either round, cylindrical, or of some intermediate contour, and similar beads were made throughout the Middle East in antiquity. Round beads of hardstone are attractive when strung, and pleasant to handle and wear, and so they have long been popular. Measurement of the round beads from a cornelian necklace known to date from the eighteenth century shows the diameter to vary by only .01 mm, so it is evident that round hardstone beads will be difficult to date.

135 Rolled cylinder bead

During the early years of the third millennium B.C. the Egyptians developed a substitute material for their favourite turquoise. They made beads of a pottery core with a blue glaze, which has unfortunately become known as 'faience', though it has no connection with the town of Faenza. These beads, of long thin shape, were made up into gorgets for funerary use, and many of them were brought out of Egypt and may be found still strung or singly. Having mastered the making of glass (see page 72), the Egyptians used it as an inlay, imitating semi-precious stones, and then for small bottles; from this it was a natural step to draw out the core-wound shape into a long cylinder and snip it into beads.

136 Segmented bead

So we arrive at the glass bead, which has been made in large quantities, in many places, from the first millennium B.C. until the present century, largely for trade with unsophisticated people in exchange for less immediately attractive but more valuable commodities, such as land and slaves. Because they have been traded so far and for so long, the identification of glass beads is difficult. Moreover the processes of manufacture are simple, and would have been available to any glassmaker in the last two thousand years and more. Glass beads may be of one colour; or the colours may be 'swirled', that is mixed as a liquid, or 'blotched', that is mixed

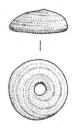

137 Bun bead

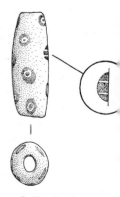

138 Eye bead

while plastic. Beads may be of 'frit', that is fragments of different coloured glass fused together. They may be made up out of glass canes, rather like sticks of Margate rock. Other colours may be applied by dipping, or by trailing on, and these trails may be rolled flat or left as applied. Finally, 'eyes' may be put on either by letting in small sections of cane, or by applying concentric dots one over another (see AMULETS). The illustrations give an idea of the possibilities and the varieties to be found, but it is quite another thing to say when and where a glass bead was made. Newer beads tend to be less well made than older ones, with slap-dash decoration.

For the last hundred years or so, spherical glass beads have been made by rolling in a heated drum, so that the glass melted sufficiently to be rounded.

Fig. 135 shows a blue glass bead which was made by rolling pad of glass round a suitable core. Figs 136 and 137 show two common shapes of ancient bead, the 'segmented' and the 'bun'. Fig. 138 is an eye bead, from which half of one of the eyes has broken and fallen out, so that you can see that it was an inlaid piece of glass. A cheaper way to achieve this effect is to dribble on concentric drops of colour and roll them flat. Fig. 139 is a selection of recent trade beads collected in Africa, and it includes swirled, blotched and fritted specimens.

Bells

Bells are basically of two types. First there is the open sort, the familiar 'church-bell' shape or less commonly like an inverted cup, which has a clapper suspended inside. This bell sounds when swung from side to side and, if made of cast bell-metal which it usually is, it may be tuned to an exact musical note. Fig. 140 shows a bell of this sort, such as might have been used by a town crier or one of a team of hand-bell ringers. The flat top is typical of a nineteenth-century bell; in the previous century the top was more domed. This 'church-bell' type ranges in size from a couple of inches high to famous huge bells such as Big Ben, and monsters like Kolokol, a Russian bell so large it was used as a chapel.

The other kind of bell is called a rumbler. It is closed at the bottom, and the clapper is a pellet, usually of iron, that is free to move within the bell. Such a bell must of course be made in two halves, and after the pellet has

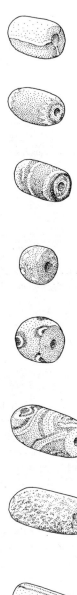

139 Swirled, blotched, and frit beads

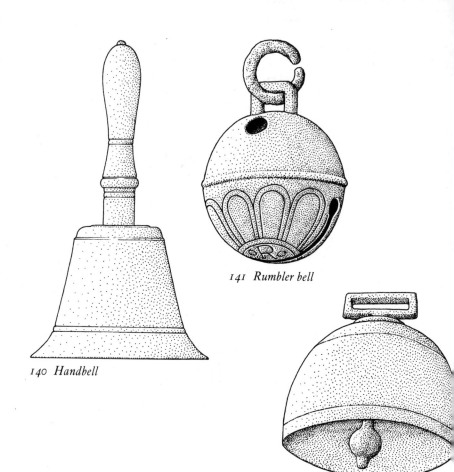

140 *Handbell*

141 *Rumbler bell*

142 *Cup bell*

been inserted the halves are joined together leaving a seam round the circumference. Unlike the church-bell, a rumbler bell sounds best when shaken rather than swung. It is seldom found much larger than a cricket ball, and it is not tunable like the church-bell type.

Both these types of bell were known to the Romans, but those we find – and they do turn up quite frequently in open country – are usually one of the following:

1. Church-bell shape, with a cast loop at the top. A group of these used to be hung in a frame over the collar of a wagon horse, to give a cheerful sound as he swayed slowly along. Similar bells, mounted on coiled springs and jangled by pulling a wire, were used to summon the servants in big houses.

2. A basically church-bell type, but made of riveted sheet metal. This is a sheep bell, called a 'cluckett'; up to the Second World War it was slung round the neck of

every sheep in a flock. The shepherd could then hear
what they were doing, even when he could not see his
sheep. Peaceful tinkling told him that they were brows-
ing; the sharper note of a single bell that one sheep was
straying; an outburst of sound that his flock was moving
in alarm.

3. Cast bell-metal rumblers, of size from a cricket ball
down to a ping-pong ball, were fixed to the head harness
of pack horses, to jingle as they jogged along. The
maker's initials were commonly cast on these bells,
which can thus be dated, some of them back to the
seventeenth century.

4. A range of small rumbler bells, made from stamped pewter or brass, were worn by men and animals,
notably by hawks, jesters, priests on their vestments,
ponies drawing sleighs, and morris dancers. According
to their various uses, these bells were called crotals,
grelots, and folly bells. Fig. 144 shows a jester's leg from
a fifteenth-century wood carving. Halves of all these

144

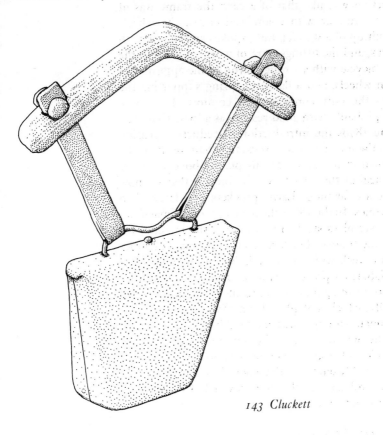

143 Cluckett

small bells may be found, and will be recognised by the loop on the top dome, or the opening along the bottom one. You may be lucky enough to find a medieval crotal, but this sort of bell is still being made in great quantity. Modern bells are flimsy, and the loop is attached without solder.

Guildford Museum, Guildford, Surrey, has some good bells and a complete frame for a cart-horse's collar.

Bicycle Parts

The most likely thing from a bicycle to be found is a lamp (see LAMPS). However the scant remains of some old machine itself may come to light, and dating is possible from materials and style.

Early in the nineteenth century the first two-wheeled vehicle recognisable as the ancestor of the bicycle might have been seen, probably being steered down a gentle slope, because it had neither pedals nor brakes. The construction was like that of a cart: the frame was of square-cut timber with chamfered edges, the wheels were built up of a wooden hub, spokes and felloes with iron tyres, and the fittings were of wrought iron. In the 1850s a bicycle with a wrought-iron frame appeared; it had iron wheels, and a flat steel spring supporting the seat was the only concession to comfort. It became known, probably with good reason, as a 'boneshaker'.

In the 1870s the introduction of reduction gearing through the now familiar sprocketed chain brought the rider down from his dangerous perch above the huge front wheel of the 'ordinary', the bicycle that we now call a 'penny-farthing'. Early sprockets were larger than modern ones. In the 1880s the development of machines to make seamless steel tube provided the material for light strong frames. The 'ordinary' had a main member of hollow steel, which was made by forging and welding – a laborious process. Another useful dating feature is the fitting of spokes at a tangent to the hub instead of radially, which took place from 1874.

The pneumatic tyre was patented by Dunlop in 1888 and in the next few years it became universal. By 1900 the bicycle had attained its modern appearance.

Glasgow Museum of Transport has a range of old bicycles, and so has the Shuttleworth Collection at Biggleswade, Herts.

Bobbins

A bobbin is a reel for holding thread, so the word is used for spools on spinning, weaving and sewing machines, but here we confine it to the bobbins for pillow-lace. The lacemaker usually works in her own cottage; on her lap is a cylindrical pillow with a canvas strip laid round it with the desired pattern outlined in pins. The necessary number of bobbins, charged with thread, are then thrown to and fro between the pins to create a strip of lace. The maximum width of the strip is the breadth of the pillow, but in practice it is seldom more than 80 mm owing to the difficulty of handling a large number of bobbins. Another lace, which has no such limitation, is known as needle-point; this is a kind of embroidery worked, as the name suggests, with a needle.

Lacemaker's bobbins turn up around the places where pillow-lace is or was made, such as in the East Midlands of England, at Honiton in Devon, and Downton in Wiltshire.

The first bobbins were simple sticks of bone, but the earliest likely to be found are the so-called wooden 'dumps' from the East Midlands, with a heavy base like bobbins from Belgium and Portugal. In the nineteenth century this bobbin became more slender, and to compensate for the loss of the heavy base a 'spangle' of beads was threaded to it. This allowed the lacemaker some identification between bobbins, though the convention of three or four square-cut beads each side of one larger spherical one somewhat limited the advantage. Old bobbins are made of hard woods with close grain such as box and fruitwood, bone, and sometimes metal. Glass bobbins are found, as are glass tobacco pipes, but neither could be used. Bobbins were decorated by carving, inlaying and inscribing. Modern bobbins are of wood, and severely practical.

Honiton bobbins have no spangle and are exceptionally light, in keeping with the gauzy Honiton lace; Downton bobbins have no spangle, but weight is given by the torpedo shape.

Luton Museum contains a lot of information about the lace of the East Midlands. See also *The Romance of the Lace Pillow* by P. P. B. Minet (Wright, Thomas, 1971) and *Pillow Lace and Bobbins* by Jeffery Hopewell (Shire, 1975).

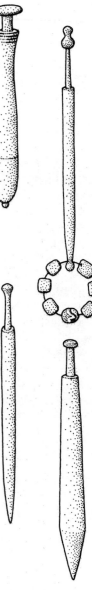

145 Dump
146 Bobbin with spangle
147 Honiton bobbin
148 Downton bobbin

Bottles

A bottle is commonly a glass vessel to hold liquid, with a narrow neck to take a stopper, and here we will consider it so to be, neglecting bottles of other materials except stoneware.

The Romans had glass bottles, but the earliest likely to be found are those for wine dating from the middle of the seventeenth century. Previously wine was kept in butts in the buttery, drawn off into bottles of pottery or leather by the butler, and thus brought to the table. The crucial invention was the cork stopper, which allowed wine to be supplied in bottles by a merchant. The corks were wired to below a ring of glass at the neck of the bottle, and this survives on modern bottles although it is not necessary except for fizzy wines such as champagne. Early wines were no doubt often still gassing a bit when bottled, and would have blown out an unwired cork. From the seventeenth to the early nineteenth century many wine bottles carried a glass seal with the name or initials of an individual, an inn, a college etc., and sometimes a date. They are called 'sealed bottles', which is confusing as one might expected this to mean a bottle with its contents still sealed in. The shape of wine bottles had progressed from a squat onion with a long neck to the modern tall cylinder by the early nineteenth century. The cylindrical shape is necessary for those wines, such as port, which became popular during the Napoleonic Wars and needed to be layed down to age for a few years. The progress of wine bottles is illustrated by

149 Bottle seal

150 Sack bottle   *151*   *152*

a seventeenth-century sack bottle, a bottle dated 1788
which was free blown and then rolled to a cylindrical
shape, and a mid-nineteenth-century mould-blown
bottle with a very late example of a seal on it. Bottles
were blown into moulds from about 1800 (Figs
150–52).

With the development of the private wine-cellar during the eighteenth century wine bottles came to be used
for storage below the house, and their contents were
decanted into a decanter for presentation at table. Thus
the wine bottle became a dispensable thing, which it
remains.

A superior form of bottle, to contain household stocks
of spirits, toilet waters or medicines, was made from the
eighteenth century until the middle of the nineteenth
century. It is square in section, with a ground glass *153 Case bottle*
stopper, and its normal position is with others of its kind
in a compartmented box. A late Georgian example is
shown. A typical feature is that the decoration, of cutting or gilding, is confined to the shoulders of these so-
called 'case bottles'.

For the supply of medicine from the apothecary small
bottles called 'vials' or 'phials' were made, and stop-
pered with corks. As the eighteenth century progressed
into the nineteenth, these phials became shorter and
broader, until the machine-made medicine bottle of
rectangular form was attained in the second half of the
last century. Figs 74 and 154 show a Georgian phial and
a late-nineteenth-century bottle. At that time bottles for
poisonous liquids were first distinguished by colouring
blue or green, or marking with ribs, or making them in a
distinctive shape. Labels on old medicine bottles are not
often preserved, but if still adhering they add to the
interest. For instance, until a few years ago the label on *154*

a certain patent medicine read 'Dr Collis Browne's Chlorodyne', but apparently this was judged to be in-accurate and it now reads 'Collis Browne's Compound Chlorodyne'.

Recent bottles are to be found on rubbish dumps, and they have been the subject of several books. Here I shall only be giving a brief history of the bottle for carbonated drinks, which is of particular interest, and illustrating a few unusual bottles.

It was late in the eighteenth century that the health-giving properties of 'mineral waters' issuing from the earth at places such as Bath and Matlock suggested that these fluids might be bottled and sold farther afield. The next step was to make up synthetic 'mineral waters', and as one popular ingredient was soda we have the origin of two expressions still current, 'minerals' for flavoured carbonated drinks, and 'soda water' for plain carbonated water. The way to dissolve carbon dioxide in water having recently been discovered, fizzy drinks could now be made, but the problem was to prevent gas escaping through the cork. The first solution was a bottle which was egg-shaped and therefore would not stand up, so the cork was kept under water and the gas retained. These 'egg' bottles date from the beginning of the nineteenth century up to the First World War, which was long after other inventions outmoded them, but they had become traditional for soda water. Up to 1850 they had a flat base at one end, with a pontil mark; after that the end is pointed. During the course of the nineteenth century they became thinner in the body, and the neck ring lengthened.

The 'globe-stoppered soda water bottle', to quote Hiram Codd's 1872 patent, is a favourite with collectors, and well documented in books on bottle collecting. It was used for beer as well as minerals, but 'Codd's wallop' did not find favour with drinkers to judge by the derisive use of the phrase today. Varieties of the globe-stoppered bottle continued in use until the 1920s, and I can remember taking them on picnics.

155

Some useful 'bottle' dates are:

1850 Invention of 'snap clip', so pontil mark disap-pears.

1859 First bottle-making machines give a regular outline, but the neck ring is still applied by hand.

1870 First upright soda-water bottles, with sloping shoulders, or like the 'egg' but with a flat base.

1877 Swing stopper introduced.

1879 Internal screw in neck introduced.

1892 'Crown cork' invented in the U.S.A., using a natural cork closure that was not entirely satisfactory.

1903 Fully automatic bottle-making machines.

1915 Granulated cork closures perfect the crown cork.

Three liquids have traditionally been supplied in stoneware bottles: ink, Dutch gin, and ginger beer. All turn up frequently, and marks impressed, inscribed or stamped enable manufacturers and retailers to be traced.

156

Finally, two unusual bottles: Fig. 155 is in fact a fire-extinguishing grenade, intended to be thrown at the seat of the conflagration. These grenades date from about sixty years ago, and may be found in remote parts of large houses; Fig. 156 shows a smelling-salts bottle, dating from about 1910, found beside the old Great Western Railway line. It is probable that the guard of the train had a stock of such bottles in case any lady passenger had an attack of the vapours.

See *Bottles and Bottle Collecting* by A. A. C. Hedges (Shire, 1975).

Boxes

A box is a small container with a lid, and is used to keep solids in. It was known to the ancient world: for example, the box from which Pandora, curious to know its contents, allowed the blessings of the gods to escape. Since those early days boxes have been made by most people of the world for small things or substances used in small quantities.

When a box is found, we want to know its purpose, unless the original contents remain. Fig. 157 shows an ivory box with four gilt metal counters in it that fit so well in size and shape that they must surely be original. If a box has contained a substance, snuff for instance, particles may remain which should be carefully examined and preferably not emptied away. Even if a box is quite empty, its shape may declare what it was for. The drawer in a medicine box (Fig. 158) is compartmented

157

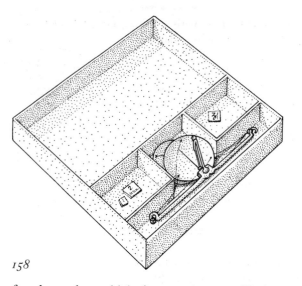

158

159 Spectacle case

for the scales, which fortunately are still there with weights on either side, and the rest of the space may be guessed to be for pills and powders. Above this drawer are eight bottles, and in the middle of them the bowl of a wine glass to measure a dose. Spectacle cases and telescope cases are obvious, and the long interior of a glove box is plain enough, though of course a box such as this may be used for other things.

Snuff boxes are frequently found, the taking of snuff being popular from the end of the seventeenth century right up to modern times. The wealthy used boxes of gold and silver embellished with gems and miniatures; merchants and professional people had boxes of hardstones, tortoiseshell, enamel or ivory; poorer people were content with papier mâché or tinplate. Fig. 161 shows a snuff box known to have been carried by a worthy citizen in the middle of the eighteenth century. It is of tortoiseshell with ormolu mounts, and was probably made in France. Fig. 90 is a humbler box of papier mâché, dating from the early nineteenth century. Notice the distinguishing feature in both: the long overlap of the lid, close fitting to prevent snuff leaking out, and the tight long hinge for the same purpose.

Boxes to contain tobacco for smoking are larger than snuff boxes, and the lid need not fit quite so closely. From the seventeenth century brass tobacco boxes were made and exported to Britain from Holland; Fig. 162 shows an example. Last century a favourite shape, con-

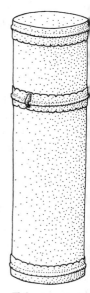

160 Telescope case

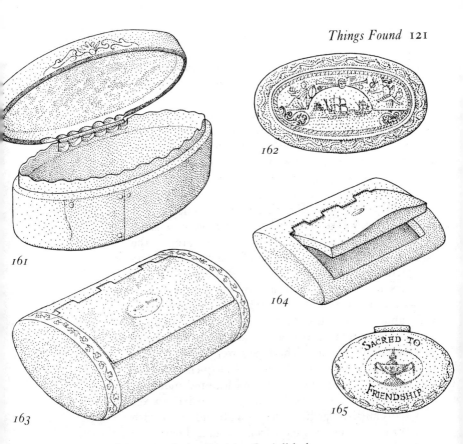

161

162

163

164

165

venient for the pocket, was a flat oval with a flush lid. An
example of walnut with silver bands is shown in Fig.
163, and Fig. 164 is of a similar snuff box.

Small and elegant boxes made for ladies in the eighteenth century contained patches for the face, possibly
to hide the marks of smallpox, or comfits, possibly to
sweeten the breath. They were of porcelain or enamel,
and the commonest of them are the late-eighteenth-
century enamel boxes (Fig. 165) made in the Birmingham area, which are decorated on a copper base with
some simple design and often a sentimental motto.
This sort of box is reproduced these days, but the
modern ones are not meant to deceive. Another kind of
small box, with a hinged grill under the lid and usually
made of silver, is the vinaigrette. In it would have been a
pad soaked in perfumed vinegar to sniff when assailed
with unpleasant smells. The vinaigrette was popular
throughout the nineteenth century.

Another interesting group of boxes are of wood or

166 *Wafer box*

occasionally ivory, with the body and lid lathe-turned and screwed together. These are seal boxes, made to contain the wafers used to close envelopes before those with adhesive flaps came in about 1840. (Fig. 166).

Among large boxes, but still within our size limit, are those made for pairs of tea caddies, often with a mixing bowl between them. These date from the days in the eighteenth and early nineteenth centuries when tea was an agreeable luxury, to be kept under lock and key and mixed by the hostess before infusion. Similar boxes were made to contain so-called 'case' bottles, that is square in section, for medicines, spirits or toilet waters. For all these, a case veneered in mahogany was usual, but the padded leather-bound boxes made around the middle of last century were useful for toilet waters expected to be taken on coach or train journeys.

Boxes are made of woods and metals of most kinds, papier mâché, ivory and tortoiseshell; these are all dealt with under MATERIALS. Japanese lacquer boxes need special mention, as until about 1900 the lacquer work was technically superb. The boxes were made of pine wood, treated with many coats of lacquer from the sumac tree, then finished with gold leaf and motifs in relief. For many centuries the Chinese have made boxes of a red cinnabar lacquer, deeply cut into relief with geometric patterns or scenes from nature. They were first used for Imperial gifts, which must have been splendid indeed to match the containers they were sent in.

See *The Collector's Book of Boxes* by M. Klamkin (David and Charles, 1972).

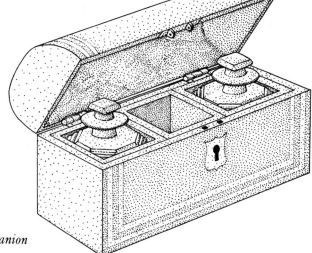

167 Toilet water box

Bracelets

The origin of the word bracelet confines it to an ornament worn on the arm; it may be in any position there, but it is usually round the wrist. The word bangle is from India: it is a form of bracelet but solid, without a clasp, and large enough to be slipped over the hand or foot. Bangles can be expensive, but a bracelet is considered superior.

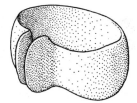

168

Wide flat bracelets were clasped round the wrists of men and women in ancient Egypt, Persia, and neighbouring countries. In the *Old Testament* the young Amalekite who killed King Saul reports to David, 'I took the crown that was upon his head, and the bracelet that was on his arm . . .'. When the ruins of these civilisations were excavated around the 1860s, it inspired a fashion for heavy gold or pinchbeck bracelets, but these were worn by women only.

In the Bronze Age, gold from Ireland became available in Britain and was used for ornaments such as the gold 'snap-on' bracelet shown.

Greek and Roman ladies wore bracelets, and during the Roman occupation of Britain bangles made from black shale were popular. These are the first likely to be found, although I once came across a piece of an ornamental bronze ring that might have been part of a Roman bracelet.

From the fall of the Roman Empire through to the middle of the seventeenth century the dress of women tended to cover arms and legs down to the hands and

169

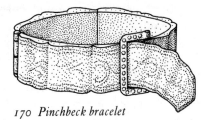

170 Pinchbeck bracelet

feet, so bracelets and bangles were out of fashion. From the 1640s onwards, when sleeves started to draw away from the wrist, bracelets were worn, but the great days of this ornament came in the nineteenth century. Matching sets of jewellery were then fashionable; a full set might include a tiara, earrings, brooch, necklace and bracelets. These followed the trends of style for personal ornaments in general, which are outlined under BROOCHES. However the following illustrations will be of interest:

Fig. 169, a bracelet of about 1870, of gold and enamel; Fig. 170, a late-nineteenth-century pinchbeck bracelet in the form of a strap with pearled buckle.

For Georgian and Victorian bracelets see *Collecting Jewellery* by Mona Curran (Arco, 1963) and *Victorian Jewellery Design* by Charlotte Gere (William Kimber, 1972).

Brooches

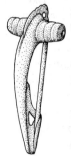

171 Early Roman

'Brooch' is the same word as 'broach', meaning a point or peg. The spelling with a double 'o' has come to mean an ornamental clasp secured to clothing by a pin: it may be for fastening or purely decorative. Brooches are now worn by women only, except in the Scottish Highlands, or among dignitaries of the church.

The first brooches appear on the dress of Ancient Greece, and were used to secure the basic garment, called a 'chiton', on the shoulders. They were of the safety-pin form known as a 'fibula', which was to continue in derivative shapes and sizes up to the Dark Ages. The brooches of the Roman Empire require some detailed attention as they are found fairly often. The Roman brooch was used to secure outer garments at the right shoulder, and was cast in bronze, with a separate pin which is often found missing. The succession of designs is shown in Figs 171 to 174.

172 Mid-Roman

The early fibulae worn by subject people of the Roman Empire were made from a piece of wire, in much the same way as a modern safety pin. Brooches of other shapes turn up wherever Rome conquered, some of them being traded from far afield, like the charming red enamelled hare from south eastern Europe shown.

The fibula of classical origin was finally taken over by the barbarian and developed into an impressive symbol of its wearer's importance. (Fig. 177).

173 Late Roman

Anglo-Saxon women wore a pair of gilt bronze saucer brooches, apparently to secure a garment such as a short cape around their shoulders. Evidence remains of an attachment for a pin at the back.

The Celts favoured a penannular brooch (in the shape of an almost complete ring) from before Roman times until well into the Dark Ages. It was first of simple form, perhaps with restrained ornamentation of curves and spirals; later it became large and impressive.

174 Late Roman

In the early Middle Ages, buttons or laces came to be used for fastening garments, and from that time brooches became mainly decorative for a while, though worn by both men and women. Thus it is difficult to distinguish them from badges, but if we accept that badges have some significance, then the brooch of the Middle Ages enters that class of rare and valuable objects which we exclude from things found.

175 Barbarian

With the increase in general wealth brought about by the Industrial Revolution, a market developed in the early nineteenth century for inexpensive jewellery. By the middle of that century, a sort of hierarchy was set up: rich and powerful ladies were adorned with precious stones; the middle classes wore semi-precious stones; the poor had to be content with glass imitations. It is the middling strata of brooches that we are most likely to encounter: those set with diamonds, emeralds and rubies are not our concern, and those with glass 'stones' will mostly have broken up and disappeared.

176 Hare brooch

178 Saxon brooch

177 Saxon brooch

179 Celtic brooch

This middle range of nineteenth-century jewellery used semi-precious stones such as turquoise and garnet, also hardstones such as jet (for mourning, notably after the death of the Prince Consort in 1861), agates and various marbles. Early Victorian brooches use the flat surfaces of hardstones to good effect, as in Fig. 180.

180

Marcasite, a variety of iron pyrites that can be cut and polished into small steely points, occurs throughout the period, and cut steel, another imitation of jewellery, was popular in the 1860s.

Coral and amber were also used, and shell cameos, which are lighter and cheaper than those made from onyx or sardonyx. An example is shown in Fig. 181.

Cameos of a uniform light grey colour are made of lava from Italy and were popular in the middle of the century. A good test of the quality of any cameo is to look at it along the edge; the faces will then be seen properly formed down to the background surface or, in cheap Victorian and later cameos, cut down like the edge of a small cliff.

During the 1860s there was a vogue for jewellery of Egyptian, Etruscan and other styles of early civilisations, inspired by the important excavations of the time in Italy, Egypt, etc (Fig. 169).

Brooches tended to be large in the middle of the century, an era of high-necked dresses, when they were used to fasten collars and fichus. Towards the end of the century they reverted to being, in the main, pieces of applied decoration, and many were small. In 1890 a patent was granted for a twisted spring pin, using the same principle as the fibula of antiquity. (Fig. 182).

There are a number of Roman brooches in the Roman Fort at South Shields, and a good selection of nineteenth-century ones in Aylesbury Museum, Bucks. See also *Collecting Jewellery* by Mona Curran (Arco, 1963) and *Victorian Jewellery Design* by Charlotte Gere (William Kimber, 1972).

182

181

The buckle was an invention of the Romans, and was used on the armour and accoutrements of their soldiers and on the harness of their horses. Buckles would not have been at all suitable for the dignified flowing robes of Roman ladies and gentlemen!

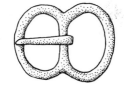

183

From these ancient times buckles have never ceased to be used and have stuck to the basic design of a frame with a bar across it, and a tongue on the bar. A development of the late Middle Ages was the symmetrical frame with a bar across the middle (Fig. 183). Most buckles will have been secured to a belt or a strap by means of a tag, called a chape, and the other end of the belt may have had a strap-end in similar style to the chape. These fitments may be found away from the parent buckle.

Buckles are usually made of metal, but some are of horn or bone or of other animal or vegetable origin.

There are some very interesting and unusual buckles to be found, as you can see from the following selection:

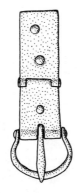

184

A Roman buckle for a soldier's cuirass. The chape is of single thickness, for riveting to armour. Similar buckles were also used on medieval armour (Fig. 184).

A Saxon belt buckle. Notice the beasts' heads on the frame biting the bar, which are typical. A waist-belt buckle is usually the only thing found in a grave from Christian Saxon times, besides the bones (Fig. 185).

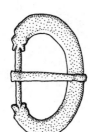

185

A fifteenth-century buckle in the shape of a contemporary capital letter 'D' (Fig. 186).

A small shoe buckle from about 1700. Shoe buckles came into fashion in the middle of the seventeenth century. Note the strongly curved shape (Fig. 187).

A large shoe buckle from the late eighteenth century. After increasing in size and ostentation throughout the century, shoe buckles gave way to laces after 1800. These 'ridiculous large buckles', as James Boswell called them, were of silver or other metal, often set with glass 'diamonds' (Fig. 188).

186

Knee buckles date from the end of the seventeenth century up to modern times. In the eighteenth century they could be made to match the shoe buckles worn with them, as shown (Fig. 189).

Wide waist-belts with long narrow buckles were fashionable on ladies' day dresses during the last twenty years of the nineteenth century (Fig. 190).

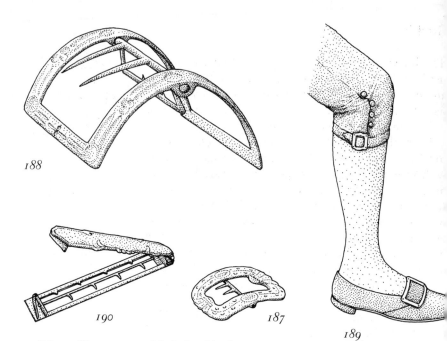

188

190　　　*187*

189

The military type of belt buckle from the last hundred years or so is made of two cast brass parts that fit together and provide a field on which the required insignia is displayed. A large rectangular loop either side allows for a wide leather belt. These buckles explain themselves as belonging to a regiment, corps, police force, the Church Lads Brigade, etc.

The buckles for animal harness, or for straps to secure luggage, are normally plainer and heavier than those for dress or armour. They would probably be of little interest if found.

The Museum of Costume at Bath has a collection of Georgian and later buckles.

Bullets

The Oxford English Dictionary defines a bullet as 'a ball of lead etc. used in firearms of small calibre; now often conical'. It differs from a cannon ball in being for a weapon held by the operator, and it is therefore smaller: a bullet is generally of lead, and a cannon ball of stone or iron.

Small round bullets, particularly if more than one is used to charge the gun, are called shot. Bullets and large shot are moulded. Figs 191 and 192 show two hand-

operated moulds, one for bullets and the other for shot.
If fresh, bullets may show a flash and a mark where the tail has been nipped off using the cutter between the grips of the mould. Small shot has been made since 1769 by dropping molten lead through a sieve at the top of a shot-tower into water. The drops of lead round up in falling and are dredged out of the water for grading. The size of pellets ranges from dust-shot for shooting humming-birds up to swan-shot and buck-shot which can be a centimetre in diameter. Before the use of cartridges by sportsmen about a hundred years ago, the shotgun was loaded from a shot-pouch which dispensed the required number of shot for each charge. A shotgun is measured by the number of single round lead shot the size of its bore that would go to weigh one pound. The favourite sizes are the 'twelve-bore' for men and the 'twenty-bore' for women and boys. Considering the amount of shot that has been discharged against game animals over the years, it is suprising that so little is found.

Turning from the shooting of animals to that of men, the size of lead ball necessary lies between one centimetre and two centimetres in diameter, according to the weapon. The bullets of Brown Bess, the famous musket of the British Army from 1795 to 1815, were around 1.8 cm and weighed fourteen to the pound, so this gun might have been called a 'fourteen-bore', and was exceptionally large. If a round lead bullet of about 1.5 cm

192

191

in diameter is found, it is likely to have been fired from a musket some time before the middle of last century, or from a pistol if about one centimetre in diameter. It is not possible to be more exact, but if the find site is a known battlefield a warrantable assumption may be made.

Up to around 1850 the normal weapon was smooth-bored and muzzle-loading. The rifle had been known since the seventeenth century, and its greater accuracy was appreciated. However there were practical difficulties in loading a rifled muzzle-loader, so it was reserved for marksmen, such as the man who shot Admiral Nelson from the fighting top of the Spanish ship alongside the *Victory* at Trafalgar.

The perfection of the breech-loading rifle, with which the French Army was first equipped in 1857, and the invention of the deep-drawn brass cartridge case in 1870, meant that by the 1880s Western armies fired conical bullets which only an expert can tell from modern ones. Indeed since 1842 the bullet had slowly and for various weapons assumed a conical shape. It was packaged with its powder into a cartridge case of cloth or paper for some years before the introduction of the brass cartridge case.

Buttons

A button is generally understood to be a small plate or dome sewn on to dress and used to fasten it round the wearer's body, but this purpose is not essential; buttons may be purely decorative.

Buttons as we know them first appeared in the thirteenth century, when they were used for fastening sleeves round the forearm. During the next two hundred years they spread to the shoulders of mantles, the fronts of jerkins and elsewhere. In the sixteenth century came the neck-to-knee coat worn distinctively by pensioners, servants, and some scholars such as Christ's Hospital 'Bluecoat boys'. The large flat buttons down the front of these coats carried the insignia of the wearer's charitable organisation, his master or his school, and they are known as livery buttons. Fig. 193 shows an early livery button with a 'crest' of three flowers dotted in by hand with a punch, and Fig. 194 a late-eighteenth-century professionally made livery button.

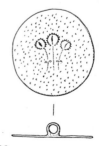

193

Brass buttons were encouraged in England by a law of
1721 forbidding the manufacture of cloth buttons, but it
was in the last quarter of the eighteenth century that the
presses of the Birmingham district started to churn out
the still familiar brass button made of a domed shell
stamped with a crest, the number of the regiment, or
whatever. At first the shank was a loop of wire brazed at
one point, but by 1780 the wire was flattened at each end
and thus brazed down. After 1840 the button has a back
and the ends of the shank pass through it and are bent out
like a split-pin. Fig. 195 shows the general arrangement
in section. During the eighteenth century many ordinary buttons were of pewter, and the rich had buttons
of silver and gold. Late in the century porcelain, enamel,
gilt, glass and cut steel buttons were fashionable: large
ones were worn on coats and smaller ones on waistcoats.
Women wore buttons on riding habits and gowns. Early
in the nineteenth century cloth covered buttons were
patented and manufactured, and by 1842 there were
buttons of paste-board edged with metal. By the middle
of the century women had accepted buttons for general
wear on all their clothes, including underclothes. The
last half of the nineteenth century was the golden age of
buttons, which were made of many materials from linen
covered cardboard to gold and precious stones. Glass
was popular; before 1920, glass buttons had metal
shanks but later the buttons and shanks are all of glass.

194

195

The latest interesting phase of buttons was around
1900, when men wore little jewelled buttons on their
waistcoats to match the studs and cuff-links worn with
their evening tail-coats.

There is a well-displayed collection of buttons in
the Museum of Costume at Bath. See also *Buttons* by
D. Epstein (Studio Vista, 1968) and *Buttons for Collectors*
by P. Peacock.

Candle Snuffers and Douters

About the year 1830 a candle wick was introduced that
bent over as it burnt, so that the 'snuff' (the charred end
of it) was consumed in a hot part of the flame. Previously
the snuff stood upright and had to be cropped from time
to time otherwise the candle smoked and gave a poor
light. The implement used to do this was called a
snuffer; if used carelessly it could 'snuff out' the candle,

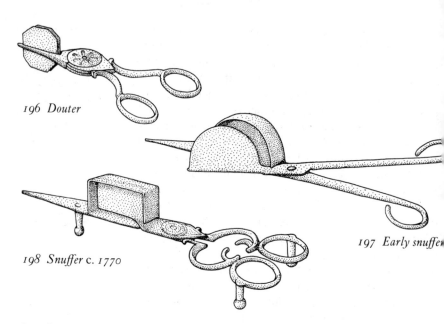

196 *Douter*

197 *Early snuffer*

198 *Snuffer* c. *1770*

but it was not designed as an extinguisher. For that purpose there was the cone-shaped extinguisher, and the less well known douter ('do-outer') shown.

Snuffers date from the late sixteenth century to the early nineteenth, when they became outmoded. Up to around 1700 they were crude wrought iron things, with the loops for the fingers forged round, and the box to retain the snuff semi-circular in outline. In the eighteenth century, they became more elegant and of cast metal, with the box rectangular by 1750. During the last eighty years of the snuffer's useful life it was the subject of some ingenious inventions to crop and retain the snuff more cleanly, but the simple scissor continued. From the earliest days to the last a point is provided on the end of the snuffer for trimming up the wick and ejecting candle stubs.

Until the middle of the eighteenth century snuffers were kept in an upright container rather like a candle-stick, but after that they were placed on a tray, and the snuffer acquired three small turned feet. These trays are sometimes found without their snuffer, but they are commonly of a waisted shape, which identifies them.

Early snuffers were of iron. In the eighteenth century many were made of steel or brass. Sometimes the handles (known as the 'bows') were of silver, or the snuffers were close-plated throughout.

199 *Snuffer tray*

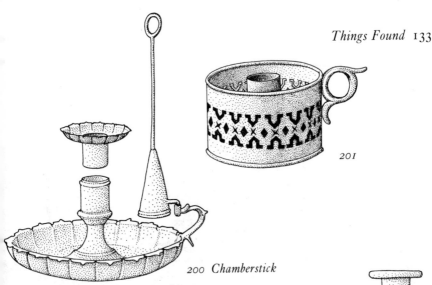

201

200 *Chamberstick*

202

Candlesticks

Basically the candle is a wick surrounded by solid fuel, whereas a lamp has a wick immersed in liquid fuel. The advantages of the candle over the lamp were the ready availability of animal tallow or beeswax, and simplicity; it needs only a socket to hold a candle. The lamp, on the other hand, although it used expensive vegetable oils, such as olive or colza, could be made to give a better light without excessive size or multiplicity. Until mineral oil became plentiful in the middle of last century, the balance of advantage lay with the candle, even for the lighting of reception rooms in the houses of the great, where a large number of candles hung in chandeliers from the ceiling, or were placed in candelabra on the walls, chimney pieces or tables. Even when the oil lamp came forward about 1850, the candlestick survived to light the way to bed or to illuminate the dark corners of sculleries, cellars and coal sheds. A 'chamberstick' is shaped like a shallow dish, for stability and to catch the drips of wax even when tilted, but ordinary candlesticks were also carried about the house, as you can see in contemporary illustrations from late-nineteenth-century books. Fig. 201 shows an early brass chamberstick, and Fig. 202 a candlestick of about 1840.

The parts of a candlestick are the base, the stem and the sconce, which is the socket for the candle and may or may not have a drip-tray round it.

204 *Early-17th-century*   205 *Late-17th-century*

206 *Sheet iron 'pig-scraper'*

The candle was known to the ancients; indeed the Romans had a goddess called Candelifera, the candle bearer, who watched over women in childbirth. Candles served to illuminate the Dark Ages as well.

Until the industrial revolution the two materials for making candles were tallow, which was cheap, smoky and smelly, and beeswax, which was expensive, but gave a fine light and had a pleasant odour. It followed that tallow candles, usually made at home by dipping a wick of worsted in a bowl of tallow, were used by the poor. Wax candles were made by a wax-chandler, using a mould, and he supplied them to churches and the houses of the rich.

The improvements to candles during the last three centuries have been:

1. About the year 1700, better preparation of beeswax made the drip-tray no longer necessary on sticks made for wax candles, so it disappeared, to reappear as a rim at the top of all candlesticks late in the eighteenth century (Fig. 203).

2. In 1825 a specially plaited wick was invented, which bent into the hot, outer part of the flame and was consumed. Previously the stump of carbonised wick stood up and had to be trimmed with snuffers from time to time, otherwise the candle smoked and gave a poor light. (See CANDLE SNUFFERS AND DOUTERS.)

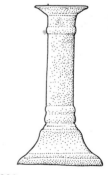

203

3. About 1850 paraffin wax became the universal material for candles, as it became plentiful, and the social distinction between beeswax for the rich and tallow for the poor faded away.

The old rhyme about 'The butcher, the baker, the candlestick maker' indicates the former importance of the craft, and indeed the making of candlesticks, mostly of brass, was an important business from the Middle Ages until the early nineteenth century. Large numbers survive, and even more are made as reproductions, to be enthusiastically collected. Fortunately most old household candlesticks have been polished over the years to a silky finish which no amount of buffing can imitate.

The sections of brass candlesticks are made up of castings or pieces formed out of sheet brass. The cast pieces are found screwed or spigoted together. If they can be unscrewed, the form of the screw will give information (see NUTS, BOLTS AND SCREWS). Often, however, the end of the screw or spigot has been hammered flat. In 1781 a patent was granted for assembling the parts of a candlestick on an iron rod, but in fact this method had been in use for some years. As to pieces formed of sheet, these may be rolled and seamed into tubes, or stamped from plate. Assembly may be by brazing or soldering, with no regard to date. The hollow casting of a candlestick in one piece, typical of those made in the nineteenth century, was not achieved in Britain until 1770, although their core-casting in two sections was mastered a hundred years before. From the sixteenth century brass candlesticks have been finished by turning, but it is not easy to decide if rings have been turned on a specimen much worn by polishing. The turned pricket candlestick in Fig. 205 was probably for chapel use.

The imposition of a tax on candles in 1704 led to the invention of the 'push-up', so that the candle could be burnt down to the last sliver of its stub. This feature is rare on silver candlesticks, whose owners would not need the extremes of economy, but it is common on the straight up-and-down sticks for humble use throughout the eighteenth and early nineteenth centuries. These are called 'pig-scrapers' because they could have been used to singe a slaughtered pig (Fig. 206).

The detachable drip-pan is a feature on good quality candlesticks of 1730 or later (Fig. 200).

Cannonballs

Guns were first made early in the fourteenth century; they were small, rare, and fired a sort of dart. Development was rapid, and by the end of that century European armies had large guns firing stone balls. Progress in iron founding during the fifteenth century substituted cast iron for stone, but the huge gun which the Turks used to batter the walls of Constantinople in 1453 used stone balls that can still be seen there.

From the fifteenth to the middle of the nineteenth century cast iron cannonballs were used, but as with bullets they cannot be dated more closely unless the find spot is a known battlefield.

A cannonball is therefore of iron or stone, and is fired from a fixed gun or one on wheels, whereas a bullet (see BULLETS) is of lead and fired from a hand-held gun. All guns are sized by reference to the weight of a single round projectile to fit their bores: thus a 'thirty-two pounder' is a cannon firing a cast iron shot weighing 32 pounds, and a 'twelve-bore' is a shot gun that fires a single round lead ball weighing twelve to the pound.

A freshly cast cannonball would show the marks of runner and seam, but those found are usually too corroded for these to be seen. Cannon were also cast and the bore machined out to size, but the difficulty was to support the boring tool rigidly down the length of the gun's bore. Improvements were made over the years, but to make sure that every ball would fit every individual gun of its size the balls were made smaller than the nominal bore of the cannon by a reduction known as 'windage'. The following table shows the diameter of English round shot for sizes of guns:

Pounder size	69	42	32	24	18	12	9
Dia. in cm.	20.2	17	15.5	13.9	12.8	11.1	10.1

Pounder size	6	3	1	$\frac{1}{2}$
Dia. in cm.	8.8	6.9	4.9	3.9

The guns of old wooden battleships were 32, 24 and 18-pounders, and guns of around these sizes would be in fortresses ashore. The Civil War of the late seventeenth century was happily the only conflict in which field guns were extensively used on English soil, and contemporary guns were as follows:

Name	Weight of Shot in kg.
Culverin	6.9
Demi-culverin	4.3
Saker	2.0
Minion	1.7
Falcon	1.2
Falconet	0.54

Grape-shot was also fired, of 2.5 to 4 cm. diameter, and hollow shot dates from this time. This was filled with gunpowder and had a projecting fuse lit from the burning propellant when the shot was fired. This was a 'bomb-shell', and we still use this word for the cause of a sudden disturbance.

The cannonballs of Civil War guns have been picked up on the battlefield of Sedgemoor, the last battle on English soil, fought in 1685.

Card Cases

You may perhaps find a decorative case big enough to hold a dozen cards 8 centimetres long by 5 centimetres broad at the back of some neglected drawer or desk. The lid will be at the shorter end, and may close with a long overlap or a hinge and a press stud. Fig. 207 shows a typical example made of wood covered with little tiles of mother-of-pearl. Others are of ivory carved with oriental scenes, or of silver, papier mâché, etc.

These cases contained the large visiting cards that ladies took with them when calling on friends last century and even as late as the outbreak of the Second World War. The etiquette of calling and leaving cards

207

was precise. It involved the card of the lady who called –
that was the large one, with only her name on it – and
her husband's card too, this being of the smaller size
used today.

The case had to be opened and closed by gloved
hands, so the simple press stud or long overlap of the lid
is distinctive.

The Buxton Art Gallery at Bideford has a collection
of card cases.

Car Parts

The parts of cars that you are likely to find, perhaps in
some neglected corner of a barn, will be either detachable items from the exterior such as wheels, lamps or
hub-caps, or frequently serviced parts from the engine
such as sparking plugs.

Early motor cars were 'coach-built', that is to say
constructed out of wooden panels and frames, no doubt
by men recruited from the coach-building trade. Coach-
built cars continued to be made until recent years, but a
'light car' industry developed in the 1900s, using metal
sheet and tubes for the bodywork and wire-spoked
wheels derived from the bicycle. The most famous early
light car was the T-Model Ford, which was produced
from 1909 to 1927, the peak years being the early 1920s.
It altered little during these years, though in 1916 the
brass radiator gave way to one of black iron.

Plain brass accessories, polished daily by the
chauffeur or proud owner, are typical of cars up to the
First World War. Heavy cast and turned hub and filler
caps in this material may be found. Brass accessories
were also nickel-plated, until in the late 1920s
chromium-plated steel became universal. This was also
when the first windscreen wipers were fitted, so that the
windscreen need no longer swing open to admit rain and
snow.

The earliest side-lights were in fact carriage lamps,
burning oil from a stalk-shaped reservoir, and the first
headlamps were oil lanterns. From around 1903 the
lights on a car consisted of two headlamps, two side-
lamps and a tail light. In 1906 acetylene-burning head-
lights appeared, but oil side-lights continued for a few
years until during the First World War electric lights
became normal on all positions on cars.

208

Up to the First World War the tyres of cars did not lodge into a recessed wheel rim but were bolted up against a so-called 'clincher' rim. In 1926 the 'balloon' tyre, of considerably larger size and lower pressure than formerly, improved road holding and reduced the danger of blowouts.

Any steering wheels found will not be older than about 1900: before then cars were steered by some form of tiller.

Just as the bodywork of early cars owed much to the craft of the coachbuilder, so the engine inherited the solid practices of the steam engineer. Thus old cars have copper pipes with nipples brazed on and screwed couplings, not the thin bell-mouthed steel or aluminium pipes of popular cars in the 1920s and later. The sparking plug is typical of progress: as late as the 1920s it was of brass, except of course where necessary for insulation; and it could be stripped down for cleaning and the replacement of worn parts.

In general the parts of old cars can be identified by their solid construction and traditional materials. If there are inscribed names and numbers on them, these can be traced through specialised literature about veteran and vintage cars.

Vintage and veteran cars are to be seen in the Montagu Motor Museum at Beaulieu, Hampshire, and at the Cheddar Motor and Transport Museum, Somerset. See also *A Pictorial History of the Automobile* by Philip Stern (Viking Press, 1953).

Cart and Carriage Parts

Bits and pieces of old horse-drawn vehicles may be found in the outhouses where they used to be kept, and it is possible to distinguish two forms of construction. 'Carriage' is a general term for a passenger vehicle of a superior kind made by a coachbuilder out of wooden panels on a framework of light timbers that have been steamed and bent into shape. Screws and glue were used. 'Cart' serves to define those vehicles made by a wheelwright out of boards and squared timbers to carry goods and passengers. He used bolts as fastenings, without any glue. Before the middle of last century, these bolts, and their square-headed nuts, were forged out of iron by the local blacksmith. He also made hinges,

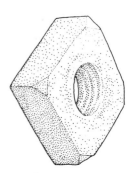

209 *Square-headed nut*

straps, and notably the 'standards' which supported the sloping sides of a wagon. These were decorative as well as functional, and supported the loads at harvest-time.

Carts had to be robust and easily repaired, hence the use of bolts and no glue so that parts could be replaced when damaged or worn. On the other hand unnecessary weight would reduce the useful load carried, so the maker lightened all exposed edges of timber with 'stopped chamfers' which are typical of a wheelwright's work. It is said that an eighth of the total weight of a wagon could be safely removed by chamfering.

The wheels of the four-wheeled wagon and the two-wheeled tumbril had iron tyres. In the old days when country roads were very bad, the wheels of carts had rims as much as nine inches broad, and their tyres were made up of lengths of iron nailed on to the felloes. Within the last hundred years cart wheels have been shod with a continuous iron tyre, as was always usual with carriage wheels.

Most carriage lamps will have been picked up and used to light the front doors of modern houses, but the lamps of humbler vehicles, for instance the gig lamp in Fig. 211, may still be found. These are commonly of sheet iron pre-1860 and sheet steel later. You might be lucky enough to find one of the cast mountings, of brass or even silver, in the form of a coronet or a crest, which distinguished the carriages of the great.

The Shuttleworth Collection at Biggleswade, Herts, and the Kirkcaldy Museum, Fife, both have old horse-drawn vehicles.

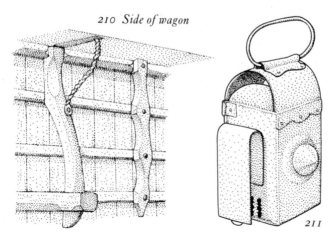

210 Side of wagon

211

Chains

The principle of making a chain by connecting links of metal to form a flexible length has been known since man first worked metals. Moreover the different shapes of link, whether plain loops, 'S' shaped, loops bent into a 'U' and then threaded, or the many other variations, are not modern developments. Even the compressed chain that looks like a snake is found in Roman jewellery. Therefore unless the links are marked, as in the case of a hall-marked gold watch chain, they are difficult to date.

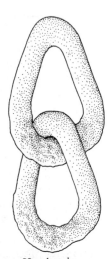

212 *Handmade iron chain*

The chains used in jewellery are too small and valuable for further attention, and many chains are too large to concern us, but between these limits lie two kinds we should consider. A chain made of iron, steel, or brass wire 'S' shaped links about an inch long has been in general use for thousands of years, at least as far back as ancient Assyria. The links are not welded, so it is easy to make up a required length by opening and closing with hand tools. Dating will depend largely on whether the wire has been hammered or drawn: drawn wire will be medieval or later. The second kind of chain is that of oval iron or steel links that have been welded. This is a chain for general use like the 'S' link type but stronger, and is used for instance to secure the brake shoe of a cart. The links may be twisted so that all lie in the same plane, but this is not essential. The making of such chain has been a speciality of the South Midlands since medieval times, and there is still one chainshop working the traditional craft. A chainshop has a coke fire with forced draft, and forging is done by an 'oliver', which is a hammer operated by a treadle. The chainmaker cuts a length of iron bar, bends it to a 'U' shape, flattens each end, threads it through an already formed link, bends round the flattened ends to lie on top of each other, and welds them together by forging. The evidence left on hand-made chain is that sometimes the diagonal line of the weld can be seen, especially on a corroded link. Machine-made chain is regular in shape, and the closure is effected by electric welding on the long side of the link, not at the end.

The Avoncroft Museum of Buildings, Bromsgrove, Worcs., has a complete chainshop with all its equipment.

Clay Pipes

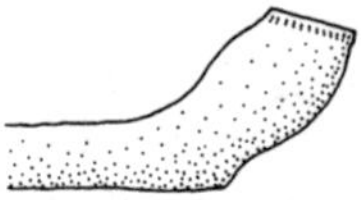

Tobacco was introduced into England in the reign of Elizabeth I. It was taken as snuff, or chewed, or smoked in pipes. The earliest pipes were of metal, but they became uncomfortably hot in use, so from about 1575 to the first twenty years of this century clay pipes were extensively used for smoking tobacco. I can remember when I was a boy in 1920 seeing elderly men smoking them. By then briar pipes were fashionable, but the 'clay' still had its devotees.

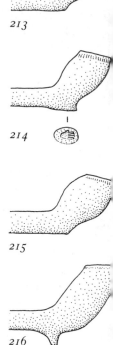

Pipes were made of a white-firing clay, the material being unchanged from first to last. Early pipes were cast solid, except that the stem hole was formed by a thin reed which burnt out in the firing. Early bowls had to be hollowed out with a knife, and their irregular surface will be seen as evidence of this. Seventeenth-century and later pipes were cast in valved moulds, but up to the early nineteenth century the outside was finished by hand, the marks of scraping to be seen and felt. In the nineteenth century pipe-making machines left seams, which were sometimes disguised by moulded design. Many of these later pipes have bowls cast with town or regimental insignia, or the bowl is in some grotesque shape.

The makers of clay pipes set up their kilns, many of which have been found, in centres of population, and supplied pipes to retailers and public houses some miles around. Clay pipes were both fragile and cheap, to the degree that they were given away with food and drink at inns. It is rare to come across a complete pipe, but bowls and stems are very common, so that the archaeologist working on a post-medieval site learns to rely on them for dating purposes.

The series is as follows:

Fig. 213 Sixteenth-century 'fairy' pipe, so called because of the small bowl, tobacco being then very expensive. There is a flat heel at the base of the bowl, but this cannot be seen in profile as it follows the line of the stem.

Fig. 214 Seventeenth century: bowl larger and heel protrudes. The maker now stamps his initials or device on the heel.

Fig. 215 Early eighteenth century: bowl still larger, and more bulbous.

Fig. 216 Late eighteenth century: the tall Dutch shape becomes fashionable, and the heel is replaced by a blunt spur. The maker's mark is now on the stem, usually as his full name.

Fig. 217 From around 1840 pipes were machine-made and lightly glazed. Early in the twentieth century the spur disappears and the shape resembles a briar pipe.

A piece of pipe stem is not possible to date unless by a happy chance the maker's name is on it. Otherwise, although the hole was normally of about the same size, centrally placed and of regular circular shape throughout the years, in early pipes it is sometimes well out of centre.

See 'Clay Pipes for the Archaeologist' by A. Oswald, *British Archaeological Report No. 14* (1975).

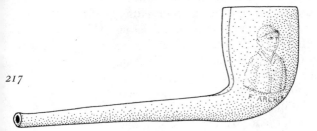

217

Coins

Most coins are small inscribed metal discs, but not all such discs are coins. They may be tokens, that is substitutes for coins in times of shortage, or counters used in games or for calculating; or more rarely coin weights used in the old days to weigh gold and silver coins.

The two sides of a coin are the obverse, usually marked with the head of a god, a ruler or some other personage, and the reverse, which carries some suitable device associated with that personage. This style was first adopted by the ancient Greeks, but the earliest coins of all were small billets of precious metal impressed with a punch. Fig. 218 shows one of these, from Lydia, dating from the ninth century B.C.

The Romans had an extensive coinage of gold, silver and copper alloy coins minted all over their dominions. The silver and bronze or brass coins are often found, and deserve some description.

218

Name	Material	Diameter in/mm	Date	Remarks
Denarius	Silver	0.7/17	Up to A.D. 250	Late ones of debased silver
Sestertius	Brass	1.1/29	From Augustus onwards	
Dupondius	Bronze	1.0/25	Early Empire	
Antoninianus	Silver	0.8/20	From A.D. 214	Late ones smaller and much debased
Follis	Bronze	1.0/25	From A.D. 295	Quickly decreases in size to 0.7/17

From the end of the third century the growing troubles of the Roman Empire were reflected in the coinage, which became debased in material and smaller in size. This gave the opportunity for counterfeiting, and many small counterfeit coins are to be found dating from the fourth century. Fig. 219 shows the design on the reverse of an antoninianus of Aurelian celebrating the defeat of Zenobia, 'Queen of the East', and Fig. 220 is of a typical small counterfeit antoninianus. Both were recently picked up in Wiltshire.

From the departure of the Romans in A.D. 418 coins are too uncommon for description here until settled conditions returned under the Plantagenet kings. Then in 1180 the short-cross silver penny was issued, replaced by the long-cross penny in 1247. The cross, though no doubt of religious significance also, enabled the penny to be cut into two halfpennies or four farthings ('fourthings'), and these may be found as well as whole coins.

The first official copper coinage in Britain was struck in the reign of Charles II in 1672. These are recognisably modern coins, with his head on one side and a seated Britannia on the other. This figure derives from Roman coins showing a captive seated on a pile of captured arms. The denominations were halfpenny and farthing, diameter 1.1in/28 mm and 0.9 in/23 mm respectively.

A distinctive change took place in British coinage in 1662, when the old method of hammering by hand between dies was superseded by the screw press hitherto used only for a few experimental issues. Now coins were notably thicker, and the edges of gold and silver ones

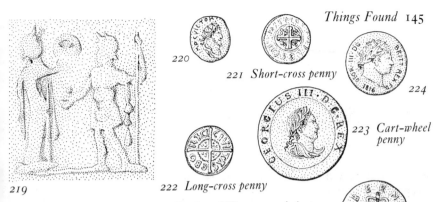

220

221 *Short-cross penny*

224

223 *Cart-wheel penny*

222 *Long-cross penny*

219

225

could be milled to discourage clipping. When examining a coin, medal or token, be sure to look at the edge, which may carry an inscription.

During the eighteenth century shillings and six-pences of silver, and halfpennies and farthings of copper were the common coins of exchange. The shilling is a little larger than the present 5p piece, and the sixpence about the size of the 1p. In the last quarter of the century shortage of coin brought about widespread counterfeiting, and it is said that only a fifth of the copper coinage was at that time genuine.

The final development to be recorded here was the copper coinage made from 1797 by Boulton and Watt in Birmingham, until the London Mint took over in the early years of the nineteenth century. The coins were well designed and finely made in steam-powered presses. The first penny was the famous 'cart-wheel' with its unusual broad rim, but wartime shortage of metal caused it to be no longer made after 1806, since when the penny has been around the size of that used until the recent decimalisation. Fig. 224 shows a George III shilling and Fig. 225 an Irish halfpenny found under the floorboards of an old house being renovated.

From the beginning of the nineteenth century the inscriptions and dating on coins will tell sufficient about them.

The British Museum has a notable collection of coins. See also *Coins* by R. A. G. Carson (Hutchinson, 1962).

Combs

Here we will consider the combs used for combing and ornamenting the hair of men and women, with a glance

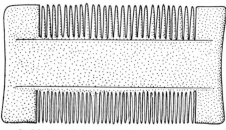

226 *Medieval comb*

227

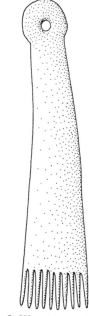

228 *Weaving comb*

at the implements also called combs used for the preparation of cloth.

The comb required accurate cutting of its prongs by a fine saw, and in ancient days it was used only by civilised people; or at least one can say that hair combs are not found on prehistoric sites in Britain. Barbarians may have made some attempt to separate their matted locks with twigs or brushes, but such implements have not survived.

Roman and medieval combs may be single or double-sided, and made of wood, antler, bone or ivory. The Vikings were notable for decorated single-sided combs. If double-sided, one side had finer teeth than the other. The teeth may be left square in section as sawn, or improved by trimming to an oval. Attribution to some particular people or date will depend on the style of decoration, if any. The comb attained its present shape at the Renaissance, and is subsequently found made of horn as well as the other materials listed above. Teeth could be either fine or coarse, but not fine at one end and coarse at the other as on modern combs.

Ornamental combs are single-sided, with a decorative top called a heading. They came into fashion during the seventeenth century and were used up to the 1920s, when the coming of short hair styles for women out-moded them. The commoner ones are from the 1870s onwards, and are made of horn, tortoiseshell or imitation tortoiseshell, often in a Spanish style. Fig. 227 shows a typical comb from the first years of this century.

Combs used on the fur of animals are called curry-combs. They are of metal, and can be made up of several rows of teeth fastened together.

Implements called combs were used for combing wool and flax before spinning, until these processes were industrialised in the eighteenth century. They look like rakes, with long sharp teeth. There is also, and of greater interest to us, the weaving comb used notably in the Iron Age to beat down the weft on an upright loom. It has recently been found that some tribes in Africa who use combs of similar pattern for weaving, also use them for combing their hair, so Iron Age combs may have been dual-purpose too. With the introduction of the weaving sword in classical times, the weaving comb went out of use.

Counters

229

The Romans were burdened with a primitive system of numbers. All but the simplest sums had to be done on an abacus, and this continued to be used in Europe until Arabic numerals slowly prevailed between the thirteenth and fifteenth centuries. The abacus remained for difficult calculations, and is still in general use in the East. However first in abbeys and then in the rising business-houses of Europe a board with counters came into use for 'casting accounts' during the fourteenth century and continued until the end of the seventeenth century. The board was checkered, the lines from bottom to top representing single numbers, tens, hundreds etc., and the counters were of metal. The city of Nuremberg supplied reckoning counters in large quantities to governments, bankers and merchants from the fifteenth to the late seventeenth century, and it is these that are often found. Such counters are usually of brass or copper, with a superficial resemblance to coins. Some are marked with the maker's name, such as Schultz, Krauwinckel and Laufer. Fig. 230 shows a typical Nuremberg counter.

230

These counters for business purposes, sometimes called 'jettons', were from time to time used as tokens (see TOKENS) or for gaming, but more convenient counters were specially made for scoring at the gambling table. These are usually of ivory, bone and mother-of-pearl. Many of them were made in China during the last two centuries, such as the fine mother-of-pearl counter with the design of a pagoda, picked up recently in a town garden (Fig. 229). Fig. 12 shows two bone fish counters, probably also Chinese-made.

The standard work is *The Casting Counter and the Counting Board* by F. P. Barnard (Clarendon Press, 1916).

Dice

Of the two 'devil's playthings', cards and dice, dice are much the older, dating from the Iron Age and used ever since. Herodotus, writing in the fifth century B.C., ascribes the invention of both dice and chess to the Lydians of Asia Minor, east of where he lived. We now know that chess originated further east, in central Asia, so perhaps that was the source of dice also.

At all events, being small and robust and needing no other apparatus than a flat surface on which to cast them, dice have always been favoured by soldiers, servants and apprentices to while away idle hours, and it is near the sites of ancient barracks, palaces and towns that they may survive to be found.

Most dice are of bone or antler, cubic in shape, and marked with the familiar dots one to six, the numbers on each of the three opposite sides adding up to seven. However there is a variant (Fig. 231), known in the ancient world before the Roman conquests and surviving through to the Dark Ages. This die has two long sides, which are usually marked with three, four, five and six dots; the square ends are unmarked. The only reason suggested for this variant is that the available material was limb bone, from which it would not be possible to make a satisfactory square die because the bone was soft or hollow in the centre.

The spots on dice are either simple depressions or 'dot and circle', easy enough to scribe with a metal bit, and so they have been made throughout the ages. One might expect to find the dots more regularly spaced on Roman dice, but otherwise dating is not possible.

231

Dolls' Heads and Limbs

Whole dolls are normally too large and fragile to reckon on finding, except for the jointed wooden 'Dutch' or 'peg-top' doll shown (this one is only six inches tall). These dolls were first made commercially in southern Germany around the year 1820 and production has continued there and elsewhere since. They are impossible to date closely unless clothed, and even then of course the garments may not be original.

The heads and limbs which we may find will have belonged to bodies of stuffed cloth or leather, long

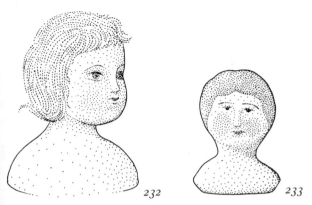

232   233

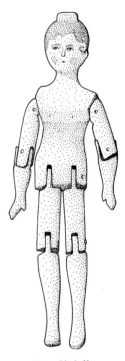

234 'Dutch' doll

perished. Wax dolls require only a mention here, as they are unlikely to survive unless carefully kept. The first wax heads were made about 1830, and production continued into the 1920s, so many people can remember their awful fate if left too near a fire. Wax dolls were expensive, with hair carefully set into the scalp, and they were richly dressed. From 1850 they had glass eyes.

As to other, more permanent materials, there was porcelain, which was used from 1840, and an unglazed pink-tinted pottery known as bisque, used from 1850, and both were used until modern times. The better quality porcelain and bisque heads had real hair, but from around 1870 the hair on cheaper dolls might be moulded as part of the head. Fig. 232 shows a bisque head of about 1880 with real hair, and Fig. 233 a porcelain head of similar date with moulded hair. Arms and legs could be extensions of the stuffed trunk, or cast of the same material as the head. Early joints were wired, but they have sockets and pins from the late nineteenth century. At this time also the first dolls with swivel eyes delighted their young owners, and there were also walking dolls with unusual metal legs.

Rubber and celluloid have been used in the making of dolls for over a hundred years, and these materials were pioneered in America.

As well as the dolls made to be children's toys, there were those for adult purposes, such as medical or surgical demonstrations, the display of fashionable clothes in miniature, the use of artists, and for witchcraft. Of these only the mannequins of the French fashion industry need further mention. These date from the eighteenth to the early nineteenth century, and their heads, of wood, do not have the infantile expression usual in children's dolls. The word mannequin, which is the same as our manikin, a little man, survived to be used for the live full-scale fashion models of the 1920s.

There are said to be a thousand dolls at Penrhyn, and other good collections are at the Bethnel Green Museum, London, at Worthing Museum, Stockport Municipal Museum, and the Warwick Doll Museum. Books include *Dolls* by John Noble (Studio Vista, 1967), *Dolls and doll makers* by Mary Hillier (Weidenfeld and Nicolson, 1968), and *Dolls* by Antonia Fraser (Octopus, 1973).

Door Fittings

These are the hinges, straps, handles and bolts on the doors of buildings and built-in cupboards: furniture fittings are dealt with separately, and so are locks and keys.

The principles of the hinge, the latch and the bolt have been known since antiquity. In the Bible it is written that the Temple built by King Solomon had doors with hinges of gold, and it is also recorded that Ammon bolted the door against Tamar.

As with many simple things, door fittings changed little from Roman times until the advent of cheap mild steel created the standard builders' fittings that are with us still.

The plain blacksmith's door fitting, such as the hasp in Fig. 53, needs no further comment, but there is a range of distinctive decorative hinges which were popular between the sixteenth and early eighteenth centuries. The most interesting is the so-called cockshead hinge, of which a seventeenth-century example is shown. The design seems to have originated in the writhing beasts of medieval strapwork on doors and chests. Later examples look more like a cock and less like a dragon. Concurrently other configurations were used, such as the 'H' hinge, one like two dovetails joined at the base, and another like a 'T' on its side with the intriguing name of cross-garnet hinge. This word may be of similar sense to the clew garnet which gathers or garners the corner of a sail to the yardarm aboard ship.

The door bolt as we know it, a round metal bar shot into a socket, first appears in the eighteenth century: the

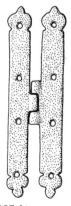

235 'H' hinge

237

doors which Ammon so unkindly shut against Tamar, and those of medieval castles, were secured with baulks of timber dropped into iron hooks.

The object in Fig. 237 is a casement latch, such as was installed from late medieval days until the eighteenth century, and many are still in use. It would be hard to identify if found away from the associated window.

An interesting old form of handle may be found (Fig. 238) which is fastened through the door with a tang, not with bolts or screws. As on furniture, this is not likely to be later than early eighteenth century.

The material used for old door fittings was iron or bronze, the smaller and better quality pieces being of the latter material.

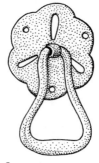

238

Drawing Instruments

A glance inside any box of drawing instruments will show two kinds of implements: varieties of rulers and varieties of compasses or dividers. Rulers will be identified by their scales, but a special form called a sector was used from the seventeenth to the middle of the nineteenth century for trigonometrical calculations and by architects and navigators. The sector is an interesting obsolete device which, I have found, can go unrecognised (Fig. 240).

But you are more likely to find compasses and div-

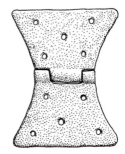

239 Dovetail hinge

iders. Nowadays these two words distinguish the 'compasses' which can draw a circle, having a pen or pencil on one arm, and the 'dividers' which have a point on both arms and are for transferring measurements, but this distinction is not soundly based. Many compasses have a point at each end, and are so depicted in medieval manuscripts showing God designing the world. Dividers were originally 'proportional dividers', that is an X-shaped instrument with a movable joint so that the span at one end can be a constant proportion of that at the other.

Medieval compasses for the use of architects and navigators are of bronze (Fig. 241), and are well and carefully made. There were also craftsmen's compasses, used for scribing as well as measuring, and these are of iron (Fig. 242) and much rougher in appearance. Of course only an iron tip would scribe a circle on the workpiece. The blacksmith made such compasses up to modern times, and it would be impossible to tell a medieval pair from one fifty years old.

It was the art and architecture of the Renaissance that brought improved drawing instruments, with points of steel and arms of finely finished and decorated bronze. These are rare things, but the steel drawing instruments of the nineteenth century are their not unworthy de-

240

241

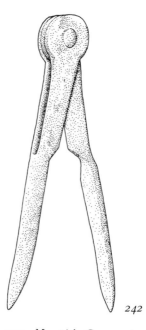

242

243

scendants, and are sometimes to be found. Fig. 243 shows a pair of compasses about a hundred years old; there is still some decoration, and you will see the joint is laminated whereas a modern instrument has a plain joint and little or no attempt at decoration. The earlier material is tool steel, but nowadays stainless steel.

The shape of the point of both compasses and dividers is important. It can be thin and sharp for piercing paper and drawing a circle round; or broad and sharp for lodging in a centre mark on metal and scribing a circle round; or comparatively broad and blunt for taking measurements off a drawing or a chart. Navigational charts in particular must not be damaged by the compasses used on them.

Earrings

The first earrings were presumably circlets, but the word now means any ornament hanging from the lobe of the ear. Earrings were known to the ancient Egyptians and to the classical world, but were not worn in the Middle Ages.

They were suspended by a wire through the lobe of the ear until screw fittings came in at the end of the nineteenth century.

Plain circular earrings are worn by men of the Romany race, and until quite recently sailors wore them in the belief that they improved the eyesight. Oriental men also wear earrings, but generally in the West the fashion has been confined to women, and their styles have varied with contemporary feminine modes.

244 Earring, 1870

Earrings were reintroduced to Europe with the Renaissance and reached England during the reign of Elizabeth I, when they were very popular. The favoured style was a pear-shaped pearl drop, which continued in fashion until the eighteenth century. Late in that century diamond-studded earrings were worn by rich ladies, and early in the nineteenth century they had earrings of gold in the Greek and Roman styles. About 1830 long drops cut from various stones were popular. By 1840 most fashionable women had their ears pierced. The operation was performed when they were young girls, and earrings of small size and simple style were made specially for them. From 1860 to 1880 were the great years for earrings of large and impressive form

(Fig. 244), which matched the brooches of those days. Studs became fashionable in the 1880s, but from then there was a decline in interest. By 1900 not all women had their ears pierced, and though screwed fittings were available, for many years the earring was of little importance in jewellery.

For Georgian and Victorian earrings see *Collecting Jewellery* by Mona Curran (Arco, 1963) and *Victorian Jewellery* by Charlotte Gere (William Kimber, 1972).

Eggs

An egg-shaped object of some interesting solid stone such as coloured marble or agate is probably purely decorative, and possibly an Easter gift. It is said that stone eggs were formerly used as hand-coolers by young ladies in the intervals at dances in the eighteenth century. A wooden egg may have been made for use while darning, instead of the more usual 'mushroom' shape.

The commonly found 'ovoid' is of pottery, approximately the size of a hen's egg, and its purpose is to encourage hens to lay by being placed in their nest boxes. An egg of chalk, about the size of a small bantam's egg, was found on the site of the abandoned town of Old Sarum, and this may have been a medieval nest-egg.

Fig. 245 shows a small egg-shaped vinaigrette, and Fig. 246 an egg-shaped silver tea-infuser. The shape lends itself as a small container for personal use.

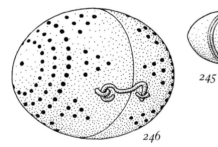

245

246

Fetters

Included under this heading are all the means of restraint used on the limbs of captives, which are variously distinguished as follows:

Fetters – for the feet.
Manacles – for the hands, now more often called handcuffs.
Shackles – properly the long link connecting fetters or manacles, but applied to restraining chains in general.
Gyves – for hands or feet; now only used poetically.

Medieval and later fetters or manacles have been found riveted round the limb bones of the skeletons of executed persons, but from early times less permanent securing devices were also available.

The Romans had a form of tubular padlock, and probably employed it on shackles – using that word now in its general sense. Fig. 247 shows a fetter ascribed to the seventeenth century, with its associated key. This form of lock was known from classical times down to the Middle Ages. The key is passed through wards at one end of the tube, and engages spring-loaded tapered pieces, pressing them inwards so that they are carried through by the key and release the hasp. Fig. 248 shows an eighteenth-century fetter working on a new principle. The two small projections on the end of the key are first used to unscrew a small cover at the end of the tubular lock. The interrupted screw at the end of the key is then inserted and screwed in to release the hasp.

Handcuffs may be a solid 'figure-of-eight' as in Fig. 249, or joined by a chain and swivel.

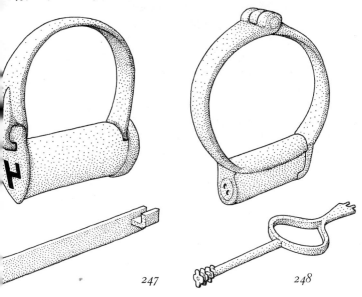

247   248

Modern forms of restraint are of plastic and not durable, unlike the fetters and manacles of old, which may turn up in the neighbourhood of former hospitals or mental institutions where people were kept against their will.

There are fetters in Wilberforce House, Hull, the birthplace of the slave emancipator William Wilberforce, and in Salisbury Museum, Wiltshire.

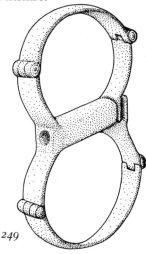

249

Firemarks

The Great Fire of London in 1666 showed very clearly the danger of conflagration in cities, but it was not until early in the next century that preventive measures were taken. The authorities then fitted fire-plugs to water-mains and provided fire engines and ladders, but made no provision for brigades except to charge constables and night-watchmen with the duty of assisting at fires. It was left to the 'fire-offices', as fire insurance companies were called, to organise their own fire-brigades, and to issue badges for affixing to premises that were insured with them. Hence the firemarks still to be seen on old houses, many in their original positions. Some, however, will have been removed, or gone into the ground when a building was demolished, so they may be found from time to time.

In London and other large cities there were a number of fire-offices, each with a fire-brigade, but in small towns and in the countryside only the major companies, of which the Sun was the largest, followed by the Phoenix and the Royal Exchange, would be represented.

250 *Early firemark*

251 *18th-century firemark*

252 *Early-19th-century firemark*

253 *Late firemark*

During the eighteenth century firemarks were of cast lead, often gilt, with the number of the policy cut into a label below the sign of the fire-office. The signs are self-explanatory, such as a sun-face (Sun), a bird arising from flames (Phoenix), a classical building (Royal Exchange), clasped hands (Hand-in-Hand). Some insurance companies still have their early records, and can recount the terms of the policy, and to whom granted, if the number is quoted.

Around the year 1800, firemarks started to be made of stamped brass, and although the labels were retained for a while, the policy number is not to be seen. Because during the eighteenth century the London fire-offices were limited to the Sun, the Phoenix, the Royal Exchange, the Hand-in-Hand, the Westminster, the London Assurance and the Union, these are the only ones for which a lead firemark may be expected.

In the middle of the nineteenth century, public fire-brigades took over from volunteers all over Britain, and firemarks ceased to have any great significance.

There is a collection of firemarks at the Chartered Insurance Institute Museum in London and in the museum at Boston, Lincolnshire. See also *Firemarks* by John Vince (Shire, 1973).

Fishing Gear

There are three methods of catching fish – by net, by spear, or by luring with a baited hook – and all three have been known since antiquity. Nets will leave little to be found except sinkers, which were of lead or stone but would be difficult to date. The familiar trident of Nep-

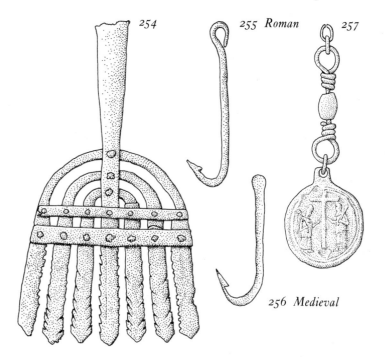

254 255 *Roman* 257

256 *Medieval*

une is a fish-spear, and it is recognisably the open, pronged and barbed weapon used against round or flat fish. In modern times a small bronze trident known as a 'fish-gig' was supplied to naval fishing enthusiasts from Royal Naval stores. Eels are thin and slippery, so they require an eel-spear of close-set prongs to hold rather than pierce. Fig. 254 shows the head of an iron eel-spear that could be about a hundred years old. Bone fish-pears, or ones of wood armed with small flints, are familiar objects from Middle Stone Age fishing sites, but are not as likely to be found casually as iron fishing gear from Roman and later times.

You are most likely to find fish-hooks, ancient ones of bone and shell, and of metal once that was available, always of the same basic shape as modern ones. A barb is not difficult to cut, and it is usually present unless it has corroded away. The end of the shank is either flattened to retain the line knotted round it, or formed into a closed eye, and both designs continue throughout history. Fig. 255 shows a Roman fish-hook with an eye, and medieval ones with a flattened shank are known.

The best source of information on early rods and reels is an illustrated copy of Isaac Walton's *Compleat Angler*. Reels were commonly of steel and brass in the eighteenth century and all of brass in the nineteenth. Rods were first made in sections connected by socket joints in the fifteenth century. Odd pieces of fishing tackle turn up near stretches of river or canal, especially the ferrules from broken and discarded sections of rod. Fig. 257 shows a brass medal which, to judge by the attached swivel, was recently used as a fishing weight.

You can see old fishing gear at the museum in Isaac Walton's cottage at Yarnfield, Staffordshire.

Flints

The commonest form of worked flint found is simply a flake struck from a lump in the process of shaping a tool. The flake will have a 'platform' on which the blow was struck to detach it, and a 'bulb of percussion' where the force of the blow was concentrated and split the stone.

Struck flakes cannot be dated unless further work has been done on them. In the Middle Stone Age, small flakes were trimmed by pressing with another piece of

258 Microlith

some suitable hard material to form the typical small sharp 'microlith' of those days. Numbers of these were set into wood or bone to make tools or weapons. Pressure flaking continued for the larger implements of the New Stone Age, and for the rare but exceptionally fine flint tools of the Bronze Age, which were probably made by specialist craftsmen, often imitating the shapes of metal artefacts. Fig. 259 shows a New Stone Age scraper, and Fig. 260 a Bronze Age knife imitating one of bronze. See also ARROWHEADS, and Fig. 112 for an Old Stone Age flint hand axe.

259

At the same time as good, evidently devoted work in flint, we also find rough and summary chipping. Comparison can be made with the carpenter and the person who sharpens a pencil: both work in wood but the aim and performance are vastly different. So there are Middle Stone Age tools flaked by striking in the Old Stone Age way, scrapers with only the minimum of secondary work to provide an edge, and some very coarse Bronze Age tools.

The Romans used flint for lathe tools, but other than them we must move forward to the invention of the wheel-lock gun in the sixteenth century before we encounter worked flints again. The wheel-lock had a flint held against a revolving steel wheel to strike a spark and ignite the priming powder. It was soon superseded by the simpler flint-lock, which had a spring-loaded hammer carrying a flint forward to strike a spark against the hinged cover of the priming pan. This mechanism was employed in pistols, hand guns and the locks of cannon until early in the nineteenth century, when the percussion lock was perfected.

260

Gun flints are rectangular in shape (Fig. 262) and quite different from any prehistoric implement or weapon, although they were likewise made from struck flakes. The size varies considerably from that for a pistol about twenty millimetres across the edge to that of a cannon-lock twice as big. Gun flints of a dark colour have always been favoured in Africa, where flint-lock guns are still in use, but in Europe and elsewhere a light-coloured flint was preferred.

262

261 *Mesolithic pick*

Footwear

There is some truth in the old joke showing an angler winding in a boot when he had hoped for a fish: leather can be preserved indefinitely if kept wet and is therefore worth considering. Some knowledge of the history of footwear will help you to identify some old and interesting things.

The Romans had sandals for wear in the home and ankle boots for outdoors; their soldiers wore a boot of open-work leather up to the calf. This *'caligula'*, from which an emperor took his name, and the civilian ankle boot, were studded with nails and cleats that must have frequently dropped off, for they are often found.

263 Roman cleat

*264 Roman shoe
nail*

It is sometimes thought that the shaping of shoes to fit the right or left foot is a modern idea, but this is not so. Some medieval shoes, of which soles but little else have been found, were so made. In those days they had two sorts of shoemaker guild: the cordwainer who used new goatskin leather from Cordova, and the cobbler who re-made shoes when they wore out. Minor repair work was done in an amateur fashion. Medieval shoes were also made of cloth.

An absurd fashion for long pointed toes reached its height in the early fifteenth century, then subsided until the shoes of 1500–1550 were square-toed. Outdoor shoes were studded with 'knobbed' nails and fitted with crescent shaped heel irons. As the use of armour declined, the boot came in for men's wear but was not important until the Civil War, when the contestants on both sides stamped about in them. The large high tongues of mid-seventeenth century shoes are also typical.

Around 1550 the raised heel came in. At first it was made of wood or cork, but by 1700 it was built of leather slices as nowadays.

Until about 1660 the normal fastening of shoes was by a strap or thong over the instep called a latchet, which was fixed in place with a button or a hook and eye.

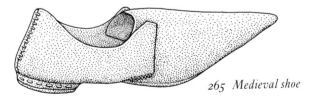

265 Medieval shoe

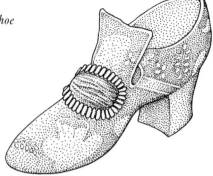

Lacing, however, was not unknown. The buckle came into fashion at the Restoration of Charles II, and remained popular until the end of the eighteenth century. (See BUCKLES.) The heels of men's shoes were medium high in the late seventeenth century, low around 1740, and then very high for the dandies of the late eighteenth century. Women's shoes of this period were decorative and made of silk, satin or cloth; the spindle-shaped 'French' heel was popular.

In the early nineteenth century men took to wearing boots almost exclusively, and continued to do so in varying styles until 1900, when shoes became tolerated for informal wear. Late in the eighteenth century the heelless sandal shoe was worn by fashionable women, but the pendulum swung to tight laced boots in the reign of Victoria.

Not until 1850 did a machine to sew leather become available, so the inexact stitching of earlier footwear should be apparent.

You can see boots and shoes in the Westfield Museum, Kettering, Northants, and in the Street Shoe Museum, Street, Somerset.

Forks

Eating forks, as distinct from the large forks used to hold meat when carving, became fashionable in the late seventeenth century as one of the elegancies of Continental life brought over by Charles II at the Restoration.

These early forks were of steel, paired with a knife, and kept as a personal possession in a double sheath, or in pouches on the side of a Scottish dirk. Fig. 267 shows a seventeenth-century steel fork with a straight stem, and Fig. 268 one of the eighteenth century with a baluster stem. This progress is typical, the baluster becoming a low swelling in the middle of the stem about 1770 and so remaining. Pairs of knives and forks continued to be made down to the early nineteenth century, some of them with folding handles. Forks of the eighteenth century are found with a pistol grip, similar to their accompanying knives which, of course, may not remain with them. All these steel forks, from beginning to end, have two prongs, like a modern carving fork. Being uncomfortably sharp, their primary purpose was to hold down meat for cutting rather than for conveying it to the mouth. (See also KNIVES.)

A separate 'race' of forks grew up, made by the

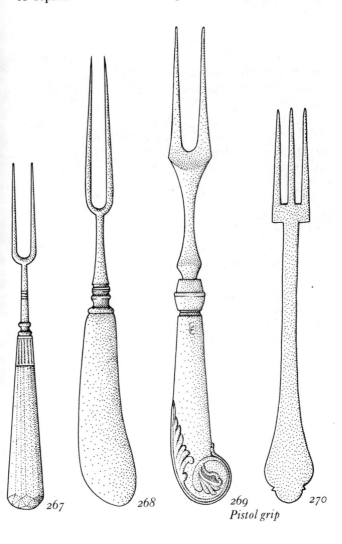

267   268   269   270
Pistol grip

silversmith to accompany the spoons he had already manufactured for centuries. Consequently silver forks follow the stylistic progress of spoons (see also). Fig. 270 shows a 'trifid' ended fork of 1680 with angular shoulders: by 1700 the shoulders sloped and have done so ever since. As to the number of prongs on a silver fork, it was normally three until the last quarter of the eighteenth century, and after that normally four.

Pewter has seldom been used in Britain for forks, because it is too soft to make satisfactory prongs. I have seen a French pewter fork with the prongs predictably bent.

Furniture Fittings

The fittings you are most likely to find are drawer handles, because they are roughly treated in use and discarded when damaged or unfashionable.

In the late seventeenth century the fashion was for hollowcast brass drop handles with round or star shaped backing plates. The handle was attached by a split tang which passed through the drawer front and was then opened out and driven into the wood. Fig. 271 shows the arrangement applied to a loose ring handle, which came in early in the next century. In the 1720s the handle became a loop, and required two small round backing plates or one large one, often engraved. At first these loops of cast brass were fixed by the old split tang method, but soon this was superseded by bolts through the drawer front with nuts on the inside. In the 1770s there was a radical change: machines were installed in the Birmingham area which stamped furniture fittings out of thin sheet brass, and from this date all backing plates except those on the grandest furniture were made by this process, often in high relief. When in the last century a plain wooden knob handle became popular, thousands of the original handles on drawers were discarded. Within the last half century, however, thousands of drawer handles have been replaced in the original style but the new ones are usually cast not stamped.

The word 'escutcheon' is given to the small plate surrounding a key-hole on furniture. It came into being in the late seventeenth century, and was of brass plate and oval in shape, with four small pierced lugs to take fixing pins (Fig. 274). Around 1750 the escutcheon

271

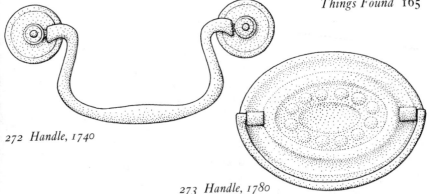

272 Handle, 1740

273 Handle, 1780

became a simple edging of key-hole shape and has so remained. Unlike handles, escutcheons are seldom replaced so are much less likely to be found.

There are some good examples of furniture fittings in *English Furniture* by J. C. Rogers (Country Life, 1959).

274

Games and Puzzles

Indoor games are of three distinct kinds: you may have a board with movable pieces, or cards of some sort which have different values or significances, or you may compete in some simple skill.

The 'board with movable pieces' type of game is of great antiquity. A set dating from the third millennium B.C. was excavated at Ur, and the method of play has been reconstructed. This was a palace game, as are those found in ancient Egyptian tombs. Much more common, and seldom leaving anything to be found, are the simple table games played on a board scratched on stone or drawn on the ground, and using pebbles as pieces. The Romans had such a game, called 'Lusoria', and 'Nine Men's Morris' is still played as it has been for centuries in Europe and Asia.

Some early games 'men' survive. The Romans used blobs of coloured glass, and there are pieces made of lead or stone, but the usual material throughout is bone. They may be distinguished from the counters used for scoring by being more substantial, and often one side is flat and the other has some simple decoration (Fig. 275).

Chess, draughts and backgammon were much played in the Middle Ages. Only chess requires special pieces. Early medieval ivory chessmen in the form of realistic

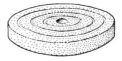

275

knights, bishops and so on are very rare: ordinary folk played chess with conventionalised pieces carved from bone. Kings and queens were suggested by a throne; the bishop was a cylinder with two 'horns' and the knight was similar but with one projection; the castle was a tapered block with cuts across the top. The early distinction between naturalistic and conventional chessmen has continued to modern times. Compare the early twentieth-century English piece with the mid-nineteenth-century Indian one (Figs 277 and 77).

276 *Chess king*

Cards are usually of paper, so most games played with those 'of different value and significance' are outside our consideration. Dominoes, however, are of this kind and deserve a word to say that they are comparatively recent, dating from the late eighteenth century. Good Victorian dominoes are of ivory and ebony but most are of bone and vulcanite or some other substitute.

Many table games require dice (see DICE) or a teetotum. Early teetotums were four-sided, with the letters A, T, N, D, or later T, P, A, N, distributed round the sides. The game was simply *Take*, *Put*, *All* or *None* according to how the teetotum fell. A, T, N, D were the Latin equivalents. Last century the teetotum developed a large number of sides with figures on them, and could be used as an auxiliary to various games.

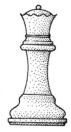

277

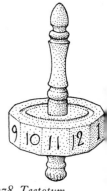

278 *Teetotum*

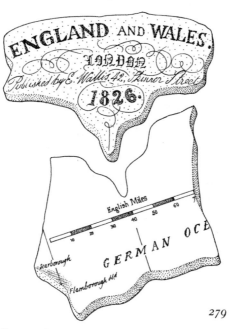

279

Finally, there are games of skill, of which spillikins is representative. The small sticks, often carved and numbered, may be found. Early ones date from the eighteenth century.

The only puzzles of any age likely to be encountered are jig-saws, which under the name of 'dissected puzzles' were first made in 1786. They can readily be dated by the picture on them, and Fig. 279 shows an example. The pieces are interlocking from about 1840.

You can see some early indoor games at Keighley Museum, Yorkshire, the Cornish Museum, Looe, and the Harris Museum, Preston, Lancashire. See also *Chessmen* by A. E. J. Mackett-Beeson (Weidenfeld & Nicolson, 1968) and *Table Games of Georgian and Victorian Days* by F. R. B. Whitehouse (Priory Press, 1971).

Glasses

The glasses discussed here are not those to improve the eyesight, for which see SPECTACLES, nor have I any more to say about glass in general, which is covered on pages 72–7. It is table glasses we will consider, as in Shakespeare's 'Glasses, glasses are the only drinking'.

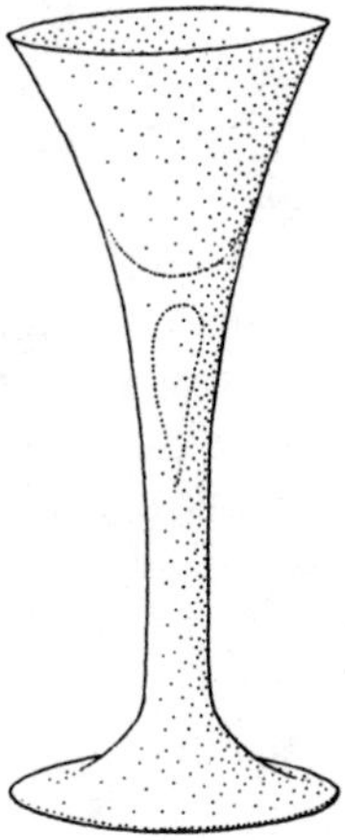

Fragments of Roman, medieval and other glass vessels up to the seventeenth century may be found. These are usually of thin blown glass, often coloured, and will be of interest to your local museum. The distinction between Roman and some much later glass is only apparent to an expert.

The sort of glass commonly found is broken pieces from drinking glasses of the eighteenth century and later, that have been thrown away. For that reason a series of typical wine glasses is shown here; candlesticks, custard glasses and other things were also made, though more rarely.

Fig. 280 Early eighteenth-century two-piece glass with enclosed 'tear'.

Fig. 281 Air-twist glass, around 1740. The spiral channels in the stem are transparent.

Fig. 282 Opaque-twist glass, around 1765. The spiral channels are white or sometimes of other colours.

Fig. 283 Glass with faceted stem, around 1780.

Fig. 284 A glass rummer of about 1815, inscribed

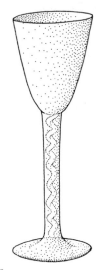

280

281

'Peace and Plenty' to celebrate the end of the Napoleonic Wars.

As well as fragmentary glasses, some complete and unusual ones turn up from odd corners where they have been put away, and a selection is shown.

Fig. 285   Early nineteenth-century glass with a deceptive bowl, called a 'Sham-dram', used by the publican when accepting a drink from a customer. A 'hokey-pokey' glass is similar but larger; the 'hocus-pocus' is a reference to the deceptive bowl.

Fig. 286   Eighteenth-century apothecary's dosing glass. The grounds from the medicine would run into the hollow tail.

Fig. 287   Eye-bath of green glass, about 1760.

In the middle of the eighteenth century the British government put a heavy duty on lead, so glasses made in England from then until 1845, when the duty was repealed, are lighter in the hand and lack the crystal brightness of the earlier glasses rich in lead.

There is a fine, well displayed collection of glass in the Pilkington Glass Museum at St Helens, Lancashire. See also *English Glass* by S. Crompton (Ward Lock, 1967).

282

283

284

287

286

285

Gun Parts

The separate parts of guns that you are likely to find are the lock, the stock, or the barrel (the word 'gun' is used in a wide sense, to include pistols).

The lock of a firearm is the mechanism that explodes the charge. In the sixteenth and seventeenth centuries there was a 'wheel-lock' in which a piece of iron pyrites was held against a revolving steel wheel to give a shower of sparks and ignite the priming powder, and there was also a 'match-lock' in which a glowing match was brought down on to the priming powder when the trigger was pulled. In the second quarter of the seventeenth century the flint-lock displaced both of these locks and lasted two hundred years until the invention of the percussion lock, which became universal in civilised countries for war and sport by 1840. So it is flint-locks that we should know a little about, and Fig. 288 is representative. A gun-lock was fitted to a large gun; the musket had a similar but smaller lock, and the pistol had a smaller one still. Pistols were first made in the days of the wheel-lock. The spring-loaded hammer of the flint-lock carries the flint forward against the steel and strikes a spark, at the same time opening the hinged pan cover to expose the priming powder. When the gun is loaded, the cover is closed to protect the priming, and the hammer must be held away from it, at 'half-cock'. If the mechanism is worn or faulty, the gun may 'go off at half-cock' (the origin of the well-known expression). The 'snap-haunce' gun, made in Southern Europe up to the early nineteenth century, has the steel and pan cover made separately.

The adoption of the brass cartridge in the third quarter of the last century eliminated the problems of gas blowing back into the lock, and made possible breech-loading and repeating firearms with complex mechanisms machined to fine limits.

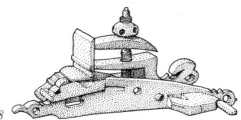

288

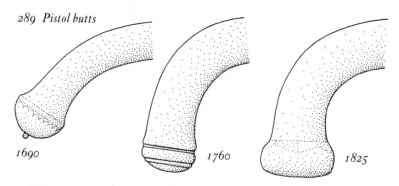

289 Pistol butts

1690   1760   1825

The stock of a pistol can, in my experience, be found detached from the lock. The progress in the shape of the pistol stock from almost straight, and at a shallow angle to the barrel, to curved at a right angle, is illustrated in Fig. 289. In general pistols were the personal arms of officers or well-off civilians, so the stock is often decorated with inlay and the butt may be ornamental, in a style helpful for dating.

The barrels of firearms, except for German sporting guns, were rarely rifled until the middle of the nineteenth century. Barrels were made by one of two processes, to give either a light, strong and expensive tube or a heavy, weak, cheap one. The expensive method was in effect a variety of pattern welding (see page 57). It gave the rope-like surface also to be seen on swords. Up to the middle of last century, the cheap method involved forming the tube from a sheet of iron with a welded seam. Later the barrels were drilled, except for the best shotguns, which are still pattern-welded.

The Armouries at the Tower of London has a large collection of firearms, and there is also a fine display in the Dick Institute, Kilmarnock, Ayrshire.

Harness

This word used to mean the armour of a knight; by extension to his steed it became the tackle strapped to a horse for riding or draught purposes, and that is the sense used here.

It was noted on page 81 that the leather of old harness seldom survives, but the buckles and rings from it are found, and also bits and stirrups. A harness buckle cannot be positively identified as such, but a strap-distributor of heavier proportions than a man might wear to gird on his sword is likely to be for a horse. Also the bronze ring shown in Fig. 290, which was found on the surface of a ploughed field, is probably from harness because of its thickness and evidence of wear.

290

The bit is an ancient piece of equipment for the control of a horse, and it is not easy to date. Both the split 'snaffle-bit' and the complex 'curb-bit' with its ability to check the ridden horse violently, were known to the Roman world. The snaffle then reappears in Saxon times, and a fully developed curb was used by the mounted knight of the Middle Ages. The craft of the lorimer, who made bits and stirrups, was important at this time.

The stirrup is a comparative newcomer, only arriving in Western Europe during the Dark Ages. Stirrups tend to follow the shape of the footwear used with them: medieval ones are broad and low, with a wide foot-rest; by the seventeenth century the arch is high, and a pivoted foot-plate is found. Seventeenth and eighteenth-century stirrups have a tread made by flattening the foot-bar (Fig. 293).

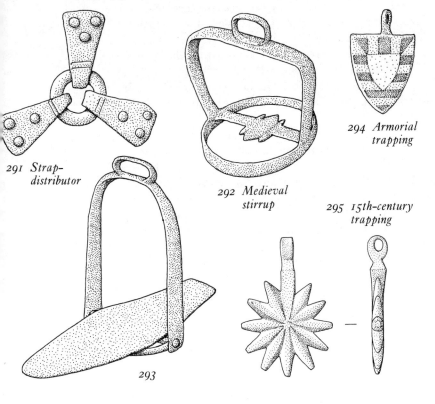

291 Strap-distributor

292 Medieval stirrup

293

294 Armorial trapping

295 15th-century trapping

Collars for draught horses were an improvement of the early Middle Ages. The hames were probably then of wood, but metal hames may survive from later times.

One particularly interesting item of harness is the 'trapping' which in medieval and later times was worn on the breast-band of riding horses, as shown in contemporary illustrations. Early ones were armorial, and late ones show their relationship to the HORSE BRASS. (See also SPURS.)

Hones and Whetstones

Hones and whetstones are both used for sharpening weapons and tools, but they do so by different means. A whetstone is made of some hard, compact but coarsely structured stone, and it sharpens by removing metal particles from the region of the blade's edge. A hone is of hard, compact and finely textured stone, and it sharpens by a polishing action, causing a minute flow of metal to improve the edge of a blade. Hones are moistened with oil and whetstones with water, though the word has no connection with 'wet'. Only very sharp edges, those of razors for instance, require to be honed, but whetstones have been used ever since metals have been known. Large and impressive whetstones were made by prehistoric people for ceremonial use: we cannot tell the reason for this, but perhaps it was because the 'terrible sharp sword' loses its power without its companion the whetstone.

296 Hone

Hones and whetstones cannot be closely dated if found casually. They come in many sizes and sections, of which Fig. 296 is typical. Small ones often have a perforation at one end, probably for suspension from the owner's belt, and some have an end shaped as though for insertion in a handle. Many of them, like modern composition whetstones, were just held in the hand. A groove may be found on whetstones where the points of knives have been sharpened.

The revolving grindstone – too large for our consideration – was an invention of the Iron Age.

Horse Brasses

The straps of a horse's harness are very suitable for decoration, in particular around the head, the breast-band and the martingale. In the Middle Ages (see HAR-NESS) trappings were worn on riding horses, and protective amulets have been placed on horses' heads since remote times. The increased availability of brass in the late seventeenth century brought into being the horse brass as we know it, which came to be worn by draught horses and occasionally by draught ponies until modern times.

The familiar brass is a plate of about four inches in diameter, with a loop for a strap at the top, but there was also a fly-terret carried on the top of the horse's head, perhaps with a hinged plate to swing and flash with its movement (Figs 297 and 298).

Until the middle of last century the only horse brass was a face-piece on the forehead; this was of the design known as a sunflash, being a dome with concentric circles. Suddenly around 1850 horse brasses became popular, and hundreds of designs were made and sold by saddlers for cart horses. Early ones were conventional, such as the crescent moon, a star, or a shield; or of local significance, such as the Staffordshire Knot; or connected with trade, such as barrels for a brewer. Many later brasses have no particular meaning. As to materials and methods of manufacture, most early brasses are cast but so are many late ones. Stamped brasses date from the 1860s: they were cheaper than the cast ones, and lighter, and could carry a more pronounced design. Brass made by the old calamine process was used on

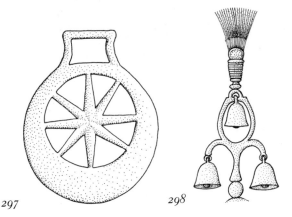

297   298

some early brasses, sometimes giving a pale colour and often a speckly pitted appearance, but the numerous reproduction brasses made since the 1920s are also of inferior metal. Old cast brasses had two projections at the back, called 'gates', to hold the brass in a vice for filing and polishing, but these gates were usually removed before the brass was sold.

The loop at the top should be smooth and worn with use, and some genuine brasses are thinned at the bottom where they have slapped against a strap over the years.

The fact is that there is no easy way of telling a horse brass that has been worn by a horse from a skilful fake, without considerable experience in handling them. You might be lucky enough to find a group of brasses attached to an old strap in the corner of a stable and then be able to say that they had certainly been made for use.

Luton Museum, Bedfordshire, has a representative collection of horse brasses. See also *Horse Brasses* by G. Hartfield (Abelard-Schuman, 1965) and *Discovering Horse Brasses* by John Vince (Shire, 1968).

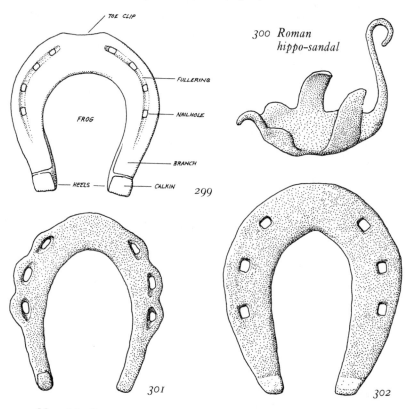

300 Roman hippo-sandal

TOE CLIP
FULLERING
NAILHOLE
FROG
BRANCH
HEELS — CALKIN
299

301

302

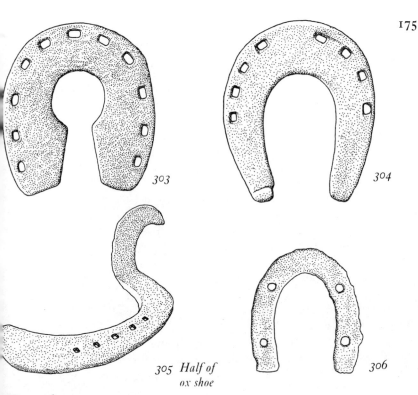

303

304

*305 Half of
ox shoe*

306

Horseshoes

The parts of a horseshoe are illustrated in Fig. 299.

The Romans had a removable iron sandal for their
horses, and by the fifth century they had adopted the
nailed shoe from their barbarian neighbours.

The oldest kind of horseshoe to be found has a wavy
edge, the calkins are made by turning back the heels, the
nail-holes are round within oval depressions, and there
is no fullering. The nail-heads are shaped like half a
cheese. This is a light shoe for a small working horse,
and was used from late Roman times to the early Middle
Ages. The wavy edge was formed when the nail-holes
were drifted through the narrow red-hot metal (Fig.
301).

Between the tenth and the fifteenth centuries the
basic 'wavy-edge' horseshoe slowly became heavier and
wider, so that the wavy edge became less and less pronounced. The nail-holes are square from the Norman
Conquest, and flat 'T'-shaped nails are used. From the
fourteenth century a more robust shoe came into use for
draught horses and the mounts of knights. Typically

this shoe has a broadly rounded rim, an arched frog, and square nail-holes. If calkins are present, they are turned down at right angles. The nails are of square section, with spiked heads, and there is no fullering (Fig. 302).

In the seventeenth century a change in the outline of the frog gives names to the 'key-hole' and the 'tongue' type of shoe. These are the first to be fullered, though not from the earliest times, and the number of nail-holes is increased up to a maximum of twenty. Calkins are usual. The key-hole shoe is dished to give a concave lower surface. See Figs 303, 304.

The typical nineteenth-century and modern horse-shoe is the one seen on stable doors; of almost constant width, it has pronounced calkins, and a toe-clip since 1830. The general tendency was towards lightness and efficiency, both draught and riding horses being of great practical importance. Surgical shoes corrected faults or eased an injury: they were of special shape, with a bar across or some other contrivance.

Oxen were fitted with shoes but their cloven hooves require them to be in two pieces, as shown in Fig. 305. The ox was used as a draught animal in England up to the First World War, and is still to be seen ploughing in Mediterranean countries.

Fig. 306 shows an early twentieth-century heel-iron from the shoe of a human, which could be mistaken for a miniature horseshoe.

Aylesbury Museum, Buckinghamshire, has a good collection of horseshoes. See also *The Village Blacksmith* by Jocelyn Bailey (Shire).

Jars

A jar is a vessel of pottery or glass with a wide mouth, suitable for the packaging of paste and jelly. It has been used throughout history for ointments and other products of similar consistency.

From the sixteenth century the Italians made fine drug jars, often of the waisted form shown, which was convenient to the hand when spooning out the contents. These jars were for permanent display in a shop, and their descendants may still be seen on the shelves of country chemists. Pottery drug jars are labelled in underglaze blue with their contents, such as 'S. Balsam', for Syrup of Balsam.

307

308

The early jar for the customer and patient's use was of similar shape but less well made and not permanently labelled.

Early in the nineteenth century a broad low jar of white-glazed earthenware, with the interior dished, was used for bear's grease, a dressing for the hair presumably favoured because a product from so notably hirsute an animal would surely promote the growth of human hair. This form of jar, printed in black, also contained tooth paste and ointments.

In the middle of the last century the lid of this kind of jar was decorated in four colours, by bat-printing, and adopted by the makers of fish paste, potted char, Gentlemen's Relish and similar delicacies. These coloured potlids, as they are now called, were made until the end of the nineteenth century, and hundreds of pictures ranging from bears on the ice to Washington Crossing the Delaware were printed on them. Reproductions abound, and are deceptive. One indication of an old potlid are dots at the edge of the picture, where the prints were adjusted into correct registration.

Large jars for coarse materials were made of brown stoneware. Fig. 309 shows a jar for boot blacking of a shape used throughout the nineteenth century.

The Pharmaceutical Society of Great Britain, 1 Lambeth High Street, London, have a fine collection of drug jars that can be seen by written application. See also *Collecting Potlids* by T. Fletcher (Pitman, 1975).

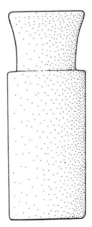

309

Kiln Furniture

This needs a word of explanation: it refers to the supports used by potters to raise pottery off the floor of the kiln, or to separate stacked pieces from each other. The purpose is to expose all the surfaces of the pots to the heat of the fire, and to prevent them sticking to each other.

Modern kiln furniture, commercially made of fireclay, is unlikely to be found, but small clay objects of pyramid and bullet shape do turn up in the ground, and may be old kiln furniture.

As to dating, unless found in a district where a pottery industry is documented, stray kiln furniture is probably from one of the medieval and post-medieval potteries which were well distributed in England wherever wood or peat was available for fuel.

From the late seventeenth century, and largely associated with the coal firing of kilns, pottery was stacked in clay drums called saggars, and saggar-pins were thrust through the sides of them to support the plates and dishes inside. The marks of saggar-pins, three scores in the glaze at angles of $120°$, may be seen on the backs of some plates, especially tin-glazed ones; and the pointed marks of the stilt, a triangular support, may be seen in an equilateral triangle on the bases of some pottery vessels.

Knives

Although a knife is an implement and a dagger a weapon, the sharp edges of both may be used for useful or murderous purposes. From early times until the beginning of the eighteenth century a knife was carried on the person, latterly in a sheath together with a fork, by men and women for the prime purpose of cutting up food.

The Romans had iron knives, either with two scales (as the halves of a knife handle are called) riveted to a broad tang, or of the familiar clasp knife pattern, but without a spring. The typical Saxon knife is broad at the back, with a flat leading down to the point and a thin tang.

Medieval knives were small and sharp pointed, with a tang the whole size of the scales, which could be of

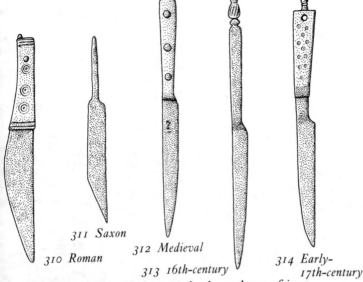

311 *Saxon*

310 *Roman*

312 *Medieval*

313 *16th-century*

314 *Early-*
17th-century

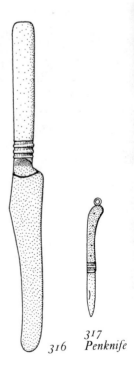

315

316

317
Penknife

wood, horn or bone. Knives made throughout of iron appear in the sixteenth century, and in the early seventeenth century the knife has a long bolster between the blade and the handle, which is slightly tapered.

The adoption of the fork late in the seventeenth century soon caused its companion knife to increase in size, and the point of the knife became blunt as it was no longer required to hold down food for cutting with another knife. From early in the eighteenth century sets of knives and forks were bought and held by householders for their family and guests. When not in use, this 'cutlery' was kept safely locked away.

A scimitar shape developed to its most pronounced in the middle of the eighteenth century and declined at the end, so that nineteenth-century knives are straight with parallel sides.

Cutlers of the eighteenth and nineteenth centuries made their knife blades of steel, welded to tanged bolsters of wrought iron; the boundary between the two materials can be seen, as indicated in Figs 315 and 316. Stainless steel knives came into general use in the 1920s.

When in the early eighteenth century knives for use at meals ceased to be carried on the person, the clasp knife returned. Also at this time the spread of literacy led to the writing of many letters, and a small sharp blade was required to cut the quill pens then in use. Early penknives and early clasp knives were single bladed, but the clasp knife with a large and a small blade, one folding into each end, is to be found from the middle of last century. It is still sometimes called a penknife.

Before the envelope came to be used with the 'penny post' about 1840, letters were folded and sealed, and a paper knife with a slender blade and a good point was needed to open the letter without damage. These early paper knives were of steel, in the form of small daggers, but the envelope yielded to a blunt paper knife, even of wood.

In the late nineteenth century and after a small clasp knife with a silver blade was carried for peeling and cutting up fruit, thus avoiding the taste of steel. These little knives may be found with a folding fork at the other end.

A small, useful booklet called *A Chronology of Cutlery* by H. R. Singleton was published by Sheffield City Museum in 1973.

Labels

It is unfortunately rare to find labels remaining on things found, but if present they should not be removed as they can be of great interest. Fig. 318 shows the label on a bottle of Camp Coffee from about twenty-five years ago, and Fig. 319 the label from a modern bottle of the same product. It is apparently not now thought proper to show an Indian as a servant bringing coffee to a European officer!

Not only bottles and jars are labelled, but furniture, and especially French furniture. Labels might be found in drawers, possibly detached.

The stock in the old shops in the Gladstone Court Museum, Biggar, Lanarkshire, is very illuminating.

Lamps

The lamp as a simple vessel of stone or pottery with replenishable fuel and a wick has been known since the Old Stone Age, but the earliest likely to be found are the small pottery or bronze lamps of ancient Rome. They are attractive things and have been extensively faked in Italy, for the benefit of tourists, over the last two hundred years.

Up to the middle of the nineteenth century the illumi-

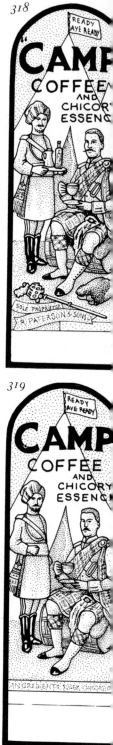

nation of buildings in the western world was chiefly by candles, because fuel for lamps was expensive. In England between 1709 and 1831 there was also a law forbidding oil lamps except those using fish oil. Open lamps of the Roman type were used for this smelly fuel, and a spout lamp from the eighteenth century is similar to the slush lamp still used out of doors by railwaymen.

When in the 1850s good mineral oil became available in quantity from the wells of Pennsylvania, lamps soon replaced candles in living rooms. Early lamps were no more than oil-supplied candles, but in a few years large lamps with double wicks were common. These gave oxygen to their flames by the induced draught of a glass chimney, but the Hitchcock lamp of 1880 had forced draught from a clockwork driven fan. Gas light, however, had been in streets and in houses since the 1820s, and it was vastly improved by the incandescent gas mantle of the 1880s. Not only that, but the electric filament lamp was invented at about the same time. As a result of this competition the oil lamp in general has survived only as a thing of simple construction for use in remote places or in emergency. If the working parts of

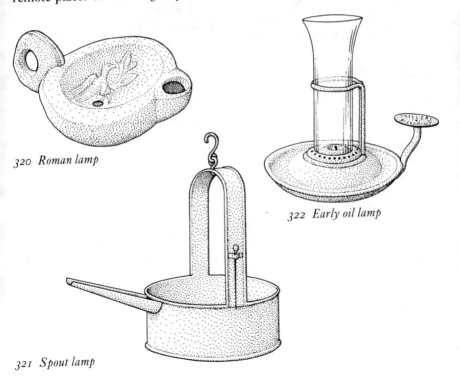

320 Roman lamp

322 Early oil lamp

321 Spout lamp

an old lamp are found they will be of brass, spun from heavier gauge metal than modern ones but otherwise similar.

A miner's safety lamp might be found, and the chronology of this useful invention is as follows:

1. From 1815 a simple round wick with wire gauze cover.

2. About 1890 the flame is surrounded with a glass cylinder, and the gauze is above it.

3. About 1900 the gauze is provided with a metal sleeve.

4. About 1920 the wick becomes double, and flat.

Finally, a few words on vehicle lamps in general. The carbide lamp appeared at the end of the nineteenth century, and was used on cars and motor cycles until after the First World War. The great name in bicycle lamps is Lucas, whose 'Silver King' models of excellent quality were first made in the 1880s. Up to about 1900 there was a roughened patch on their bases to strike a match on. A spring bracket was supplied with carbide lamps.

The museum at Cyfarthwa Castle, South Wales, has a series of miners' lamps. See also *Lighting* by W. T. O'Dea (HMSO, 1967) and *Discovering Oil Lamps* by C. A. Meadows (Shire, 1972).

Locks and Keys

The principle of the lock and key has been known to man since early antiquity, and is also found in nature: the sexual organs of certain spiders incorporate a key held by the male to fit a lock in the female so that only those of the same genus can mate.

The first locks had a number of pins of different height and a key with pins on it to align them, in much the same way as a Yale lock. The Romans employed this pattern, and also had locks with 'wards', which are circumferential strips in the way of the turning key so that, in theory, only the correctly cut key can pass them and engage the notch in the bolt to shoot it.

The keys you may find from medieval times to the eighteenth century will be warded with increasing complexity, but dating depends largely on style.

Fig. 323 is a thirteenth-century bronze key made for a coffer. Keys for chests and coffers, which have only to be

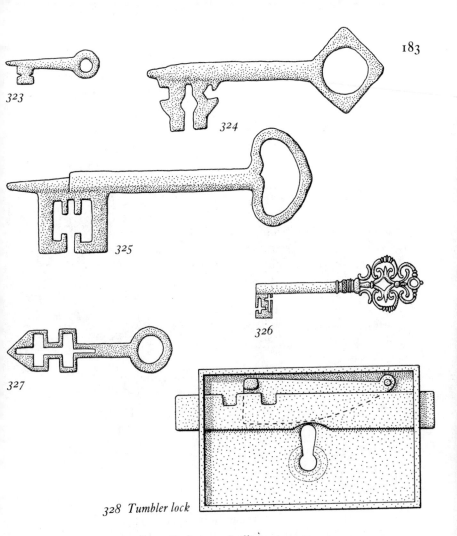

323

324

325

326

327

328 Tumbler lock

operated from one side, usually have a hollow stem to engage in a pin of the same size and thus provide added security. Door keys must be operable from both sides, so their stems are solid and the two sides of the bit are symmetrical.

Fig. 324   A late Gothic key of the fourteenth century.

Fig. 325   A typical fifteenth-century door key with an extended stem and kidney bow.

Fig. 326   A seventeenth-century key, finely made in the Renaissance style.

A variant in shape is the latch key (Fig. 327), which was inserted into a horizontal opening and turned upright to lift the spring-loaded latch of a door. Like all

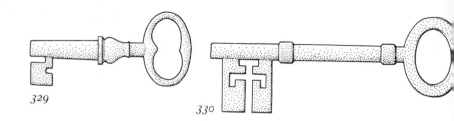
329

330

door keys the wards are symmetrical, so that it can be used from inside and outside the house.

Late in the eighteenth century a new principle, that of the tumbler lever, was introduced into general use. In its simplest form the key is required to lift a single lever an exact amount before the bolt will move. Soon the tumblers were multiplied, so that, for example, 'Secure Two Lever' may be seen inscribed on locks. If there is more than one tumbler, the nose of the key will be stepped. This feature gives rise to the common belief that the bit of an old key is shaped on the sides, and that of a later one on the end.

331 Padlock

The late eighteenth century was a time of invention in locks and keys (see specialist literature). The Bramah lock dates from 1784, and the Yale cylinder from 1848, early examples having a flat key, which was later corrugated.

Fig. 329 An eighteenth-century steel key with a nicely turned stem.

Fig. 330 A nineteenth-century key, also of steel, but less robust and having a standardised air.

It remains to mention the tubular padlock, which has been described under FETTERS. Other early padlocks work in the same way as the locks on chests. Eighteenth-century ones came to be heart-shaped.

Willenhall Lock Museum, Staffordshire, has a fine collection of the work of locksmiths in that area of the Midlands, and there is also a good collection in Weston-super-Mare Museum, Avon. See also *Locks and Keys Throughout the Ages* by V. J. M. Eras (Bailey Bros. and Swinfen, 1974).

Loom-Weights

The warp threads of a vertical loom are each held taut by a weight tied to their ends, and loom-weights are frequently found where this kind of loom has been in use.

A horizontal loom stretches the warp threads between rollers, or by some other means, and so has no need of loom-weights.

In the ancient world the vertical loom was prevalent in the Middle East and Europe. Fig. 332 shows a Bronze Age loom-weight of terracotta found in southern Turkey. It is typical, with a hole near the top, and is of a size to be held in the palm of the hand. Fig. 333 shows a large pyramidal weight of chalk from the British Iron Age. Others may be of stone, and disc or quoit shaped with a central hole.

The horizontal loom was known in ancient Egypt, and in a developed form it took over in the early Middle Ages as the loom for professional weaving in Europe. In remote places, however, the vertical loom, which is simple to construct and takes up less floor space, has survived to the present day, so a modern loom-weight might be found.

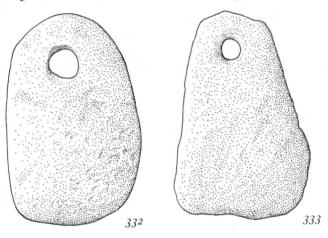

332   *333*

Marbles

The game of marbles has been played with much the same rules for many centuries, and mostly by boys. It is unique in one way: the playing pieces are themselves at stake, and change hands between the players. Thus a confident player will risk a favourite 'ally', as a choice large marble is called; others may venture a lesser 'taw', the name for an ordinary marble and for the game itself.

334

As to the materials, the name suggests that they were made of marble, and the fine painted ally in Fig. 334 appears to be so. Its decoration suggests an early nineteenth-century date. It is said that ally is short for alabaster, and an ally of alabaster was found at Old Sarum in Wiltshire. No doubt stone marbles were rolled in a tumbling machine to round them up. Common taws were made of glazed pottery. The first glass marbles were the stoppers from mineral water bottles of the Codd variety (see BOTTLES), but from the late nineteenth century glass marbles with a spiral coloured twist have been made in a 'bead-furnace'. Pieces of glass cane are heated and tumbled together so that they change to a spherical shape by the same process that makes glass beads.

335 *Ally with coloured twist*

The glass ally has never been cheap: in my youth each one cost 3d, a week's pocket money.

There are modern plastic marbles simulating the old glass ones.

Mechanical Toys

The toys you are most likely to find, often incomplete and seldom in working order, are those made of thin stamped and enamelled tinplate, with the pieces clipped together in characteristic fashion. Many incorporate a clockwork motor, and some toy vehicles in the 1920s had a geared flywheel.

These mechanical toys are the cheap mass-produced relations of 'automata' first made in the eighteenth century in Switzerland and popular until early in the present century. An automaton is greatly superior, having a complicated body mostly composed of wood and metal limbs, levers, cranks, scroll-plates etc., and being properly clad in clothes or fur as appropriate. The clockwork, which is well made by a clocksmith, causes the automaton to perform suitable actions, such as juggling with plates, dancing, or whatever.

The great industrial city of Nuremberg, long famous for fine metalwork, led the way in supplying the western world with mechanical toys of great ingenuity, from the late nineteenth century to the outbreak of the First World War, and through the 1920s. The toys are often marked, the most important early names being Lehmann, Bing, Marklin and Carette. Fig. 336 shows a walking figure dressed in the style of 1910 and marked 'Lehmann' on the base of the body, between the legs. I was a child in the 1920s and was given toy railway

336

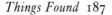

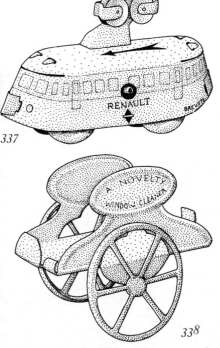

337

338

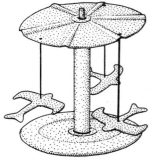

339

engines made by Bing. They were cheap, thinly made and easily damaged: the front of one boiler came off, to show a printed design on the inside advertising coffee. It must have been made from a tin can.

The French, the British, the Americans and latterly the Japanese also made mechanical toys. Fig. 337 is of an elevated railway car made by 'Renault' and possibly intended for the American market. The French were well known for mechanical toys of good quality, in which some parts are die-cast. Fig. 338 illustrates a British ladder cart, such as was used by window cleaners.

The dating of these toys will depend largely upon style, unless some particular detail gives it away. For instance, the little aircraft with 'Taube' shaped wings on a model roundabout, places it almost certainly as around the Second World War and German (Fig. 339).

You can see mechanical toys at the Grange Museum, Rottingdean, Sussex, the Playthings Past Museum, Beconwood, Worcestershire, and the Bethnel Green Museum, London. See also *The Golden Age of Toys* by J. Remise and J. Fontin (Patrick Stephens, 1967) and *Discovering Toys and Toy Museums* by Pauline Flick (Shire, 1977).

Medals

The word medal is simply a variant of 'metal'. A medallion is a large medal, and a medalet is a small one, but the terms are not exact.

Military medals as we know them date from the early nineteenth century: those awarded for service in the Napoleonic Wars were issued many years after the conflict ended, although a medal for all who fought at Waterloo was struck in 1816. The idea of military medals may have been inspired by the medallions awarded to Roman soldiers for courage in the field, although their highest award was not a medal but a crown of oak leaves. British military campaign medals up to and including the First World War were inscribed round the edge with the name of the recipient. It is not unknown for the original name to be removed and a more illustrious one engraved instead. Careful measurement will detect this fake.

340

One foreign medal often brought back as a souvenir is the German 'Iron Cross'. Fig. 340 shows an example from the First World War. That from the 1939–1945 war is marked with a swastika.

341

Medals granted for services are worn on the person, and have some means of suspension. There are also commemorative medals, made simply to be acquired. Of this kind the most important are the portrait medals of famous people made throughout Europe from the fifteenth century and often engraved by well-known artists. Early medals were cast, but from the seventeenth century they were 'struck' from dies, like coins. Most medals are of gold, silver or bronze, but brass and white metal ones are known. Being commemorative, they explain themselves in their inscriptions provided, of course, the inscription can be read.

342

343

The illustrations show the variety of occasions on which medals are struck.

Fig. 341 A royal event: the jubilee of George III.

Fig. 342 A social event: the medal of a Friendly Society.

Fig. 343 A grim act of justice: the hanging in chains of a murderer.

Fig. 344 A trades' exhibition, at which medals are given for excellence in the products displayed.

344

The Royal Hospital at Chelsea, London, has a good

display of British medals, and so does the Imperial War Museum, London. See also *Orders, Medals and Decorations* by P. Hieronymussen (Blandford Press, 1967).

Metal Toy Figures

The expressions 'lead soldier' or 'tin soldier' are more usual, but small figures cast from lead-tin alloy are not all military.

In the Middle Ages a technique was developed for casting pilgrim badges (see BADGES) using shallow moulds of stone, and the first metal toy figures were made by the same means at Nuremberg in the eighteenth century. These so-called 'Nuremberg flatties', which are no more than a millimetre thick, continued in production until early this century, and the old moulds are now being used again. Early figures are high in tin, and so harder and shinier than the lead-rich later ones. Some figures were coloured. From 1848 a height of 30 mm for standing figures was standard. Fig. 345 shows a chef of about 1880.

In the 1870s figures known as 'semi-solids' were first made. These, as the name suggests, are intermediate between the 'flatty' and a fully rounded figure. Fig. 346 shows a semi-solid policeman which is probably German but made for the British market. German metal toy figures were popular in Britain, particularly in the early years of this century.

British metal figures start with William Britain, who invented hollow-cast figures in 1893. The principle was simple: hot liquid metal is poured into a two-piece mould which, after a carefully judged pause, is emptied to leave a solid crust forming the figure. Britain's figures are 'solid' as regards proportions, and arms hinged at the shoulders are usual from 1911. Fig. 348 shows a soldier

345

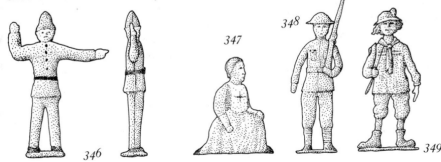

346

347

348

349

in First World War uniform; the legs bound in puttees are typical of the time. Fig. 347 shows a nurse; she is probably from an ambulance unit set, in which she might be kneeling by a wounded soldier on a stretcher. Fig. 349 is of a well modelled and amusing yokel from the farm figures which were popular in the 1930s and soon after the Second World War. It is marked on the base 'Britain – Made in England – Copyright'.

Plastic figures were introduced in 1954, and by 1960 metal figures were a thing of the past.

Worcestershire County Museum, Hartlebury, has toy soldiers, and so does the Grange Museum, Rottingdean, Sussex. See also *Collecting Old Toy Soldiers* by I. Mackenzie (Batsford, 1975).

Nails

Large nails are called spikes, and small ones brads or tacks. The interest in nails arises from their methods of manufacture and their variety of forms for different purposes. Almost all nails are made of iron or mild steel, though the upholsterer 'gets down to brass tacks'.

The so-called 'wrot' nails were made by hand from ancient days until 1950, when the last 'nailing shed' in England closed. The nailer had a forge in which to heat his iron stock. He sharpened its end with a hammer, cut the nail to length over a hardie, then dropped the half-made nail into a bored hole of suitable depth and size before forging the head and ejecting the completed nail from below.

'Cut' nails are cut from rolled plate. Modern ones are cut to the finished shape and are therefore flat. The heads of early cut nails, from about 1800, were forged to shape.

'Wire' nails have been completely machine-made from 1850, but drawn wire has been used as the stock for some hand-made nails from about 1800.

It will be seen, then, that a nail that appears to have been entirely forged by hand is likely to be of the eighteenth century or earlier, but it is not possible to be certain.

This is no place to detail the myriad kinds of nails, but a few definitions will be useful.

Rose-nail: a nail with a faceted head, more or less decorative, for exterior work.

350 Clasp-nail

351 Clench-nail

Clout-nail: a nail with a flat round head, first used for nailing cloth ('clout') on to wood.

Clasp-nail: a nail with opposite points on the head, which sink into the wood and give added security.

Clench-nail: a nail with a flat or chisel end, which is driven through two or more thicknesses of wood and clenched or riveted over a washer called a 'rove'.

Clench-nails are employed to secure the strakes on the sides of boats. They are usually found in a used condition. The door nail in the expression 'dead as a door nail' is also of this type. It was clenched after being driven through the upright planks of a medieval door and through cross-pieces at the back; so it was dead in the sense of being immovable, like a dead-lock.

Medieval nails were large and crudely made, and were used mostly in the building of houses for the fixing of floors, roof-planks, and so on. These nails, which rate as 'spikes' by their size, are often found. The main constructional members of wooden-framed houses were fastened by tapered wood pins called 'tree-nails'. These could be driven out again and the valuable heavy timber re-used. Early furniture also was pegged; nails were first used for making up drawers in the middle of the seventeenth century. They continued in use for coarse furniture, the better sort of furniture being dove-tailed and morticed from the late seventeenth century.

The nails for reinforcing a surface, rather than for use as fastenings, will be large-headed and short shanked. Such are the studding-nails used on the bottoms of wooden ships, and the nails through the iron tyres of carts until the tyre became a continuous hoop by the middle of the last century.

Finally, Fig. 352 shows a special nail called a tenterhook, for stretching out broadcloth on frames after fulling. It is proverbially uncomfortable to be on tenterhooks, and one can see why.

The Avoncraft Museum of Buildings, Bromsgrove, Worcestershire has a nailer's shop, and there is a good display of nails in Salisbury Museum, Wiltshire.

352

Needles

A needle is here defined as a small sharp instrument with an eye at the other end, used for piercing and sewing cloth and leather. There are other types of needles, such as the magnetised ones in the mariner's compass and the needles in old electric telegraphs which spelt out the morse code.

The first needles were of bone, and primitive societies used this material up to and including the time of the Saxons in England. Bronze needles are found on Roman and medieval sites. The first steel needles came from the needlesmiths of south Germany in the late fourteenth century. The eyes of these were formed by a closed hook. The first needles with punched eyes were made in the Low Countries during the next century. It should be possible to distinguish a punched eye from a closed hook under a magnifying glass: a long oval hole was left by the punches, the first of which formed the sloping sides of the eye while the second pierced it.

The needle industry at Redditch in Worcestershire was founded in the fourteenth century, according to local tradition. It expanded greatly in the eighteenth century, and is still going strong today. The raw material used has always been steel.

Manufacture was divided into eight processes, each done by a separate workman. The final stage applied a fine polish to the needles. Early needles were individually pointed by filing, but from about 1850 they were spun in a chuck and ground to a point. An early book of Redditch needles should therefore show some variation in the shape of the points.

The ordinary sewing needle is straight, but the sailmaker uses a large curved needle for thrusting through canvas, and the upholsterer has a round needle for quickly working his seams.

The thatcher's needle is huge in comparison to all others, and it not infrequently turns up where it has been mislaid in the thatch of roofs and haystacks. It is proverbially difficult to find, however.

Nuts, Bolts and Screws

The principle of the screw was discovered by Archimedes in the third century B.C., and applied to lift water and to press grapes and olives. However it is not these uses that concern us, but the screw thread used in fastenings. This was not fully developed until later.

The first practical problem was to cut a thread on a bar. The ancients did this by wrapping a right-angle-

353 Medieval needle

354 Sailmaker needle

355 Thatcher's needle

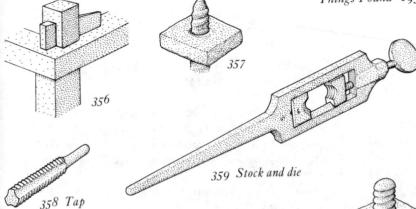

356

357

358 Tap

359 Stock and die

360

triangle-shaped piece of some suitable material round the bar and scribing along the hypoteneuse. They then chiselled and filed along this line, no doubt helped by a template cut to the required thread form. The completed thread could then be used to tap its own interior thread in wood.

It was much more difficult to cut the interior thread in a nut. Until the eighteenth century large nuts were laboriously threaded by routing out and hand chasing to fit an individual bolt. It is not surprising that through the Middle Ages and later the usual machinery fastening was a cotter-pin. Fig. 356 shows one on the fourteenth-century clock in Salisbury Cathedral.

Early nuts and bolts have a coarse thread and a hand-made air, as in Fig. 357, which shows the bolt on a bell trunnion which is probably from the sixteenth century, when the bell was installed.

The late seventeenth century was a time for technical improvements, and screwing-tackle as we know it now was invented then. Screws were cut in a lathe using a lead-screw, which left its mark on Charles II furniture by popularising the spiral twist on chair legs. Bolts, however, were, and still are, usually threaded by means of a stock and die. Nuts are cut with a tap, or rather a series of taps each cutting deeper. This tap is somewhat like a bolt, but of tool steel, and the thread is interrupted to expose the cutting edges. Fig. 360 shows a bolt from a fire engine dated 1760; the thread is finer than that on the bell trunnion, and looks to be die-cut.

Furniture screws came into use late in the seventeenth century, but it was not until the Industrial Exhibition of 1851 that the gimlet-headed wood screw made its appearance.

In 1841 Joseph Whitworth read a paper on 'A Universal System of Screw Threads', and a few years later his threads were adopted throughout Britain. Previously there had been local standards, and earlier still every engineer had his own screwing tackle. One could learn a lot from detailed examination of the thread forms on old machinery, but this would be beyond our simple resources.

The Museum of Science and Industry in Birmingham is the authority on screw threads. See also *Iron and Steel* by M.K.V. Gate (Longmans).

Pens

The only writing implement from the ancient world you might find is a stylus, used in the time of the Romans for writing on wax tablets. As you will see the business end is pointed, and the other flat for use as an eraser.

The word 'quill' first meant a stalk, and many peoples besides the Chinese have written with pens of reed or similar vegetable material. However in Europe from the sixth century A.D. the large feathers of geese, swans and other big birds have been used for writing. They still carry sufficient prestige to be employed in select merchant houses and by splendidly old-fashioned people, as well as calligraphers.

From the late seventeenth century ordinary people took to writing, whereas previously it had been a thing for clerks, scriveners and poets. They needed a pen-knife (see KNIVES) to cut their quill pens until around the middle of the last century, when the metal nib, still dipped in an ink bottle, gradually took over. The first steel nibs, made in 1828, were copies in metal of the quill, with a single cut down to the tip, but soon there were improvements to suit the new material. In 1830 a hole at the top of the slit was introduced, and a few years later some nibs had additional slits at each side of the point. Stainless steel nibs date from 1926. In general the more like a quill in size and shape it is, the older a nib will be. Fig. 362 shows a typical nib about seventy years old.

361 Stylus

362

The first practicable fountain pen was produced in the United States of America in 1884. Until the 1920s many fountain pens were filled by means of a glass dropper, but the side lever and interior sac 'self-filling' type then prevailed, with some that filled by plunger action like garden syringes or a bicycle pump.

The ball-point pen was invented in 1944.

Pins

The word pin is used, generally, to mean any small pointed length without an eye but usually with a head. Special pins, such as belaying pins aboard sailing ships and cotter pins in machinery, will not be considered here.

The parts of a pin are its head, shank and point. The uses of pins are manifold, but they are usually for temporarily fixing together textiles or documents, or for dressing the hair.

Bone pins first appear in the Stone Age and continue through all ages, being used even now in remote parts of the world. Light in weight and not too sharp, they have been favoured for hairdressing purposes, for securing loose textured clothing, or for closing leather bags provided with suitable holes. Bronze pins were used in ancient and medieval days for many purposes, including eating shellfish and cleaning the finger-nails.

The heads of two medieval pins are shown. The early pins of bone and bronze, being simple objects made with simple tools, are dateable only if found in sealed deposits.

The long thin steel hat pin, as we know it, was an invention of the eighteenth century, and was used to secure together the large hats and elaborate hair-styles of the period as mentioned in Boswell's *Life of Johnson*. Hat pins continued in use through the next century and up to modern times, their heads following the trends of fashion.

Men used similar decorative pins to fix down their cravats and neck-ties. The heads of these are designed to be seen from the side, whereas a hat pin is made for an all-round view. Cravat pins are larger than tie pins.

The thin sharp disposable pin was first made in the fifteenth century when drawn brass wire became available in quantity. Brass was the preferred material for

363 Neolithic bone pin

364 Bronze pin

365 Medieval pin

pins, being strong in the hard drawn condition and resistant to corrosion after the finished pins had been tinned. Inferior pins were made of iron, also tinned. Cheap steel was not obtainable for pins until the middle of the nineteenth century, and even so this material took a long time to be accepted, so that brass pins were still being made well into the twentieth century.

In Shakespeare's time the common pin was well known, and he uses it to typify something small or of little value, as we do. In his play *King Richard III* there is a reference to a row of pins, so apparently they were already being put up for sale pinned on to papers. Also in his time pins with fancy heads could be obtained; they were like a modern hat pin and no doubt used for a similar purpose. It was these decorative pins that women bought with their allowance of 'pin money'.

366
Medie
pin

367

368

From the fifteenth to the middle of the nineteenth century so-called 'spun-head' common pins were made as follows:

1. The shank was prepared from drawn and straightened brass wire, cut to length and pointed.

2. Wire for the head, also of brass but thinner, was closely coiled on to a revolving shaft of the same diameter as the shank of the pin. It was withdrawn from the shaft, and snipped into heads of exactly two coils each.

3. A head was then threaded on top of a shank and placed in a horizontal die, to be forced into shape by the descent of a pedal-operated ram.

Fig. 367 illustrates a faulty pin, with the head on the shank but never struck, to show the appearance of the two coils, which are still to be seen to some degree on a finished pin (Fig. 368).

The spun-head, horizontally struck pin continued to be made until the 1850s: those made in London, Gloucester and Bristol had a wide reputation and, particularly during the eighteenth century, were extensively exported to Europe and America.

The weakness of this pin was that the head was not positively secured to the shank. During the early years of the nineteenth century progress was made towards a machine that would strike the pin vertically, so as to shape the head and raise a securing collar on the shank at one blow. Such a machine was first made in the 1830s, and pins made by it have a wedge-shaped head.

All that remained was to make a machine that would

form the head out of the shank, like a nail, and this was also achieved in the 1830s, though it was twenty years before the spun-head pin was completely outmoded. These one-piece machines gave pins a rivet-shaped head with a small 'pip' on top of it.

When pins are found in old textiles or documents, examination under a magnifying glass will show up the distinctions outlined above and assist in dating.

Gloucester City Museum has pin-making machinery and pins.

Pipe Stoppers

The tobacco in a clay pipe required to be tamped down carefully with something of the same size as the interior of the bowl otherwise it could easily be broken. Hence the pipe stopper, with its round flat base and decorative head, looking somewhat like a seal.

369
About 1640

Pipe stoppers may be broadly dated from the size of the base, which became progressively larger as the bowl of the tobacco pipe (see CLAY PIPES) increased in size. The subject and style of the handle will also help; for instance, the head of the Duke of Wellington suggests an early nineteenth-century date. It was he who imposed controls on smoking in barracks, so he was in another sense a 'pipe stopper'.

Pipe stoppers are rare earlier than the eighteenth century or later than 1850. No doubt tobacco in the pipes of seventeenth-century smokers required tamping, but they must have used whatever came to hand before plentiful brass became available for the casting of stoppers. In the late nineteenth century the clay pipe was no longer smoked in polite society, so the 'purpose-made' pipe stopper fades out of use.

370
About 1840

Examples in wood, bone and other non-metallic materials are known, but brass has always been favoured. The seventeenth and nineteenth-century pipe stoppers shown are typical examples showing variation in the size of the base.

Fig. 371 shows a piece of carved bone found on a beach, with brown staining at the neck end to show it had been used as a pipe stopper, but it was probably not made for that purpose.

Wells Museum, Wells, Somerset, has a special collection of pipe stoppers.

371

Pots and Pans

Until kitchen ranges of cast iron were made in the early years of the last century, cooking in all but great houses was on an open fire; indeed open fire cooking proceeded well into the second half of the nineteenth century, as readers of Charles Dickens will know.

The utensils of the open fire are made to stand on the hearth, more or less in the fire as required, or to hang over it. Early footed skillets of bronze were cherished and are often mentioned in wills. Medieval cooking pots of pottery largely gave way in the seventeenth century to a metal pot hanging on a so-called crane over the fire, accompanied by a kettle. It is these two, equally discoloured by constant exposure to smoke, who call each other black in the proverb. The material of the pot and kettle was copper, or cast iron from early in the eighteenth century.

Cooking at a 'down-hearth' was basic. You stewed meat, if you had it, in the pot, with vegetables slung in nets at the side. You could roast meat in the direct heat of the fire, using some form of jack, such as the bottle-jack turned by clockwork, common during the late eighteenth and early nineteenth centuries. Built into the side of the hearth there might be an oven for bread and bakemeats.

Saucepans and frying pans are associated with the sophisticated cookery possible on the cooking range, installed in great houses since the seventeenth century. These utensils, of heavy copper well-made and inwardly

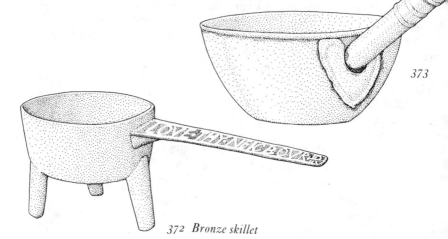

373

372 Bronze skillet

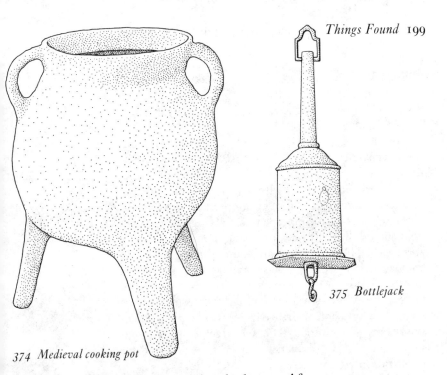

374 Medieval cooking pot

375 Bottlejack

tinned, survive from the last two hundred years. After the First World War cast aluminium was used for kitchen pots and pans, followed in the early 1930s by stainless steel. Fig 373 shows a pan of welded stainless steel plate from that time. The spinning of copper had long been practiced to give light, cheap pans, and from before the Second World War it was also employed on stainless steel and aluminium. Better kitchenware continues to be of cast metal.

Old-fashioned kitchen utensils can be seen in the Geffreye Museum, London, Guildford Museum, Ford Green Hall, Stoke-on-Trent, and Ludlow Museum, Salop. Many country houses open to the public also have special displays in their old kitchens.

Printing Blocks

The blocks found will probably be of metal, but a wood-block could survive under favourable circumstances.

The characteristics of all printing blocks are the same: their surfaces are accurately flat, and cut or dissolved away to leave lines or areas that compose a picture. A seal may look at first glance like a printing block, but they can be distinguished by the depth of the design, which is more or less constant in a printing block but shaped in a seal.

Early books were illustrated with woodcuts, the pictures being formed by cutting away the areas not to be inked. This is essentially the same process as for lettering, so woodcuts were set among type and the two inked and printed together. In the seventeenth and early eighteenth centuries the prints of most books came to be made chiefly on copper plates by various processes which drew on the metal with instruments or acid, and woodcuts were relegated to cheap publications such as *Comic Cuts*. These copperplate engravings or etchings held the ink in their lines or prepared areas, and their surfaces had to be wiped clean before printing, so unlike woodcuts they could not be set among type. The significance of this for us is that small woodcut blocks of various proportions were made, but copperplates were commonly of whole or half-page size. The page size of books ranged from about 8 cm by 13 cm to about 23 cm by 38 cm. Old copperplates are sometimes re-used for other purposes, and these can be interesting.

In the 1820s steel plates started to be used instead of copper ones, the advantage being the greater number of impressions to be got from the harder material without excessive wear. Being hard, steel was difficult to engrave, but that was overcome in the middle of the century by electroplating with steel the completed engraving made on copper.

Querns, Pounder Stones and Mortars

This extended title covers the various primitive implements used for crushing and grinding raw materials.

One of the earliest handiworks of man must have been the preparation of food by pounding with a piece of stone or wood, or grinding it between two stones. A further step would be to pound and grind coloured earths for pigments, which were needed as long ago as the Old Stone Age for cave paintings; and a very early use of red ochre was to paint the bones of the dead, presumably to restore some mystic life in them.

From the Bronze to the Iron Age, a prehistoric quern is shaped like a saddle, and the operator worked to and fro on it with a rubbing stone. These stones, in shape like

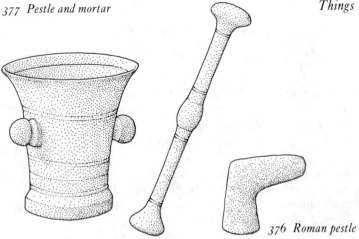

376 Roman pestle

a small loaf, can in my experience be found in dry-stone walling of later date. From the days of the Romans the rotary quern has been the standard form in remote communities, with most grinding performed in mills turned by wind or water. Querns were made of some hard rough stone, often traded far afield from its place of origin, so a broken quern or rubbing stone may stand out as a stranger among the native rocks. Some grit would get into the flour from the quern, and the teeth of elderly people were ground down by it, but in the process their teeth would be kept clean and healthy.

As to pounder stones, naturally shaped ones can only be fairly claimed as such if stained by pounding up colours, or battered by pounding other stones. The one shown is a carefully made Roman pounder stone which might be called a pestle, as it was probably for use with a pottery 'mortarium' in preparing food.

The word mortar has several meanings, but we are concerned only with the mortars used by alchemists and others to pound up the materials for experiments, medicines, and dry compounds generally. The drawing shows a typical mortar of this kind, with its pestle. The bell-founder made mortars, as their shape suggests, and he used his common alloy bell-metal for them. Both the mortar illustrated and its pestle are marked with the number '7', presumably to avoid contamination by keeping pairs together.

Razors

One of the decisions to be made by the human male is whether to wear his beard or shave it off. The beard is a 'secondary sexual characteristic' and thus to be encouraged, but it needs a lot of attention to keep clean and more important it provides a hand-hold for your enemy in battle. Consequently the fashion for a full beard or a clean-shaven face has veered from one to the other through history, taking in moustaches and whiskers of all kinds.

In the Stone Age it seems that men shaved with sharp flints or sea-shells. In the Middle Bronze Age they had bronze razors which must have been hafted for use. The Romans suffered themselves to be shaved by a barber, who wielded an iron razor with no soap. Finally the Emperor Hadrian allowed his beard to grow, it is said to hide the scars left by shaving. This example was followed by some of his subjects, but shaving continued through to the Middle Ages, and was no doubt still a painful experience. Moreover one did not get a close shave, as we know from Chaucer, who wrote 'He kissed her . . . with thick bristles of his beard unsoft, for he was shaven all new'. Shakespeare, however, could write 'keen as the razor's edge invisible', so there must have been some improvement by the sixteenth century.

Earlier razors seem to have disappeared, but those of the seventeenth century turn up: they were made heavy in the blade, like the scissors of those times. In the late eighteenth century good razors of crucible steel from Sheffield must have helped to maintain the fashion for a clean-shaven face which lasted all through that century. In the nineteenth century the blade of the razor was

378 Bronze Age razor

380 19th-century razor

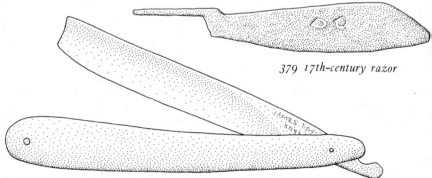

379 17th-century razor

hollow ground, allowing for a very keen edge. The end
remained square-cut until early this century, when the
open razor became of modern shape. But of course the
safety razor popularised by Gillette in the early twentieth century, and the electric shaver which was first on
the market in 1931, have made the old 'cut-throat'
almost obsolete.

Rings

A ring is the most personal of ornaments. Necklaces
and pendants may tell of wealth, honours and status;
brooches are but decorative fasteners; earrings frame a
pretty face; but a ring on the finger carries the signet
of its owner, or it may be the gage of true love, the memor-
ial of a friend, a protection against evil, a token of high
ecclesiastical office.

381 *Fede ring*

Wedding rings were known in the ancient world, and
some of the Roman rings we find may have been given
and accepted in marriages. Only Romans of the upper
classes were permitted to wear gold rings, which were
set with jewels, sometimes cut as seals. Rings of iron or
bronze were worn by anyone. In the late Middle Ages
and up to the eighteenth century, a girl would accept
from her lover a 'posy' ring, which could be a plain or
decorated hoop; the essential thing was a suitable senti-
ment inscribed inside the ring. This was sometimes in
rhyme, such as 'My hart and I, untill I dy', hence the
name 'posy' or 'poesie', but 'I like my choice' would do
as well. A posy of flowers was given with the ring, and
the name somehow got transferred to the bouquet. In
the seventeenth century the 'fede' ('faith') ring was
popular, with crowned clasped hands and hearts on it.
The one illustrated is similar in form to the variety
known as a 'gemel' ring, which was made in two or three
parts and split between the lovers. The plain middle
portion, if any, was retained by a witness, and the whole
contraption was assembled again when the couple came
together for their wedding.

382 *Mourning ring*

383 *15th-century
signet ring*

384 *Purse ring*

From the sixteenth to the early nineteenth century it
was customary to present rings, or money to buy them,
to friends who came to a funeral. These were sombre in
appearance, with deaths-heads or perhaps black enamel
bands.

The protection aspect has been discussed under

AMULETS. A special case is the ring of plain metal which, in the Middle Ages and up to the sixteenth century, was especially blessed by the King or Queen of England and presented as a remedy for cramp. These 'cramp rings' will not be easy to recognise unless by some happy chance there is some note of explanation found with them.

High dignitories of the Church wore rings, usually large and imposing, which are mentioned here for the sake of completeness but are not very likely to be found.

Signet rings are a large class of interesting rings. The earliest you are likely to come across are merchants' rings from the fifteenth century with their marks engraved, or rings with crests or initials from medieval to modern times. Some medieval rings, presumably used as a seal like other signets, are engraved with the figures of saints.

An object which may be mistaken for a finger ring is the plain metal ring, not always waisted in outline, used to secure money in stocking purses last century.

Scissors

The first scissors appear in Dark Age graves, and it is believed that they were not known earlier. Scissors were developed from shears by some unknown genius, but until the late Middle Ages small domestic shears (see SHEARS) were more usual around the house than scissors, which were in general a tradesman's implement. In the fourteenth century a man who went to topple one of the standing stones at Avebury was not quick enough, and it fell on him. He was a tailor, and among his bones they found a pair of scissors like those in Fig. 385. Notice the loops forged from the solid, of circular shape and in line with the handles. This is typical up to the seventeenth century, when the loops were forged as a 'closed hook' like the loops on contemporary snuffers. It was in the sixteenth century that scissors became used domestically instead of shears, though the barber used shears to cut hair for another hundred years. There is only one mention of 'scissars' in Shakespeare, and that seems to refer to a servant unskilfully cutting some man's hair.

In the eighteenth century the loops of scissors are again forged from the solid, and the shape of the imple-

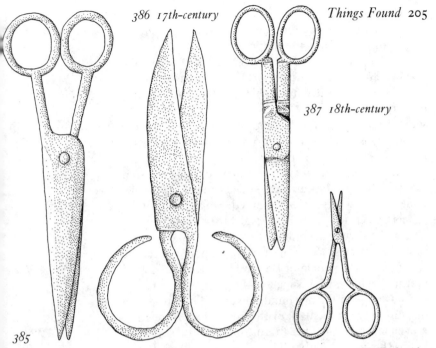

386 17th-century

387 18th-century

385

388 Embroidery scissors

ment becomes more modern, often with chiselled decoration.

The nineteenth century was a popular time for embroidery, and the small sharp scissors used by ladies for this work may be found. Other scissors were made in a range of sizes and qualities, as they are now.

Seals

To be accurate, a seal is the impression made by a matrix (with its Latin plural matrices), but in common language we call the implement itself a seal, so let us do so here.

The first seals were of cylindrical shape, rather like miniature garden rollers, were made of some decorative stone, and dated from 3,500 B.C. in Mesopotamia. Later came the stamp seal, which lasted through classical antiquity and survived the Dark Ages in courts and monasteries. The Chinese have used seals for thousands of years too, the chief characteristic of them being that they are used with ink and the lettering is incised, so the impression shows the letters in white on a coloured background.

The prime purpose of a seal is to confer security, whether it be rolled on the clay envelope of a cuneiform tablet, impressed on the stopper of a jar of wine or stamped in wax on a folded letter. A seal also certifies the authority of a document, as in 'Our King has written a braid letter, and sealed it with his hand'. In government, documents were either 'patent', that is open for all to see, as in the expression 'patently obvious', or they were 'close'. The seal had no security function on a 'letter patent', but did have authority.

389
Ecclesiast
seal

The seals and impressions we may find will be from the Middle Ages onward, the seals of metal. As a rule, ecclesiastical seals were of a pointed oval shape until the sixteenth century, and later oval but with no points. Other seals were round. Seals are not easy to date accurately, unless the subject of the impression can be related to some person or event. The retaining loop of Gothic 'trefoil' shape suggests the thirteenth century, but was popular for two hundred years. The alternative of a raised bar at the back, with a round hole through it, is even less helpful. The lettering on medieval seals may be in Roman or Lombardic capitals, with Black Letter from the second half of the fourteenth century.

390
Medieval
seal

391 Medieval seal

From the beginning of the eighteenth century to the 1830s fob-seals were worn by gentlemen on a ribbon or chain hanging from a watch in the small fob-pocket at the top of the waistband, or by ladies together with keys, scissors and other things on a so-called chatelaine hanging from the belt. These seals were of gold or pinchbeck, with hardstone 'matrices', and they conform in style to that of their period. Fig. 392 shows an example from about 1800. After 1830 the desk seal came into fashion, and remained so throughout the century. There are impressive large ones cut with family crests, but also small ones for ladies, sometimes having replaceable matrices with fancy designs and mottoes engraved on them.

392 About 18

Shears

Shears have been continuously used since the Iron Age, and have differed little in design over two thousand years. Very large shears, over four feet long, were used from the time of the Romans to crop the surface of cloth during its manufacture; medium sized shears were for the shearing of sheep; and small ones were for various

393 Desk seal

domestic uses in the Middle Ages and later, as described under SCISSORS.

Although the basic design has altered little, there are distinctions in detail between the shears of different peoples and times. The shears of the Dark Ages were as simple as could be, but around the twelfth century the loop started to develop a key-hole shape, which was most pronounced in the late Middle Ages. In the Middle Ages, also, the root of the blades became indented so that the aperture had a Gothic outline. In the fifteenth century this was elaborated. In the sixteenth century scissors took over from small domestic shears, but large shears continued in use for sheep shearing, the cropping of cloth, for gardening and other outdoor work. Now powered machines have largely taken over, but shears are not yet entirely things of the past.

Shell Cases

Here we consider the cases of deep-drawn brass made for so-called 'fixed' ammunition of all sizes, ranging from bullets to shells of a calibre up to ten centimetres and more. Above that size the shell is provided separately, and one or more cartridges of propellant loaded into the gun after it. Not only would it be difficult to make a very large shell case in brass, but it would be beyond the strength of a man to carry it when full of propellant and topped with a shell. It is useful to remember that a projectile of fifty kilograms weight is the heaviest that a strong, trained man can lift and load by hand.

The deep drawing of brass was perfected about a hundred years ago, so brass shell cases date from that time.

Empty shell cases are frequently found, usually having been converted for use, the larger ones cut down for ash trays, the smaller ones to hold spills, pens, pipe cleaners etc.; bullet cases may have been turned into cigarette lighters.

The main interest for us lies in the base, which is marked with letters and figures known as 'headstamps'. Inserted into the base will be found the fuse, with two or three depressions round its edge to take the special spanner used to screw it into place. In the middle of the fuse should be another depression, where the firing pin

394
Dark Age
shears

395
Medieval
shears

396
15th-century

struck it. Headstamps, found on the shell itself and on the fuse, are generally not difficult to read. They may give some or all of the following information:

1. The type and mark of gun for the ammunition, e.g. 'Two pounder Mk. I–III and VI Guns'.
2. Dates, maker's name, batch numbers, modifications.
3. The stamps of inspectors, usually as initials.

Shell cases were recovered to be used again, and thus may bear a considerable number of headstamps, some of them cancelled by a line through them. Fig. 397 shows the headstamps on a large German shell case of the First World War now cut down to form a capacious ash tray.

This is the place to warn the reader against having any contact with unexploded ammunition: in particular with German shells and bombs from the Second World War, which are now unstable and very dangerous. Finds should be reported to the police.

Shell and cartridge cases can be seen in most military museums such as the Imperial War Museum, London, and the museum of the South Wales Borderers at Brecon. There is no popular book on the subject, but if you can get hold of them, *The Cartridge Headstamp Guide* by H. D. White and B. D. Marshall (H. P. White Laboratory, U.S.A.) and *Cartridges of the World* by Frank Barnes (Follett Publishing Co., Chicago) are useful.

Skates

Bone skates were used in northern Europe, including Britain, probably from very early times until the fourteenth century. The raw material was the leg bone of some suitable animal, be it horse, cattle or red deer, and the skate was provided with holes at the ends to fasten it over the instep or ankle, or both. Bone skates when found will probably have retained the smooth under-surface acquired in use. The example shown is typical and presumably medieval: close dating is not possible. These bone skates would provide little or no push–off, so the skater propelled himself with an iron shod pole.

Wood skates date from the late Middle Ages, but it was not until the late eighteenth century that they were provided with iron runners, and the first skating races in this country date from about that time. The steel skate was introduced in 1850. Some twenty years after that the artificial ice rink was invented, and as a consequence figure skating developed. The skate for this has a hollow ground blade with some lengthwise curvature (known as 'rock'), and it curves sharply up at the front end to finish in a short array of teeth, upon which the skater can stop and balance. All other skates, old and new, are longer than those for figure skating and flat. Modern ones are particularly thin.

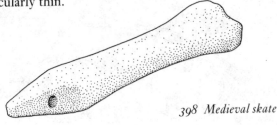

398 Medieval skate

Spectacles

Pairs of spectacles are quite often found, for the good reason that they are useless to the owner or anyone else once his eyes have progressed beyond the power of their lens to correct them.

It seems probable that lens of rock crystal were used in the ancient world as magnifying glasses for minute work on jewellery and engraved gems. The first mention of glasses to correct the vision is by Roger Bacon, who wrote a treatise on optics in 1268 and advised the use of lens by aged people. Spectacles are shown in late medi-eval carvings and pictures. Shakespeare has King Lear say 'If it be nothing I shall not need spectacles', and by 1618 they were commonplace enough to be listed as an item of trade with Japan.

Early spectacles have round lens set into rims and a

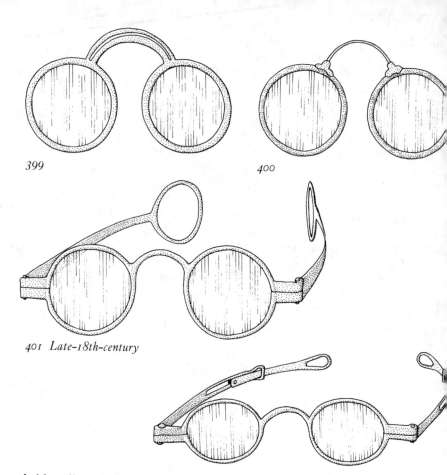

399   400

401 *Late-18th-century*

402 *About 1850*

403

bridge all made from one piece of horn or tortoiseshell; these materials gave sufficient spring for the glasses to perch on the nose of the wearer. Fig. 399 shows a seventeenth-century example, and Fig. 400 a mid-eighteenth-century pair improved by a steel bridge. Metal frames, with the side pieces known as 'bows', appeared in the eighteenth century; the bows are quite short and the lens still large. In the early nineteenth century the lens became smaller and the bows larger. In the middle of that century the lens are commonly oval, and the bows are made to extend round to the back of the head, where they may be tied together. From the late nineteenth century recognisable modern spectacles with thin metal frames were used, or so-called 'pince-nez' without frames and made to grip the nose. About 1914 the lens became large and round again, with a vogue for artificial tortoiseshell rims and bows in the 1920s which

is still with us. A single lens with a rim and a holder, of
which Fig. 403 shows an example from about 1860, may
have been used to assist the vision or intimidate an
opponent, as may a monocle, which dates from within
the last hundred years.

Spears

The weapon called a spear may be thrust or thrown; a
javelin or lance is usually of light construction, for
throwing; a pike is a heavy weapon for thrusting, or it
may be ornamental, as for example the Sheriff's pike
shown. Ornamental heads of spear form are also made
on metal palings, and when found detached they may be
mistaken for real spears. However an ornamental spear-
head is coarse and heavy in construction, and may even
be made of some impractical material such as cast iron.
Moreover the blade edges will be blunt, with no sign of
ever having been sharpened.

In general the throwing spear is for the independent
fighting man, and the thrusting weapon for he who
stands or advances shoulder to shoulder with his com-
panions.

Although arrow heads were made of flint and bone
before the age of metals, it takes metal to make a satisfactory spear. Bronze Age spearheads fall into a well-
known series, the late ones being hollow cast like later

404 Pike head
405–9 Bronze Age
410 Saxon

404   405   406   407   408   409   410

axes. The leaf-shaped Late Bronze Age type, with its cutting edges showing evidence of careful sharpening, must have been made in considerable quantities, as it is often found on or near the surface in open country.

The sword was a more important weapon than the spear in the Iron Age, but the Roman legionary carried an ingenious variety of spear nearly seven feet long and so made that it bent at the join between the iron shaft and wood extension if it stuck in an enemy's shield, thus hindering his movements. This was a *pilum*; the spear called a *hasta*, which is early encountered by those trying to learn Latin, was a light javelin carried by skirmishers.

The spear was an important weapon in the armoury of the Saxons. The size and section of the head varies much between different specimens, but a constant feature is the split socket, shown in Fig. 410 with a typical blade. The Vikings had a spear for war with characteristic straight sides. They also had a hunting spear which had wings, presumably on the same principle as the broad hunting arrow, which disables but does not of necessity kill outright.

Early medieval spears are similar to Saxon ones, but with the development of plate armour in the thirteenth century a stout needle shape developed.

Modern foreign spears, which in the past have been brought back as souvenirs from Africa and elsewhere, are often taken to museums for identification. They are usually broader and bigger than European medieval or earlier spearheads and, most significantly, they look and feel new.

Spindle Whorls

The simplest way to spin the raw materials for textiles, be they wool, flax, cotton or other threads, is by means of a spindle as shown in Fig. 414. The operator pulls out a strand from a combed supply of the basic fibre, lays it alongside the end of the already spun yarn from which the spindle hangs, and twirls the spindle to incorporate the added length. When the yarn becomes too long, some from the lower end is wound round the spindle. The success of this simple process in producing a yarn of more or less constant character depends on the fact that once a certain degree of twist is obtained at some point along the yarn, the twisting action ceases there, so the

411
Viking war spear

412 *Viking hunting spe*

413 *Late medieval*

whole length eventually comes to the same degree of twist. The critical factor is what we would call the angular momentum of the spindle whorl, the pierced circular weight at the bottom of the spindle. Of course the 'spinster' only knew that a certain size and weight of whorl made a satisfactory yarn, but what it means to us is that we find spindle whorls, from all times and peoples, varying around 5 cm in diameter according to the density of their material and the kind of fibre for which they were intended.

Spindle whorls date from Neolithic times, and are still in use among primitive peoples. The material of whorls may be a natural stone, chalk, pottery or lead. Rock crystal beads have been found in the graves of Saxon women, together with large important brooches. It seems possible that these 'beads' were ceremonial spindle whorls, only to be owned and used by some important female member of the community. Clearly the operation of spinning was important, or the word 'spinster' would not have survived.

414

415 *Chalk whorl*

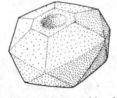

416 *Rock crystal bead*

Spoons

The knife, the spoon and the fork are the three implements used by civilised man to prepare his food and convey it from plate to mouth. Of these the spoon is the most ancient, dating back to Egypt of the pharaohs. Before the seventeenth century A.D., the majority of western people lived on porridges and broths of vegetable ingredients, scooped out of bowls, for which a spoon was sufficient. Only the rich could afford meat, which was put before them on a plate or a slice of bread, there to be cut up with the aid of knives carried on the person, aided by fingers which, as we still remind ourselves, were made before forks. Thus until forks came into common use at the end of the seventeenth century, the spoon was the only table implement in household possession, and we still speak of 'counting the spoons' after an untrustworthy visitor has left. To provide for

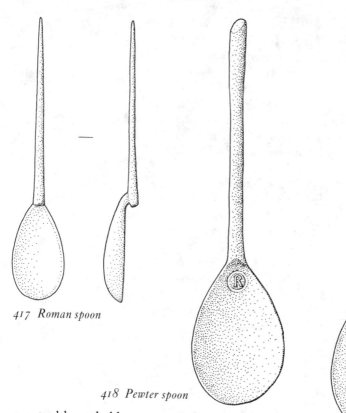

417 Roman spoon

418 Pewter spoon

419 Latten spoon

eventual household use, spoons have long been a popular christening gift, either singly or in sets, and fortunate is he who is 'born with a silver spoon in his mouth'.

Ancient Roman spoons are occasionally found, some of a distinctive stepped shape with a drop shaped bowl as also in medieval and later spoons, which are the earliest spoons likely to be discovered. They were made of silver, latten or pewter. The illustrations show a pewter spoon of about 1450 and a latten one of about 1650. If silver could not be afforded, latten, often silvered or tinned, was preferred to pewter because of its superior strength. The bowl and stem of these spoons were made from a single piece of metal. It is a common forgery to make one from an old, hall-marked stem with a new bowl soldered on, but the join should be apparent as well as the discontinuity of shape. The finials of early spoons were separately made in various forms, the one everyone knows being the apostle spoons provided in sets of twelve and the Master. An oval shape of bowl

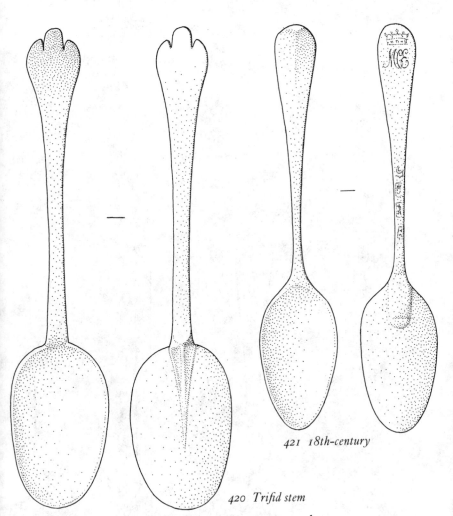

421 *18th-century*

420 *Trifid stem*

developed soon after the middle of the seventeenth century, and with a square-ended stem is known as a Puritan spoon. A few years later the trifid stem, with a 'rat tail' at the back of the bowl, made its appearance. From the early years of the eighteenth century spoons became essentially modern in shape. In the second half of the eighteenth century various patterns of cutlery were made, and a variety of silver spoons for special purposes, including marrow scoops and sugar sifters as well as the now familiar salt and mustard spoons, and caddy spoons for measuring out tea. Nineteenth-century tableware is either ornate or more or less faithful copies of eighteenth-century patterns. Some eighteenth-century spoons were converted into 'berry' spoons.

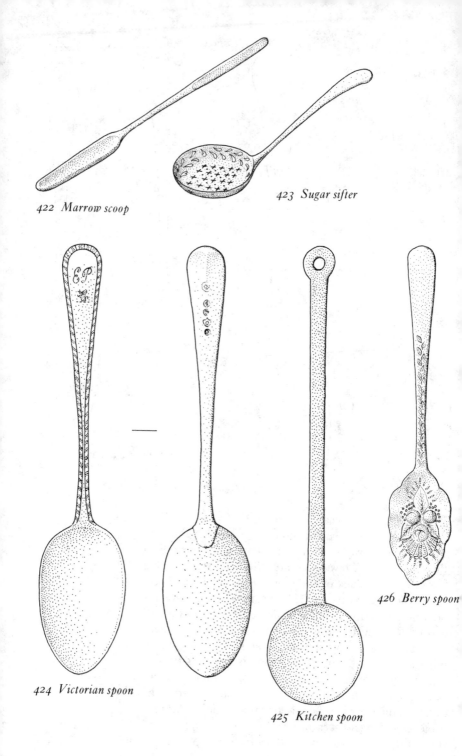

422 *Marrow scoop*

423 *Sugar sifter*

424 *Victorian spoon*

425 *Kitchen spoon*

426 *Berry spoon*

It is remarkable how few spoons of materials other than silver have survived between the latten spoons of the seventeenth century and late-nineteenth-century ones of Electro-plated Nickel Silver. Pewter spoons of the eighteenth century are met, but base metal spoons, and forks for that matter, of the first half of the last century have disappeared, presumably into the melting pot. Among fragments of nineteenth-century pottery found in a town garden bed, the badly corroded bowl of a large spoon turned up. Under the rust it appeared to be of iron, and there is no reason why tinned iron spoons should not have been used last century. The commercial application of electro-plating in the 1840s is said to have been applied first to brass and copper, then to Britannia metal, and finally to nickel silver. Some spoons of the first three metals must surely remain in out of the way corners, to be found and identified.

Handsome large spoons of brass were made for kitchen use in the eighteenth century. The one shown was made from two pieces of sheet joined by silver soldering half-way along the stem. The piece from which the bowl has been beaten out is slightly thicker, giving a good balance to this humble implement. Such refinement is seldom found except in things made in the eighteenth century.

Dover Corporation Museum, Kent, has a good collection of spoons.

Spurs

The Romans had a light spur of bronze with a simple point. This so-called 'prick' spur carries through to the thirteenth century when rowels (spiked revolving discs) first appear. These considerably intensified the persuasion to increase speed which could be brought to bear on a large horse by its armoured rider, just as the sophisticated curb bit of those days could be made forcibly to decrease the horse's speed.

By the fourteenth century the rowel spur was universally adopted, and during the next two centuries the spur increased in two dimensions. Firstly the sides or 'bows' became broader to accommodate the heavy armour sabbatons on the feet of mounted knights in the later years of chivalry. Secondly the spur developed a long neck so that an armoured rider could reach the

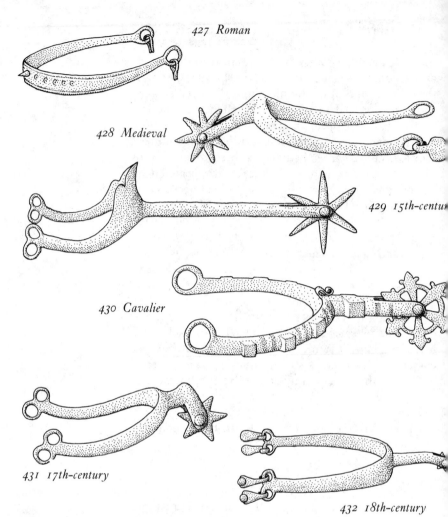

427 Roman

428 Medieval

429 15th-centur

430 Cavalier

431 17th-century

432 18th-century

horse's flank more easily. The illustrations show an early
medieval spur and a fifteenth-century one. In the seventeenth century Cavaliers wore ostentatious spurs with
large rowels, and another more practical type developed,
with a characteristic drop neck, which was possibly
favoured by Roundheads. In the eighteenth century
decorum prevailed, and small rowels were general, but
with widespread bows to clasp the heels of large riding
boots.

In the last half of the nineteenth century spurs came
to be made universally of mild steel, in place of the iron,
brass or bronze of former centuries, and this material is
still used.

Thimbles

The word thimble is associated with the thumb, and indeed thimbles have been worn in that position for the tougher kinds of needlework by sailmakers, leather-workers and hatters.

We tend to think of a thimble as made of metal, but they can be of leather, wood, bone, or even of jade. The typical thimble of the Middle Ages was of leather. How-ever the Romans had bronze thimbles similar in form and function to our own. Bronze thimbles reappeared in the fifteenth century. By the seventeenth century silver was already a popular material judging by the Royalist name for the Roundheads, 'Thimble and Bodkin Army', which implied that they were supported by gifts of such small trinkets. Fig. 434 shows a brass thimble of about that time, with indentations punched by hand. In the late seventeenth century a machine was invented for the multiple casting of thimbles, which no doubt made them more plentiful but would have left no evidence of the new process. Then in the middle of the eighteenth century the punching of the indentations was mechan-ised, so that henceforward they are of even size and regularly placed, as in the late-eighteenth-century thimble shown in Fig. 435.

433 *Roman*

434

435

Cheap eighteenth-century thimbles are of brass, bronze, and pewter, but in the last half of the century highly decorative porcelain and enamel ones were made, more for show than use. There were also fine thimbles of precious metal with bands of inlay or gems below the rim. From the last century to modern times, however, most women have preferred a plain silver thimble for needlework in the house, and a steel one for workshop use.

Tiles

Tiles may be laid to make a serviceable floor; walls may be clad with them on the inside to keep out the damp from bathrooms, or on the outside to keep out the weather; and they have been specially appreciated on and around stoves, being decorative and easy to keep clean.

A mosaic is made up of small tiles called 'tesserae', which we will also consider here.

Clearly the field is large, and we must restrict ourselves to the sort of interesting tile that might be found
in the western world. Firstly, then, we have those from
the floors of Roman buildings, the walls of which may
have disappeared though under the ground lies a mosaic
or tile pavement, perhaps to be turned up by unusually
deep ploughing.

The tesserae from Roman mosaic floors are cubic, and
between one and two cm wide, the smaller ones for fine
work in palaces and temples. They are of various plain
coloured stones, or of red terracotta. They were laid in
patterns, either geometric or figurative. Larger tesserae,
now to be called tiles, were laid to compose conventional
patterns which experts call by names starting 'opus';
thus, for example, 'Opus Alexandrinum' is of black and
red on a white ground.

In the Middle Ages from the twelfth to the fifteenth
centuries, a distinctive sort of inlaid tile was used on the
floors of important churches and secular buildings. A
typical one is Fig. 436. The body is normally of red
pottery, which was impressed with a wooden stamp and
the depression filled with a clay which, after the tile had
been covered with glaze and fired, showed a contrasting
colour, normally yellow. In general the depression on
early tiles, if it can be seen across a break, will appear
deeper than on later ones, but dating depends chiefly on
style. The making of such tiles, now called 'encaustic',
was revived in the middle of the last century, using
machines and metal dies. These reproductions have
none of the charm of the originals; no more need be said
as they may be seen in the chancels of most restored or
modern churches.

Another kind of tiles are those of tin-glazed earthenware, decorated in blue and other high-temperature
colours, made in Holland since the end of the sixteenth
century and in Britain since the late seventeenth century. The first Dutch tiles were in polychrome, in the
Spanish style, and not much exported to this country. In
the middle of the seventeenth century Dutch tiles decorated in blue became very popular in England, and
late that century their manufacture started in London
and Bristol. Fig. 437 shows a late-seventeenth-century
tile, which is probably English. It is 7 mm thick: later
tiles became progressively thinner. By the middle of the
eighteenth century tiles painted in polychrome were

popular, but then printing instead of painting restored monochrome work on British tiles, first in black and then in blue or manganese purple. The distinction between early Dutch and English tiles is largely based on style. Fig. 438 shows one which surely must be English, and Fig. 439 can be nothing but Dutch.

The commercial manufacture of decorative tiles started in the middle of the last century, the basic material being compressed clay dust, which gave harder and thinner tiles than those from earlier centuries. Advanced techniques were used on their surfaces, and many different colours in various styles, but plant forms were most popular.

See *Mosaics in Roman Britain* by A. Rainey (David and Charles, 1971), *Dutch Tiles* by C. H. de Jonge (Pall Mall, 1971), and *Victorian Ceramic Tiles* by Julian Barnard (Studio Vista, 1972).

Tins

It has been explained on page 63 how improvements in the rolling of mild steel plate and the invention of a process to apply labels and patterns in lacquer colours to tinplate allowed shaped tins and the bodies of mechanical toys to be manufactured in the last quarter of the nineteenth century.

The heyday of shaped tins was the first thirty years of this century, when fanciful creations such as attaché cases, Chinese vases and stacks of books served to contain biscuits and sweets. The example shown is typical, and was clearly intended for milk chocolates.

A second group of interesting tins are those specially made to enclose gifts. They may be found marked with the name of a brewer or tobacco firm and containing, for example, a set of dominoes. They were given to publicans by salesmen on their rounds. Particularly attractive because their dates are evident are the small flat boxes of cigarettes or sweets given in the name of royalty or heads of state to members of the armed forces in time of war. Very rarely these survive with their original contents intact, which greatly adds to their interest, but more often they were emptied and kept for sentimental reasons. The tin decorated with the heads of General and Mrs Smuts was presented to me at the beginning of the Second World War.

440

441

Toilet Instruments

Nowadays we rely on the services of 'beauticians' to remove our unwanted hair; from time to time we have our ears syringed by a doctor or nurse; and we may employ a manicurist or look after our nails ourselves. In the old days, however, ear scoops, tweezers, and small pointed instruments for cosmetic purposes were all personal possessions dating from Roman times to the nineteenth century. Bronze tweezers, ear scoops and pins, sometimes separate and sometimes wired together, are mostly found from the years between the first and the fifteenth centuries.

Tweezers appear to have been used by men as well as women, and have been found in the graves of Saxon warriors and the drains of medieval monasteries. Possibly they were needed to supplement the shaving gear of

442 Medieval tweezers

443 Saxon ear scoops and pins

those days (see RAZORS), and they would have been useful to both sexes for the removal of thorns.

Tokens

The token described here is a metal disc like a coin, made as a substitute for it in times of shortage of small change. Counters may circulate as coin, or tokens be used as counters, but the purpose for which each were made is what defines them.

444 *Charles I farthing*

The first tokens we may find are copper farthings from the reign of Charles I. These are tokens in the sense that they were made under Government authority to be redeemed for silver farthings which, due to inflation, had become too small to mint. Redemption was, however, comparable to the writing on present-day banknotes which says 'I promise to pay the bearer on demand the sum of . . .'. In 1645 these token farthings were withdrawn following the execution of Charles I, and a spate of private and municipal tokens took their place. Some farthing and whole penny tokens were issued, but they were mostly halfpennies, many of them brass as well as copper and bronze. No doubt the pro-

445 *17th-century token*

verbially valueless 'brass farthing' dates from these times. A typical token is shown: on one side is some suitable device according to the business of the issuing concern – a Turk pouring coffee, a shuttle, a man making candles. Municipal tokens bore, as might be expected, the arms and name of the city, the token value and the date. In 1670 the issue of token money was made illegal, and in 1672 the first copper coinage of England was issued.

446 *18th-century*

In the second quarter of the eighteenth century the amount of legal small change became quite inadequate for the rapidly increasing population of Britain, and now it was industrial concerns that produced token pennies and halfpennies for the pay packets of their workpeople. A penny token of the Parys Mines Company is shown. These later tokens circulated freely in industrial areas and were readily accepted as substitutes for coins, being of better quality than the counterfeit coins also in circulation at that time. In 1817 the law again made token money illegal. Nevertheless from about 1840 to 1890 public houses and some other concerns issued 'trade checks', of 1d to 6d value, with the name of the concern on one side and the value on the other. These were given as part of their wages to staff, and they circulated in coaching houses.

Most provincial museums have collections of tokens with local associations, notably Newport Museum, Gwent, and the Victoria Art Gallery, Bath. See also *Trade Tokens* by G. C. Williamson (Seaby, 1967) for seventeenth-century tokens, and for later ones *Tradesmen's Tickets and Private Tokens* by R. C. Bell (Corbitt and Hunter, 1966).

Tools

Hand tools are of two kinds: those that cut and those that deform. Thus a chisel cuts, but a planishing hammer flattens without removing or separating material. Hammers and mallets may also be used as auxiliaries, for instance to strike the end of a chisel.

On finding a tool, the first thing to decide is into which group it falls. If it is sharp, study of its edge or edges will tell you something of the material it was made to cut. Figs 447 and 448 show a simple comparison between the stout, wide-angled edge of a chisel for metal, and the thin sharp edge of one for wood. When you come to less simple tools such as reamers, the purpose of which is to clean up a round hole already drilled, this difference should be remembered. In my experience a cruel looking 'knuckle-duster' made by a criminal was thought to be armed with metal-working reamers, whereas in fact they could only have been used on some softer material such as wood or leather. The difference might have been important to the police.

447

448

The second group of tools, those that deform, includes crushers and pounders (see QUERNS). All 'deforming' tools tend to develop a characteristically smooth working surface, which is often a wide one. Leather is worked by wooden tools such as the saddler's 'smasher' shown in Fig. 449.

There is a distinction to be observed between, at one end of the scale, large rough outdoor tools such as the stonemason's axe, and at the other delicate workshop tools such as a gold-leaf burnisher (Figs 125, 85). Between these we find a host of tools which by their style and material will tell us something. In general the worker in metals uses tools chiefly made of metal, and the carpenter favours wood for tool handles.

The dating of tools is no easy task. For one thing they remain very similar once a satisfactory pattern has evolved: a Roman butcher's cleaver looks much like one from the butcher's shop just down the road. For another, their methods of manufacture did not change: in the museum at Gloucester is a tilt hammer which was used to make edge tools for two hundred years, powered consecutively by water, steam, and electricity but having throughout the same working parts.

A point to note is that the joiner's brace and bit, though unaltered in style since the Middle Ages, had the brace and bit permanently fixed together until the early nineteenth century, when it was provided with a latch to allow the bit to be changed.

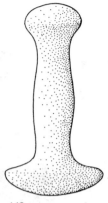

449

The finest collection of woodwork and allied tools is undoubtedly that in St Albans City Museum, Herts. For hand tools in general you should visit the Science Museum, London, or the Museum of Science and Industry, Birmingham.

Traps

Traps divide into three kinds, none of them pleasant to contemplate. The least offensive is that which secures a creature alive and uninjured, for the preservation of its species, for transfer elsewhere, or for scientific study. Then there is the trap that kills outright, usually by crushing. Finally the least acceptable trap catches the animal by a limb and retains it alive until the trapper arrives. It is this last sort of trap that humane people seek to eradicate, and it is also the kind that we may most expect to find – hopefully no longer in use. The gin trap got its name from 'engine' in the sense of being a contrivance. These traps were formerly used to catch small game and vermin, but have been illegal in Britain for over twenty years. There was a round variety, called a pole trap, which was set on top of a pole where some unfortunate bird might alight. This device has been outlawed since 1906.

The 'breakback' spring trap, baited with cheese and of a size for either rats or mice, is still a familiar object and need not detain us. Another trap of the instant fatal variety, however, that could have been seen in kitchens and larders last century, employed a block of wood

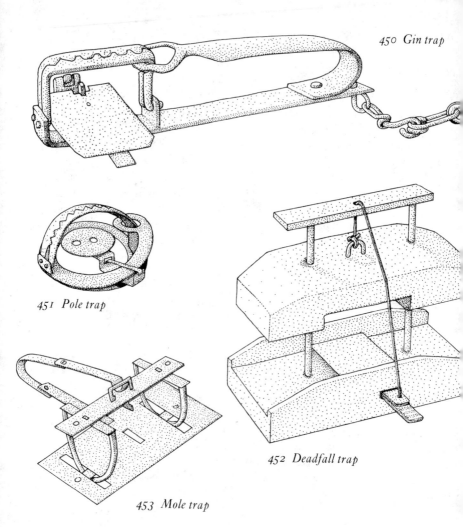

450 *Gin trap*

451 *Pole trap*

452 *Deadfall trap*

453 *Mole trap*

tripped by the mouse when attempting to eat the bait. The block then fell and crushed the unfortunate rodent. It looks as though this trap was effective but messy.

Also dating from the last century were ingenious traps that lured mice up on to a platform and then precipitated them into a tin of water by means of a tilting platform.

The old form of mole trap shown was set in their runs like the modern scissor-shaped one. The old trap was probably as ineffective as a modern one in deterring moles once they have decided to inhabit the ground under the lawn.

You are likely to come across only two sorts of weights. Firstly there are those of cup or disc shape graduated in the avoirdupois scale and used by retailers and domestically to weigh household commodities. Secondly there are smaller, rectangular weights in the apothecaries' scale, used by apothecaries and in the home to weigh medicines.

We are moving towards the metrication of all things, which is in some ways to be regretted, but few will shed tears for the passing of Troy weight. Although painfully learnt at school, it was seldom met in normal life so remained incomprehensible to many people. The root of our difficulties lay in a statute of Elizabeth I, which required 'bread, gold, silver and electuaries' to be weighed in Troy. Let us analyse this strange assortment. Bread was a most important diet in the Middle Ages, for which we still pray daily, and it was controlled by the government in England before the avoirdupois scale was established, hence it came to be weighed in Troy. The 'Assize of Bread' dates from the thirteenth century right through to 1815. Those who deal in precious metals have always clung to Troy weight, despite official attempts to abolish it, and even today the advertisements for issues of commemorative medals specify their weights in Troy ounces, which are slightly larger than the ounce avoirdupois. Finally 'electuaries', that is to say drugs in the pharmacist's sense, were conveniently weighed in Troy because that scale was based on the weight of a grain of wheat 'taken from the middle of the ear, well dried', so that actual grains could, and probably were, used to weigh doses of drugs. The apothecaries' scale was:

20 grains	=	1 scruple
3 scruples	=	1 drachm (or dram)
8 drachms	=	1 ounce (Troy)

In 1864 the scruple was abolished, and the Troy pound was outlawed in 1878, but despite these knocks the scale has survived.

Fig. 454 shows three apothecaries' weights of the early nineteenth century. The symbol ℈ will be found for scruple, and note that the number of grains is indicated by punch marks.

454

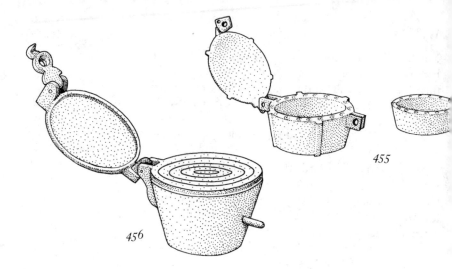

455

456

The pound avoirdupois, which came through unchanged in Europe from Roman times, was first used for imports to Britain in the thirteenth century. It came to be employed, with its familiar divisions and multiples of ounces, stones, etc., for everything other than bread, precious metals and pharmacist's drugs. Fig. 455 shows a medieval weight and Fig. 456 a nest of official avoirdupois cup weights dated 1820. The better known flat weight, with a raised edge to allow stacking, dates from the sixteenth century.

The Avery Historical Museum, Birmingham, specialises in weights and weighing machines.

Whistles

A whistle is properly an instrument without stops or other means of changing its note, but the word is also used for the simple stopped flutes we will consider here.

The numberless flutes of perishable material such as reed, which country folk have cut for themselves since Pan first taught them how, have left no trace. Occasionally an example made of bone may survive, and Fig. 457 shows one formed from the leg bone of a swan which may be medieval.

To produce a note, a stream of air must be directed against an orifice in the side of the instrument. In the side-blown flute this is done directly against a hole from outside. In the end-blown flute the air is constricted at the mouthpiece so that it impinges on the edge of a hole

from inside, like an organ pipe. The mouthpiece may be
partly closed with the lips, or the lower half of it may be
plugged with some suitable material, which may or may
not survive.

No doubt a musicologist could tell us much about the
origin of any flute by analysis of its musical scale, but
they are otherwise difficult to date.

The boatswain's call, of which Fig. 458 shows a
specimen, was used aboard Naval ships from the late
fifteenth century until a few years ago. It is held with the
spherical part, known as the 'buoy', in the palm of the
hand, and the note is varied by opening and closing
the fingers, and also by trilling with the tongue.

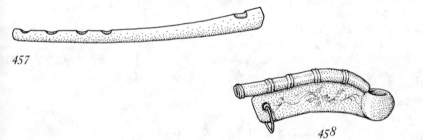

457

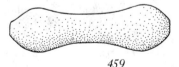

458

Wig Curlers

A side-line by the manufacturer of clay pipes was the
making of wig curlers, small waisted sausages of pipe-
clay. They vary slightly in size, but the one shown is
typical.

The wearing of wigs as a male fashion dates from the
late seventeenth century to the early nineteenth century,
so most wig curlers would be from the eighteenth century. However wigs may be worn in any age by men or
women with the misfortune to lose their own hair, so
these dates are not certain.

459

Further Reading

Ash, D., *Dictionary of British Antique Silver* (Pelham, 1972)

Barton, L., *Historic Costume for the Stage* (A. & C. Black, 1937)

Bedford, John, *The Collecting Man* (Macdonald, 1968)

Biggs, John, *The Story of the Alphabet* (Oxford University Press, 1968)

Blandford, R. W., *Country Craft Tools* (David & Charles, 1974)

Bridgeman, Harriet and Drury, Elisabeth (Ed), *Encyclopaedia of Victoriana* (Country Life, 1975)

Childe, Gordon, *Prehistoric Communities of the British Isles* (W. & R. Chambers, 1940)

Cunnington, C. W. and P. E., and Beard, C., *A Dictionary of English Costume* (A. & C. Black, 1960)

Douglas, R. W. and Frank, S., *A History of Glassmaking* (G. T. Foulis, 1972)

Edlin, H. L., *What Wood is That?* (Thames & Hudson, 1969)

Fletcher, E., *A Treasure Hunter's Guide* (Blandford Press, 1975)

Gentle, R. and Field, R., *English Domestic Brass* (Elek, 1975)

Godden, G. A., *British Pottery* (Barrie & Jenkins, 1974)

Hodges, Henry, *Artifacts* (John Baker, 1964)

Hume, I. Noel, *All the Best Rubbish* (Gollancz, 1974)

Mackay, J., *An Encyclopaedia of Small Antiques* (Ward Lock, 1975)

Metcalfe, O. K., *General Principles of English Law* (Cassell, 1975)

Metz, R., *Precious Stones* (Thames & Hudson, 1964)

Needham, J., *Clerks and Craftsmen in China and the West* (Cambridge University Press, 1970)

Palmer, Liddesdale, *English Social History in the Making* (Nicholson & Watson, 1934)

Perry, E. M., *Collecting Antique Metalware* (Hamlyn, 1974)

Plenderleith, H. J., *The Conservation of Antiquities and Works of Art* (Oxford University Press, 1956)

Rogers, J. C., *English Furniture* (Country Life, 1959)

Quennell, M. and C. H. B., *A History of Everyday Things in England* (Batsford, 1934)

Savage, G., *A Concise History of Bronzes* (Thames & Hudson, 1968)

Trevelyan, G. M., *English Social History* (Longman, Green 1944)

Tylecote, R. F., *History of Metallurgy* (The Metals Society, 1976)

Untracht, O., *Metal Techniques for Craftsmen* (Doubleday, 1968)

Ware, D. and Stafford, M., *An Illustrated Dictionary of Ornament* (Allen & Unwin, 1977)

Wilkinson, F., *Militaria* (Ward Lock, 1969)

Wright, L., *Home Fires Burning* (Routledge & Kegan Paul, 1964)

The Collector's Encyclopaedia (Collins, 1974)

Complete Encyclopaedia of Antiques (The Connoisseur, 1975)

Index

Forka, 162–4
Fossils, 10
France, 62; glassware, 74; lacquered
tinware, 62; mannequins, 149–50;
mechanical toys, 187; tortoiseshell
veneering, 80
Franks, 104
Furniture, 24; inlaid, 41; nails for,
191; screws, 194; woods used, 58,
82–3
Furniture fittings, 164–5
Fyrkat, 20, 21

Games and puzzles, 165–7
Germany, 39; black letter
inscriptions, 32; 'Dutch' dolls,
148; Iron Cross, 188; silver, 67;
steel needles, 192
Glass, 72–7
Glasses, table, 167–8
Glassware, makers' markings, 29;
engraved, 32; tools and methods
used, 73; Roemers, 74; bull's eyes,
74; vessels, 75–6, 116; faked,
76–7; conservation, 91
Glazes, 71
Gold, hallmarking, 26–7; use of
chasing, 40; beads, 109; coinage,
143; rings, 203; snuff boxes, 120
Gothic style, 19–20, 206, 207
Greece, classical, 46; bracelets, 123;
brooches, 124; coins, 143; dice,
148; principle of the screw, 192
Gun-metal, 47
Guns, 136–7, 160, 169–70

Hallmarks, 26–7
Hardstones, 86–9, 110; jewellery,
126 see also Jade
Harness, 170–3 see also Horse
brasses
Heraldry, 27–8
Hittites, 53
Hones, 172
Horn, 78, 79, 80; articles made from,
79–80, 101, 146, 210; imitation
tortoiseshell, 81
Horse brasses, 172, 173–4
Horse-drawn vehicles, 139–40
Horseshoes, 54, 174–6
Huguenots, 41

Idols, 45
Industrial archaeology, 35

Industrialization, 22–3
Inlaying, 41, 86, 170
Inscriptions, 26–30, 32; dating by
style, 30, 33; interpretation, 92;
amulets, 98; coinage, 145; medals,
188; pewterers, 64–5
Ireland, glassware, 32, 75–6; gold
from, 123
Iron, forging, 39; early history, 53;
technology, 53; alloys, 59–60;
conservation, 91
Iron Age, 53, 54, 56; axes, 103–4;
weaving combs, 147; dice, 148;
grindstones, 172; loom-weights,
185; shears, 206
Ironmasters, 58
Italy, 68; drug jars, 176
Ivory, 41, 78; origins, 78; carving
and staining, 78; boxes, 119, 120,
122; counters, 147; chessmen, 78,
165–6

Jade, 86, 87; Chinese, 87–8; axes,
102, 103
Japan, 61
Japanese, inlaid armour, 41; high
carbon steel, 58; lacquerwork
boxes, 122; mechanical toys, 187;
spectacles, 209; swords, 57
Japanning, 84
Jars, 176–7
Jewellery, 21, 41, 86, 203; brass, 50;
paste, 72; talismanic import, 98;
white metal, 66 see also Bracelets,
Brooches, Earrings, Rings
Jig-saws, 166, 167
Jodrell Laboratory, 35
Jutes, 109

Kelly's Directory, 29
Keys, 10, 14, 182–4
Kiln furniture, 178
Knives, 178–80, 194, 213; and forks,
163

Labels, 63, 180; for medicine
bottles, 117–18
Lacemaking, 115
Lacquer, 62–3, 84, 122
Lamps, 133, 180–2; carriage, 138,
140; gig, 140
Latten, 51, 214, 217
Law, on things found, 16–17; of
trespass, 17